Networking Essentials
The Cram Sheet

This Cram Sheet contains the distilled, key facts about Networking Essentials. Review this information last thing before you enter the test room, paying special attention to those areas where you feel you need the most review. You can transfer any of these facts from your head onto a blank sheet of paper before beginning the exam.

STANDARDS AND TERMINOLOGY

1. Know the various names and uses for each of the seven layers of the OSI Reference Model:
   - **Application layer** Provides a set of interfaces for applications to use to gain access to networked services.
   - **Presentation layer** Converts data into a generic format for network transmission; for incoming messages, it converts data from this format into a format that the receiving application can understand.
   - **Session layer** Enables two parties to hold ongoing communications—called sessions—across a network.
   - **Transport layer** Manages the transmission of data across a network.
   - **Network layer** Handles addressing messages for delivery, as well as translates logical network addresses and names into their physical counterparts.
   - **Data Link layer** Sends special data frames from the Network layer to the Physical layer and handles physical addresses.
   - **Physical layer** Converts bits into signals for outgoing messages, and signals into bits for incoming messages.

2. About disk striping with parity:
   - All members of a set equal in size.
   - Partitions must be on different physical disks.
   - 3 drives minimum; 32 drives maximum.
   - Slower than striping without parity, faster than mirroring.
   - If one drive in set fails, missing data can be rebuilt from remaining devices and parity info.

3. If you lose a member of a volume set or stripe set without parity, everything is lost!

4. Neither boot nor system partitions can reside on a volume set or disk stripe set, even with parity.

5. RAID levels and details:

Type	Fault Tolerant?	Speed	Includes:
RAID 0	No	Fastest	Disk striping without parity, volume sets
RAID 1	Yes RAID	Slowest	Disk mirroring (slower), disk duplexing (faster)
RAID 5	Yes	Intermediate	Disk striping with parity

39. Look at Memory: Pages/Second in Performance Monitor to decide whether more RAM is needed.

40. Know how to troubleshoot the following:
    - User and account management
    - Performance tuning
    - Network operations
    - Network modeling
    - Physical plant, including cabling, data, and telecommunications
    - Security policies and auditing
    - Disaster planning and recovery
    - Capacity planning
    - Software/hardware upgrades and maintenance

41. The Event Viewer can monitor such activities as unsuccessful logon attempts, but you must enable logon auditing first. You can see a report of unsuccessful logon attempts from Event Viewer's Security log.

42. In an SNMP environment, the agent is the program loaded on a client machine or a networked device to monitor network traffic and to report events to the management program console.

43. Primary defense against data loss is implementation of an effective, efficient backup system with appropriate scheduling and methodology. Use fault-tolerant systems, such as RAID 1 or RAID 5, in addition to—not to exclusion of—data backups.

Certification Insider™ Press
© 1999 The Coriolis Group.
All Rights Reserved.

Networking Essentials

Microsoft Certified Systems Engineer

Adaptive Testing Edition

Ed Tittel, Kurt Hudson,
James Michael Stewart

MCSE Networking Essentials Exam Cram, Adaptive Testing Edition
© 1999 The Coriolis Group. All rights reserved.

This book may not be duplicated in any way without the express written consent of the publisher, except in the form of brief excerpts or quotations for the purposes of review. The information contained herein is for the personal use of the reader and may not be incorporated in any commercial programs, other books, databases, or any kind of software without written consent of the publisher. Making copies of this book or any portion for any purpose other than your own is a violation of United States copyright laws.

Limits Of Liability And Disclaimer Of Warranty
The author and publisher of this book have used their best efforts in preparing the book and the programs contained in it. These efforts include the development, research, and testing of the theories and programs to determine their effectiveness. The author and publisher make no warranty of any kind, expressed or implied, with regard to these programs or the documentation contained in this book.

The author and publisher shall not be liable in the event of incidental or consequential damages in connection with, or arising out of, the furnishing, performance, or use of the programs, associated instructions, and/or claims of productivity gains.

Trademarks
Trademarked names appear throughout this book. Rather than list the names and entities that own the trademarks or insert a trademark symbol with each mention of the trademarked name, the publisher states that it is using the names for editorial purposes only and to the benefit of the trademark owner, with no intention of infringing upon that trademark.

The Coriolis Group, LLC
14455 N. Hayden Road, Suite 220
Scottsdale, Arizona 85260

602/483-0192
FAX 602/483-0193
http://www.coriolis.com

Tittel, Ed
   MCSE networking essentials exam cram / by Ed Tittel, Kurt Hudson, and James Michael Stewart. --Adaptive testing ed.
      p. cm.
   Includes index.
   ISBN 1-57610-445-1
   1. Electronic data processing personnel--Certification.
   2. Microsoft software--Examinations--Study guides. 3. Microsoft Windows NT. 4. Computer networks. I. Hudson, Kurt. II. Stewart, James Michael. III. Title.
QA76.3.T5745   1999
004.6--dc21   99-10840
                                                      CIP

Printed in the United States of America
10 9 8 7 6 5 4 3 2 1

Publisher
Keith Weiskamp

Acquisitions Editor
Shari Jo Hehr

Marketing Specialist
Cynthia Caldwell

Project Editors
Meredith Brittain
Jeff Kellum

Technical Editor
Deborah Lupica

Production Coordinator
Kim Eoff

Cover Design
Jody Winkler

Layout Design
April Nielsen

14455 North Hayden, Suite 220 • Scottsdale, Arizona 85260

The Smartest Way To Get Certified ™

Thank you for purchasing one of our innovative certification study guides, just one of the many members of the Coriolis family of certification products.

Certification Insider Press™ was created in late 1997 by The Coriolis Group to help professionals like you obtain certification and advance your career. Achieving certification involves a major commitment and a great deal of hard work. To help you reach your goals, we've listened to others like you, and we've designed our entire product line around you and the way you like to study, learn, and master challenging subjects. Our approach is *The Smartest Way To Get Certified*.

In less than a year, Coriolis has published over one million copies of our highly popular *Exam Cram*, *Exam Prep*, and *On Site* guides. Our *Exam Cram* books, specifically written to help you pass an exam, are the number one certification self-study guides in the industry. They are the perfect complement to any study plan you have, as well as to the rest of the Certification Insider Press series: *Exam Prep*, comprehensive study guides designed to help you thoroughly learn and master certification topics, and *On Site*, guides that really show you how to apply your skills and knowledge on the job.

Our commitment to you is to ensure that all of the certification study guides we develop help you save time and frustration. Each one provides unique study tips and techniques, memory joggers, custom quizzes, insight about test taking, practical problems to solve, real-world examples, and much more.

We'd like to hear from you. Help us continue to provide the very best certification study materials possible. Write us or email us at **craminfo@coriolis.com** and let us know how our books have helped you study, or tell us about new features that you'd like us to add. If you send us a story about how an *Exam Cram*, *Exam Prep*, or *On Site* book has helped you, and we use it in one of our books, we'll send you an official Coriolis shirt for your efforts.

Good luck with your certification exam and your career. Thank you for allowing us to help you achieve your goals.

Keith Weiskamp
Publisher, Certification Insider Press

About The Authors

Ed Tittel is a 20-year veteran in the computing business who owes his high-tech career to a continuing love for the beautiful city of Austin, Texas. Ed covers lots of Windows NT subjects, with over 20 NT-related titles to his credit. He is also a member of the Networld+Interop trade show faculty, where he teaches on Windows NT security and performance topics. Prior to going out on his own in 1994, Ed worked at Novell for six years, where he began as a field engineer and left as the company's director of technical marketing.

Ed has contributed to over 85 computer books, including many in the *Exam Cram* and *Exam Prep* series, for which he is also the series editor. Ed has also written articles for publications that include the late *Byte*, *InfoWorld*, *LAN Magazine*, *Windows NT Magazine*, and *PC Magazine*.

In his spare time, Ed likes cooking homemade stock and all the good stuff that comes from it, playing pool, and walking his dawg, Blackie. You can reach Ed by email at **etittel@lanw.com** or on the Web through **www.lanw.com/staff/etbio.htm**.

Kurt Hudson, president of HudLogic, Inc, has earned MCSE, MCSE + Internet, MCT, and A+ Certified Technician ratings. He began his technical career with the U.S. Air Force, earning medals for systems efficiency, training excellence, and national security. He has worked for Unisys, where he helped launch two Windows 95 support operations for Microsoft and Compaq, and for Productivity Point International, where he trained hundreds of computer support engineers and system administrators. Today, he writes commercial technical publications, trains computer professionals, and troubleshoots networking problems. He has authored or co-authored several publications, which are listed at **www.hudlogic.com**. You can reach Kurt via email at **kurt@hudlogic.com**.

James Michael Stewart is a full-time writer focusing on Windows NT and Internet topics. Most recently, he has worked on several titles in the *Exam Cram* and *Exam Prep* series. Michael has been developing Windows NT 4 MCSE-level courseware and training materials for several years, including both print and online publications, as well as classroom presentation of NT training materials. He has been an MCSE since 1997, with a focus on Windows NT 4. You can reach Michael by email at **michael@lanw.com**, or through his Web page at **www.lanw.com/jmsbio.htm**.

Acknowledgments

Thanks to Keith Weiskamp, the publisher at The Coriolis Group, for backing the *Exam Cram* concept, for starting Certification Insider Press, and for giving us the chance to revisit, revise, and expand on our original Core Four *Exam Crams*. We've created an industry phenomenon and launched a real brand name. Thanks a million!

Thanks also to the folks who helped turn our bright ideas into real books and marketing plans. On the LANWrights side, my special thanks go out to Dawn Rader, project manager and editor extraordinaire; James Michael Stewart, Windows NT wizard and collaborator nonpareil; Mary Burmeister, Goddess of Glossaries; Kyle Findlay, our handyman around the office; and Dr. Bill Brogden, the man who built the test engine that made so much of our work possible. You guys are the greatest! Thanks also to my Core Four co-authors, James Michael Stewart and Kurt Hudson. At Coriolis, special thanks go to Shari Jo Hehr, our acquisitions editor and den mother; Sandra Lassiter, queen of production and editing; Paula Kmetz, managing editor; Meredith Brittain, Dan Young, and Jeff Kellum, our project editors for these titles; and Kim Eoff and Jon Gabriel, our production coordinators for these titles. We'd also like to thank Cynthia Caldwell, Deanna Gogol, Anne Tull, Neil Gudowitz, Richard Flowers, and many more, for their outstanding efforts in marketing and selling these books.

Finally, thanks to my family for being there when I needed them. Mom and Dad: You've been a source of inspiration, challenge, and friendship. Kat, Mike, and the gang: You've helped remind me why I'm doing all this. To Tressa and the kids: Hang in there, the sun's breaking through the clouds. Last, thanks to Blackie (my giant and enthusiastic eight-month-old black labrador) for pulling me away from the keyboard and out into the real world on occasion.

—*Ed Tittel*

I would like to thank the following people for their professional contributions to this book: Julie A. Hudson, Doug Dexter, and Lori Marcinkiewicz.

—*Kurt Hudson*

Acknowledgments

Thanks to my boss and co-author, Ed Tittel, for including me in this book series. Thanks to Dawn Rader; without you, this book would never have been complete. A warm howdy to Mary Burmeister (our other work slave). To my parents, Dave and Sue: Thanks for always being there and making it clear how much you care. To Dave and Laura: Buy the $20,000 home theater and I'll camp on your couch and cook your meals! To Mark: The cult of the Pocketgods will come back to haunt you—it is already noted in your permanent record. To HERbert: Please stop digging your claws into the back of my neck while I'm asleep. And finally, as always, to Elvis—I've been looking high and low for a glittery white jumpsuit of my own, but it seems that Wal-Mart is always sold out!

—*James Michael Stewart*

Contents At A Glance

Chapter 1 Microsoft Certification Exams

Chapter 2 Networking Concepts And Terms

Chapter 3 Network Protocols

Chapter 4 Cabling And Interfaces

Chapter 5 Network Hardware And Topologies

Chapter 6 Network Planning And Design

Chapter 7 Network Operations

Chapter 8 Network Administration And Support

Chapter 9 Network Naming And Security

Chapter 10 Wide Area Networks

Chapter 11 Problem Diagnosis And Resolution

Chapter 12 Sample Test #1

Chapter 13 Answer Key #1

Chapter 14 Sample Test #2

Chapter 15 Answer Key #2

Table Of Contents

Introduction .... **xv**

The MCSE Exam Cram Self-Assessment .... **xxix**

Chapter 1
Microsoft Certification Exams **1**
    Assessing Exam-Readiness 2
    The Exam Situation 3
    Exam Layout And Design 5
    Recognizing Your Exam Type: Fixed-Length Or Adaptive 7
    Exam-Taking Basics 9
    Question-Handling Strategies 10
    Mastering The Inner Game 10
    Additional Resources 11

Chapter 2
Networking Concepts And Terms **13**
    Basic Terminology 14
    What Is A Network? 18
    Choosing A Network 23
    Practice Questions 25
    Need To Know More? 28

Chapter 3
Network Protocols **29**
    The OSI Reference Model 30
    Protocols 38
    Practice Questions 40
    Need To Know More? 44

Chapter 4
Cabling And Interfaces 45
    Cable Types 46
    Wireless Technologies 54
    Cabling Considerations 55
    Understanding NDIS And ODI 56
    Practice Questions 58
    Need To Know More? 66

Chapter 5
Network Hardware And Topologies 67
    Networking Components 68
    Network Topologies 76
    Networking Standards And Technologies 82
    Practice Questions 90
    Need To Know More? 98

Chapter 6
Network Planning And Design 99
    Network Layout Principles 100
    Topology Requirements 102
    Selecting A Network Architecture 104
    Network Design Principles 108
    Planning For Successful Deployment 110
    Practice Questions 113
    Need To Know More? 121

Chapter 7
Network Operations 123
    Network Operating Systems 124
    Installing A NOS 127
    Network Services 129
    Network Printing 130
    Implementing Networked Applications 131
    Practice Questions 132
    Need To Know More? 135

Chapter 8
Network Administration And Support 137
    Managing Networked Accounts   138
    Managing Network Performance   144
    Practice Questions   150
    Need To Know More?   153

Chapter 9
Network Naming And Security 155
    Network Naming Schemes   156
    Planning For Network Security   160
    Security Models   163
    Additional Security Considerations   165
    Disaster Recovery   170
    Practice Questions   178
    Need To Know More?   184

Chapter 10
Wide Area Networks 185
    WAN Terminology   186
    Analog Connectivity   188
    Digital Connectivity   189
    Packet Switching   190
    Practice Questions   201
    Need To Know More?   206

Chapter 11
Problem Diagnosis And Resolution 209
    Approaches To Network Management   210
    Prevention Through Planning   215
    Troubleshooting Networks   221
    Troubleshooting Hardware Problems   224
    Troubleshooting Software Connection Problems   225
    Handling Network Performance Problems   226
    Practice Questions   227
    Need To Know More?   233

Chapter 12
Sample Test #1 235
    Questions, Questions, Questions   236
    Picking Proper Answers   236
    Decoding Ambiguity   237
    Working Within The Framework   238
    Deciding What To Memorize   239
    Preparing For The Test   239
    Taking The Test   240
    Sample Test #1   241

Chapter 13
Answer Key #1 261

Chapter 14
Sample Test #2 275

Chapter 15
Answer Key #2 297

Glossary 313

Index 389

Introduction

Welcome to *MCSE Networking Essentials Exam Cram, Adaptive Testing Edition*! This book aims to help you get ready to take—and pass—the Microsoft certification Exam 70-058, titled "Networking Essentials." This introduction explains Microsoft's certification programs in general and talks about how the *Exam Cram* series can help you prepare for Microsoft's certification exams.

Exam Cram books help you understand and appreciate the subjects and materials you need to pass Microsoft certification exams. *Exam Cram* books are aimed strictly at test preparation and review. They do not teach you everything you need to know about a topic (such as the impedance of 10BaseT cables, nor all the nitty-gritty details involved in using a time domain reflectometer, or TDR). Instead, we (the authors) present and dissect the questions and problems we've found that you're likely to encounter on a test. We've worked from Microsoft's own training materials, preparation guides, and tests, and from a battery of third-party test preparation tools. Our aim is to bring together as much information as possible about Microsoft certification exams.

Nevertheless, to completely prepare yourself for any Microsoft test, we recommend that you begin by taking The MCSE Exam Cram Self-Assessment included in this book immediately following this introduction. This tool will help you evaluate your knowledge base against the requirements for an MCSE under both ideal and real circumstances.

Based on what you learn from that exercise, you might decide to begin your studies with some classroom training or some background reading. On the other hand, you might decide to pick up and read one of the many study guides available from Microsoft or third-party vendors on certain topics, including The Coriolis Group's *Exam Prep* series (for which a title on Networking Essentials is also available).

We also strongly recommend that you install, configure, and fool around with the software that you'll be tested on, because nothing beats hands-on experience and familiarity when it comes to understanding the questions you're likely to encounter on a certification test. Book learning is essential, but hands-on experience is the best teacher of all!

The Microsoft Certified Professional (MCP) Program

The MCP Program currently includes eight separate tracks, each of which boasts its own special acronym (as a would-be certificant, you need to have a high tolerance for alphabet soup of all kinds):

- **MCP (Microsoft Certified Professional)** This is the least prestigious of all the certification tracks from Microsoft. Passing any of the major Microsoft exams (except the Networking Essentials exam) qualifies an individual for MCP credentials. Individuals can demonstrate proficiency with additional Microsoft products by passing additional certification exams.

- **MCP+I (Microsoft Certified Professional + Internet)** This midlevel certification is attained by completing three core exams: "Implementing and Supporting Microsoft Windows NT Server 4.0," "Internetworking Microsoft TCP/IP on Microsoft Windows NT 4.0," and "Implementing and Supporting Internet Information Server 3.0 and Microsoft Index Server 1.1" or "Implementing and Supporting Microsoft Internet Information Server 4.0."

- **MCP+SB (Microsoft Certified Professional + Site Building)** This certification program is designed for individuals who are planning, building, managing, and maintaining Web sites. Individuals with the MCP+SB credential will have demonstrated the ability to develop Web sites that include multimedia and searchable content and Web sites that connect to and communicate with a back-end database. It requires one MCP exam, plus two of these three exams: "Designing and Implementing Commerce Solutions with Microsoft Site Server, 3.0, Commerce Edition," "Designing and Implementing Web Sites with Microsoft FrontPage 98," and "Designing and Implementing Web Solutions with Microsoft Visual InterDev 6.0."

- **MCSE (Microsoft Certified Systems Engineer)** Anyone who has a current MCSE is warranted to possess a high level of expertise with Windows NT (version 3.51 or 4.0) and other Microsoft operating systems and products. This credential is designed to prepare individuals to plan, implement, maintain, and support information systems and networks built around Microsoft Windows NT and its BackOffice family of products.

  To obtain an MCSE, an individual must pass four core operating system exams, plus two elective exams. The operating system exams require individuals to demonstrate competence with desktop and server operating systems and with networking components.

You must pass at least two Windows NT-related exams to obtain an MCSE: "Implementing and Supporting Microsoft Windows NT Server" (version 3.51 or 4.0) and "Implementing and Supporting Microsoft Windows NT Server in the Enterprise" (version 3.51 or 4.0). These tests are intended to indicate an individual's knowledge of Windows NT in smaller, simpler networks and in larger, more complex, and heterogeneous networks, respectively.

Note: The NT 3.51 version is scheduled to be retired by Microsoft sometime in 1999.

You must pass two additional tests as well. These tests are related to networking and desktop operating systems. At present, the networking requirement can be satisfied only by passing the Networking Essentials test. The desktop operating system test can be satisfied by passing a Windows 95, Windows NT Workstation (the version must match the NT version for the core tests), or Windows 98 test.

The two remaining exams are elective exams. An elective exam may fall in any number of subject or product areas, primarily BackOffice components. These include tests on Internet Explorer 4, SQL Server, IIS, Proxy Server, SNA Server, Exchange Server, Systems Management Server, and the like. However, it is also possible to test out on electives by taking advanced networking topics like "Internetworking with Microsoft TCP/IP on Microsoft Windows NT 4.0" (but here again, the version of Windows NT involved must match the version for the core requirements taken). If you are on your way to becoming an MCSE and have already taken some exams, visit **www.microsoft.com/mcp/certstep/mcse.htm** for information about how to proceed with your MCSE certification.

Whatever mix of tests is completed toward MCSE certification, individuals must pass six tests to meet the MCSE requirements. It's not uncommon for the entire process to take a year or so, and many individuals find that they must take a test more than once to pass. Our primary goal with the *Exam Cram* series is to make it possible, given proper study and preparation, to pass any related Microsoft certification test on the first try. Table 1 shows the required and elective exams for the MCSE certification.

➤ **MCSE+I (Microsoft Certified Systems Engineer + Internet)** This is a newer Microsoft certification and focuses not just on Microsoft operating systems, but also on Microsoft's Internet servers and TCP/IP.

Table 1 MCSE Requirements*

Core

All 3 of these are required	
Exam 70-067	Implementing and Supporting Microsoft Windows NT Server 4.0
Exam 70-068	Implementing and Supporting Microsoft Windows NT Server 4.0 in the Enterprise
▶ Exam 70-058	Networking Essentials
Choose 1 from this group	
Exam 70-064	Implementing and Supporting Microsoft Windows 95
Exam 70-073	Implementing and Supporting Microsoft Windows NT Workstation 4.0
Exam 70-098	Implementing and Supporting Microsoft Windows 98

Elective

Choose 2 from this group	
Exam 70-088	Implementing and Supporting Microsoft Proxy Server 2.0
Exam 70-079	Implementing and Supporting Microsoft Internet Explorer 4.0 by Using the Internet Explorer Administration Kit
Exam 70-087	Implementing and Supporting Microsoft Internet Information Server 4.0
Exam 70-081	Implementing and Supporting Microsoft Exchange Server 5.5
Exam 70-059	Internetworking with Microsoft TCP/IP on Microsoft Windows NT 4.0
Exam 70-028	Administering Microsoft SQL Server 7.0
Exam 70-029	Designing and Implementing Databases on Microsoft SQL Server 7.0
Exam 70-056	Implementing and Supporting Web Sites Using Microsoft Site Server 3.0
Exam 70-086	Implementing and Supporting Microsoft Systems Management Server 2.0
Exam 70-085	Implementing and Supporting Microsoft SNA Server 4.0

* This is not a complete listing—you can still be tested on some earlier versions of these products. However, we have included mainly the most recent versions so that you may test on these versions and thus be certified longer. We have not included any tests that are scheduled to be retired.

To obtain this certification, an individual must pass seven core exams plus two elective exams. The core exams include not only the server operating systems (Windows NT Server and Server in the Enterprise) and a desktop OS (Windows 95, Windows 98, or Windows NT Workstation), but also include Networking Essentials, TCP/IP, Internet Information Server (IIS), and the Internet Explorer Administration Kit (IEAK).

The two remaining exams are elective exams. These elective exams can be in any of four product areas: SQL Server, SNA Server, Exchange Server, or Proxy Server. Table 2 shows the required and elective exams for the MCSE+I certification.

▶ **MCSD (Microsoft Certified Solution Developer)** The MCSD credential reflects the skills required to create multitier, distributed, and COM-based solutions, in addition to desktop and Internet applications, using

Table 2 MCSE+Internet Requirements*

Core

All 6 of these are required	
Exam 70-067	Implementing and Supporting Microsoft Windows NT Server 4.0
Exam 70-068	Implementing and Supporting Microsoft Windows NT Server 4.0 in the Enterprise
▶ Exam 70-058	Networking Essentials
Exam 70-059	Internetworking with Microsoft TCP/IP on Microsoft Windows NT 4.0
Exam 70-087	Implementing and Supporting Microsoft Internet Information Server 4.0
Exam 70-079	Implementing and Supporting Microsoft Internet Explorer 4.0 by Using the Internet Explorer Administration Kit
Choose 1 from this group	
Exam 70-064	Implementing and Supporting Microsoft Windows 95
Exam 70-073	Implementing and Supporting Microsoft Windows NT Workstation 4.0
Exam 70-098	Implementing and Supporting Microsoft Windows 98

Elective

Choose 2 from this group	
Exam 70-088	Implementing and Supporting Microsoft Proxy Server 2.0
Exam 70-081	Implementing and Supporting Microsoft Exchange Server 5.5
Exam 70-028	Implementing a Database Design on Microsoft SQL Server 7.0
Exam 70-029	System Administration for Microsoft SQL Server 7.0
Exam 70-056	Implementing and Supporting Web Sites Using Microsoft Site Server 3.0
Exam 70-085	Implementing and Supporting Microsoft SNA Server 4.0

* This is not a complete listing—you can still be tested on some earlier versions of these products. However, we have included mainly the most recent versions so that you may test on these versions and thus be certified longer. We have not included any tests that are scheduled to be retired.

new technologies. To obtain an MCSD, an individual must demonstrate the ability to analyze and interpret user requirements; select and integrate products, platforms, tools, and technologies; design and implement code and customize applications; and perform necessary software tests and quality assurance operations.

To become an MCSD, you must pass a total of four exams: three core exams and one elective exam. Each candidate must also choose one of these two desktop application exams—"Designing and Implementing Desktop Applications with Microsoft Visual C++ 6.0" or "Designing and Implementing Desktop Applications with Microsoft Visual Basic 6.0"—*plus* one of these two distributed application exams—"Designing and Implementing Distributed Applications with Microsoft Visual C++ 6.0" or "Designing and Implementing Distributed Applications with Microsoft Visual Basic 6.0."

Note: Microsoft is planning to release desktop application and distributed application exams on Visual J++ and Visual FoxPro in the spring of 1999.

Elective exams cover specific Microsoft applications and languages, including Visual Basic, C++, the Microsoft Foundation Classes, Access, SQL Server, Excel, and more.

➤ **MCDBA (Microsoft Certified Database Administrator)** The MCDBA credential reflects the skills required to implement and administer Microsoft SQL Server databases. To obtain an MCDBA, an individual must demonstrate the ability to derive physical database designs, develop logical data models, create physical databases, create data services by using Transact-SQL, manage and maintain databases, configure and manage security, monitor and optimize databases, and install and configure Microsoft SQL Server.

To become an MCDBA, you must pass a total of five exams: four core exams and one elective exam. The required core exams are "Administering Microsoft SQL Server 7.0," "Designing and Implementing Databases with Microsoft SQL Server 7.0," "Implementing and Supporting Microsoft Windows NT Server 4.0," and "Implementing and Supporting Microsoft Windows NT Server 4.0 in the Enterprise."

The elective exams that you can choose from cover specific uses of SQL Server and include "Designing and Implementing Distributed Applications with Visual Basic 6.0," "Designing and Implementing Distributed Applications with Visual C++ 6.0," "Designing and Implementing Data Warehouses with Microsoft SQL Server 7.0 and Microsoft Decision Support Services 1.0," and two exams that relate to NT: "Internetworking with Microsoft TCP/IP on Microsoft Windows NT 4.0" and "Implementing and Supporting Microsoft Internet Information Server 4.0".

➤ **MCT (Microsoft Certified Trainer)** Microsoft Certified Trainers are individuals who are deemed able to deliver elements of the official Microsoft curriculum, based on technical knowledge and instructional ability. Thus, it is necessary for an individual seeking MCT credentials (which are granted on a course-by-course basis) to pass the related certification exam for a course and complete the official Microsoft training in the subject area, and to demonstrate an ability to teach.

This latter criterion may be satisfied by proving that one has already attained training certification from Novell, Banyan, Lotus, the Santa Cruz Operation, or Cisco, or by taking a Microsoft-sanctioned workshop on instruction. Microsoft makes it clear that MCTs are important cogs in the Microsoft training channels. Instructors must be MCTs before Microsoft will allow them to teach in any of its official training channels, including Microsoft's affiliated Authorized Technical Education Centers (ATECs), Authorized Academic Training Programs (AATPs), and the Microsoft Online Institute (MOLI).

Certification is an ongoing activity. Once a Microsoft product becomes obsolete, MCPs typically have 12 to 18 months in which they may recertify on current product versions. (If individuals do not recertify within the specified time period, their certifications become invalid.) Because technology keeps changing and new products continually supplant old ones, this should come as no surprise.

The best place to keep tabs on the MCP Program and its various certifications is on the Microsoft Web site. The current root URL for the MCP program is **www.microsoft.com/mcp/**. But Microsoft's Web site changes frequently, so if this URL doesn't work, try using the Search tool on Microsoft's site with either "MCP" or the quoted phrase "Microsoft Certified Professional Program" as a search string. You will then find the latest, most accurate information about their certification programs.

Taking A Certification Exam

Alas, testing is not free. Each computer-based MCP exam costs $100, and if you don't pass, you may retest for an additional $100 for each additional try. In the United States and Canada, tests are administered by Sylvan Prometric and by Virtual University Enterprises (VUE). Here's how you can contact them:

- ▶ **Sylvan Prometric** Sign up for a test through the company's Web site at **www.slspro.com**. Or, register by phone at 800-755-3926 (within the United States or Canada) or at 410-843-8000 (outside the United States and Canada).

- ▶ **Virtual University Enterprises** Sign up for a test or get the phone numbers for local testing centers through the Web page at **www.microsoft.com/train_cert/mcp/vue_info.htm**.

To sign up for a test, you need a valid credit card, or contact either company for mailing instructions to send them a check (in the U.S.). Only when payment is verified, or a check has cleared, can you actually register for a test.

To schedule an exam, call the number or visit either of the Web pages at least one day in advance. To cancel or reschedule an exam, you must call before 7 P.M. pacific standard time the day before the scheduled test time (or you may be charged, even if you don't appear to take the test). When you want to schedule a test, have the following information ready:

- ▶ Your name, organization, and mailing address.

- ▶ Your Microsoft Test ID. (Inside the United States, this means your Social Security number; citizens of other nations should call ahead to find out what type of identification number is required to register for a test.)

- ▶ The name and number of the exam you wish to take.

▶ A method of payment. (As we've already mentioned, a credit card is the most convenient method, but alternate means can be arranged in advance, if necessary.)

Once you sign up for a test, you'll be informed as to when and where the test is scheduled. Try to arrive at least 15 minutes early. You must supply two forms of identification—one of which must be a photo ID—to be admitted into the testing room.

All exams are completely closed-book. In fact, you will not be permitted to take anything with you into the testing area, but you will be furnished with a blank sheet of paper and a pen or, in some cases, an erasable plastic sheet and an erasable pen. We suggest that you immediately write down on that sheet of paper all the information you've memorized for the test. In *Exam Cram* books, this information appears on a tear-out sheet inside the front cover of each book. You will have some time to compose yourself, to record this information, and even to take a sample orientation exam before you begin the real thing. We suggest you take the orientation test before taking your first exam, but because they're all more or less identical in layout, behavior, and controls, you probably won't need to do this more than once.

When you complete a Microsoft certification exam, the software will tell you whether you've passed or failed. Results are broken into several topic areas. Even if you fail, we suggest you ask for—and keep—the detailed report that the test administrator should print for you. You can use this report to help you prepare for another go-round, if needed.

If you need to retake an exam, you'll have to schedule a new test with Sylvan Prometric or VUE and pay another $100.

The first time you fail a test, you can retake the test the next day. However, if you fail a second time, you must wait 14 days before retaking that test. The 14-day waiting period remains in effect for all retakes after the first failure.

Tracking MCP Status

As soon as you pass any Microsoft exam other than Networking Essentials, you'll attain Microsoft Certified Professional (MCP) status. Microsoft also generates transcripts that indicate which exams you have passed and your corresponding test scores. You can order a transcript by email at any time by sending an email to mcp@msprograms.com. You can also obtain a copy of your transcript by downloading the latest version of the MCT Guide from the Web site and consulting the section titled "Key Contacts" for a list of telephone numbers and related contacts.

Once you pass the necessary set of exams (one for MCP, six for MCSE, or nine for MCSE+I), you'll be certified. Official certification normally takes anywhere from four to six weeks, so don't expect to get your credentials overnight. When the package for a qualified certification arrives, it includes a Welcome Kit that contains a number of elements:

- An MCP, MCSE, or MCSE+I certificate, suitable for framing, along with a Professional Program Membership card.

- A license to use the MCP logo, which permits you to use that logo in advertisements, promotions, and documents, and on letterhead, business cards, and so on. Along with the license comes an MCP logo sheet, which includes camera-ready artwork. (Note: Before using any artwork, individuals must sign and return a licensing agreement that indicates they'll abide by its terms and conditions.)

- A subscription to *Microsoft Certified Professional Magazine*, which provides ongoing data about testing and certification activities, requirements, and changes to the program.

- A one-year subscription to the Microsoft Beta Evaluation program. This subscription will get you all beta products from Microsoft for the next year. (This does not include developer products. You must join the MSDN program or become an MCSD to qualify for developer beta products.)

Many people believe that the benefits of MCP certification go well beyond the perks that Microsoft provides to newly anointed members of this elite group. We're starting to see more job listings that request or require applicants to have an MCP, MCSE, MCSE+I, and so on, and many individuals who complete the program can qualify for increases in pay and/or responsibility. As an official recognition of hard work and broad knowledge, one of the MCP credentials is a badge of honor in many IT organizations.

How To Prepare For An Exam

Preparing for any Windows NT Server-related test (including Networking Essentials) requires that you obtain and study materials designed to provide comprehensive information about the product and its capabilities that will appear on the specific exam for which you are preparing. The following list of materials will help you study and prepare:

- The exam prep materials, practice tests, and self-assessment exams on the Microsoft Training And Certification Download page (www.microsoft.com/train_cert/download/downld.htm). Find the materials, download them, and use them!

In addition, you'll probably find any or all of the following materials useful in your quest for Networking Essentials expertise:

- **Microsoft Training Kits** Microsoft Press offers a Self-Study Kit for Networking Essentials, now in its second edition. For more information, visit: **http://mspress.microsoft.com/prod/books/1051.htm**. This training kit contains information that you will find useful in preparing for the test (a deluxe multimedia version is also available).

- **Microsoft Readiness Review** Microsoft also offers a CD with practice exams to assess your test readiness for Exam 70-058. Visit **http://mspress.microsoft.com/prod/books/2413.htm** for more details.

- **Microsoft TechNet CD** This monthly CD-based publication delivers numerous electronic titles on topics relevant to Networking Essentials on its Technical Information (TechNet) CD. Its offerings include product facts, technical notes, tools and utilities, and information. A subscription to TechNet costs $299 per year, but it is well worth it. Visit **www.microsoft.com/technet/** and check out the information under the "TechNet Subscription" menu entry for more details.

- **Study Guides** Several publishers—including Certification Insider Press—offer Networking Essentials titles. The Certification Insider Press series includes:

    - The *Exam Cram* series These books give you information about the material you need to know to pass the tests.

    - The *Exam Prep* series These books provide a greater level of detail than the *Exam Cram* books and are designed to teach you everything you need to know from an exam perspective. *MCSE Networking Essentials Exam Prep* is the perfect learning companion to prepare you for Exam 70-058, "Networking Essentials." Look for this book in your favorite bookstores.

    Together, the two series make a perfect pair.

- **Classroom Training** ATECs, AATPs, MOLI, and unlicensed third-party training companies (like Wave Technologies, American Research Group, Learning Tree, Data-Tech, and others) all offer classroom training on Networking Essentials. These companies aim to help you prepare to pass the Networking Essentials test. Although such training runs upwards of $350 per day in class, most of the individuals lucky enough to partake (including your humble authors, who've even taught such courses) find them to be quite worthwhile.

> **Other Publications** You'll find direct references to other publications and resources in this book, but there's no shortage of materials available about Networking Essentials. To help you sift through some of the publications out there, we end each chapter with a "Need To Know More?" section that provides pointers to more complete and exhaustive resources covering the chapter's information. This should give you an idea of where we think you should look for further discussion.

By far, this set of required and recommended materials represents a nonpareil collection of sources and resources for Networking Essentials and related topics. We anticipate that you'll find that this book belongs in this company. In the section that follows, we explain how this book works, and we give you some good reasons why this book counts as a member of the required and recommended materials list.

About This Book

Each topical *Exam Cram* chapter follows a regular structure, along with graphical cues about important or useful information. Here's the structure of a typical chapter:

> **Opening Hotlists** Each chapter begins with a list of the terms, tools, and techniques that you must learn and understand before you can be fully conversant with that chapter's subject matter. We follow the hotlists with one or two introductory paragraphs to set the stage for the rest of the chapter.

> **Topical Coverage** After the opening hotlists, each chapter covers a series of topics related to the chapter's subject title. Throughout this section, we highlight topics or concepts likely to appear on a test using a special Exam Alert layout, like this:

> This is what an Exam Alert looks like. Normally, an Exam Alert stresses concepts, terms, software, or activities that are likely to relate to one or more certification test questions. For that reason, we think any information found offset in Exam Alert format is worthy of unusual attentiveness on your part. Indeed, most of the information that appears on The Cram Sheet appears as Exam Alerts within the text.

Pay close attention to material flagged as an Exam Alert; although all the information in this book pertains to what you need to know to pass the exam, we flag certain items that are really important. You'll find what appears in the meat of each chapter to be worth knowing, too, when preparing for the test. Because this book's material is very condensed, we recommend that you use this book along with other resources to achieve the maximum benefit.

In addition to the Exam Alerts, we have provided tips that will help you build a better foundation for Networking Essentials knowledge. Although the information may not be on the exam, it is certainly related and will help you become a better test-taker.

This is how tips are formatted. Keep your eyes open for these, and you'll become a Networking Essentials guru in no time!

➤ **Practice Questions** Although we talk about test questions and topics throughout each chapter, this section presents a series of mock test questions and explanations of both correct and incorrect answers. We also try to point out especially tricky questions by using a special icon, like this:

Ordinarily, this icon flags the presence of a particularly devious inquiry, if not an outright trick question. Trick questions are calculated to be answered incorrectly if not read more than once, and carefully, at that. Although they're not ubiquitous, such questions make regular appearances on the Microsoft exams. That's why we say exam questions are as much about reading comprehension as they are about knowing your material inside out and backwards.

➤ **Details And Resources** Every chapter ends with a section titled "Need To Know More?". This section provides direct pointers to Microsoft and third-party resources offering more details on the chapter's subject. In addition, this section tries to rank or at least rate the quality and thoroughness of the topic's coverage by each resource. If you find a resource you like in this collection, use it, but don't feel compelled to use all the resources. On the other hand, we recommend only resources we use on a regular basis, so none of our recommendations will be a waste of your time or money (but purchasing them all at once probably represents an expense that many network administrators and would-be MCPs, MCSEs, and MCSE+Is might find hard to justify).

➤ Your authors have also prepared three adaptive exams for Networking Essentials that are available online. To take these practice exams, which should help you prepare even better for the real thing, visit **www.coriolis.com/cip/core4rev/** and follow the instructions from there. Pick the Networking Essentials book, and when prompted for a password, enter the string NEPTOL61982.

The bulk of the book follows this chapter structure slavishly, but there are a few other elements that we'd like to point out. Chapters 12 and 14 each include a sample test that provides a good review of the material presented throughout the book to ensure you're ready for the exam. Chapter 13 is an answer key to the sample test that appears in Chapter 12; likewise, Chapter 15 has the answer key to the sample test in Chapter 14. We suggest you take the first sample test when you think you're ready, and take the second one after studying some more if you don't get at least 70 percent of the questions correct. Additionally, you'll find the Glossary, which explains terms, and an index that you can use to track down terms as they appear in the text.

Finally, the tear-out Cram Sheet attached next to the inside front cover of this *Exam Cram* book represents a condensed and compiled collection of facts and tips that we think you should memorize before taking the test. Because you can dump this information out of your head onto a piece of paper before taking the exam, you can master this information by brute force—you need to remember it only long enough to write it down when you walk into the test room. You might even want to look at it in the car or in the lobby of the testing center just before you walk in to take the test.

How To Use This Book

If you're prepping for a first-time test, we've structured the topics in this book to build on one another. Therefore, some topics in later chapters make more sense after you've read earlier chapters. That's why we suggest you read this book from front to back for your initial test preparation. If you need to brush up on a topic or you have to bone up for a second try, use the index or table of contents to go straight to the topics and questions that you need to study. Beyond helping you prepare for the test, we think you'll find this book useful as a tightly focused reference to some of the most important aspects of Networking Essentials.

Given all the book's elements and its specialized focus, we've tried to create a tool that will help you prepare for—and pass—Microsoft Exam 70-058, "Networking Essentials." Please share your feedback on the book with us, especially if you have ideas about how we can improve it for future test-takers. We'll consider everything you say carefully, and we'll respond to all suggestions.

Send your questions or comments to us at **craminfo@coriolis.com** or to our series editor, Ed Tittel, at **etittel@lanw.com**. He coordinates our efforts and ensures that all questions get answered. Please remember to include the title of the book in your message; otherwise, we'll be forced to guess which book you're writing about. And we don't like to guess—we want to *know*! Also, be sure to check out the Web pages at **www.certificationinsider.com** and **www.lanw.com/examcram**, where you'll find information updates, commentary, and certification information.

Thanks, and enjoy the book!

The MCSE Exam Cram Self-Assessment

Based on recent statistics from Microsoft, as many as 250,000 individuals are at some stage of the certification process but haven't yet received an MCP or other Microsoft certification. We also know that three or four times that number may be considering whether or not to obtain a Microsoft certification of some kind. That's a huge audience!

The reason we included a self-assessment in this *Exam Cram* book is to help you evaluate your readiness to tackle MCSE (and MCSE+I) certification. It should also help you understand what you need to master the topic of this book—namely, Exam 70-058, "Networking Essentials." But before you tackle this self-assessment, let's talk about concerns you may face when pursuing an MCSE, and what an ideal MCSE candidate might look like.

MCSEs In The Real World

In the next section, we describe an ideal MCSE candidate, knowing full well that only a few real candidates will meet this ideal. In fact, our description of that ideal candidate might seem downright scary. But take heart: Although the requirements to obtain an MCSE may seem pretty formidable, they are by no means impossible to meet. However, you should be keenly aware that it does take time, requires some expense, and consumes substantial effort to get through the process.

More than 90,000 MCSEs are already certified, so it's obviously an attainable goal. You can get all the real-world motivation you need from knowing that many others have gone before, so you will be able to follow in their footsteps. If you're willing to tackle the process seriously and do what it takes to obtain the necessary experience and knowledge, you can take—and pass—all the certification tests involved in obtaining an MCSE. In fact, we've designed these *Exam Crams*, and the companion *Exam Preps*, to make it as easy on you as possible to prepare for these exams. But prepare you must!

The same, of course, is true for other Microsoft certifications, including:

➤ MCSE+I, which is like the MCSE certification but requires seven core exams, and two electives drawn from a specific pool of Internet-related topics, for a total of nine exams.

- MCSD, which is aimed at software developers and requires one specific exam, two more exams on client and distributed topics, plus a fourth elective exam drawn from a different, but limited, pool of options.
- Other Microsoft certifications, whose requirements range from one test (MCP or MCT) to many tests (MCP+I, MCP+SB, MCDBA).

The Ideal MCSE Candidate

Just to give you some idea of what an ideal MCSE candidate is like, here are some relevant statistics about the background and experience such an individual might have. Don't worry if you don't meet these qualifications, or don't come that close—this is a far from ideal world, and where you fall short is simply where you'll have more work to do.

- Academic or professional training in network theory, concepts, and operations. This includes everything from networking media and transmission techniques through network operating systems, services, and applications.
- Three-plus years of professional networking experience, including experience with Ethernet, token ring, modems, and other networking media. This must include installation, configuration, upgrade, and troubleshooting experience.
- Two-plus years in a networked environment that includes hands-on experience with Windows NT Server, Windows NT Workstation, and Windows 95 or Windows 98. A solid understanding of each system's architecture, installation, configuration, maintenance, and troubleshooting is also essential.
- A thorough understanding of key networking protocols, addressing, and name resolution, including TCP/IP, IPX/SPX, and NetBEUI.
- A thorough understanding of NetBIOS naming, browsing services, and file and print services.
- Familiarity with key Windows NT-based TCP/IP-based services, including HTTP (Web servers), DHCP, WINS, DNS, plus familiarity with one or more of the following: Internet Information Server (IIS), Index Server, and Proxy Server.
- Working knowledge of NetWare 3.x and 4.x, including IPX/SPX frame formats, NetWare file, print, and directory services, and both Novell and Microsoft client software. Working knowledge of Microsoft's Client Service for NetWare (CSNW), Gateway Service for NetWare (GSNW), the NetWare Migration Tool (NWCONV), and the NetWare Client for Windows (NT, 95, and 98) is essential.

Fundamentally, this boils down to a bachelor's degree in computer science, plus three years of work experience in a technical position involving network design, installation, configuration, and maintenance. We believe that well under half of all certification candidates meet these requirements, and that, in fact, most meet less than half of these requirements—at least, when they begin the certification process. But because all 90,000 people who already have been certified have survived this ordeal, you can survive it too—especially if you heed what our self-assessment can tell you about what you already know and what you need to learn.

Put Yourself To The Test

The following series of questions and observations is designed to help you figure out how much work you must do to pursue Microsoft certification and what kinds of resources you may consult on your quest. Be absolutely honest in your answers, or you'll end up wasting money on exams you're not yet ready to take. There are no right or wrong answers, only steps along the path to certification. Only you can decide where you really belong in the broad spectrum of aspiring candidates.

Two things should be clear from the outset, however:

➤ Even a modest background in computer science will be helpful.

➤ Hands-on experience with Microsoft products and technologies is an essential ingredient to certification success.

Educational Background

1. Have you ever taken any computer-related classes? [Yes or No]

   If Yes, proceed to question 2; if No, proceed to question 4.

2. Have you taken any classes on computer operating systems? [Yes or No]

   If Yes, you will probably be able to handle Microsoft's architecture and system component discussions. If you're rusty, brush up on basic operating system concepts, especially virtual memory, multitasking regimes, user mode versus kernel mode operation, and general computer security topics.

   If No, consider some basic reading in this area. We strongly recommend a good general operating systems book, such as *Operating System Concepts*, by Abraham Silberschatz and Peter Baer Galvin (Addison-Wesley, 1997, ISBN 0-201-59113-8). If this title doesn't appeal to you, check out reviews for other, similar titles at your favorite online bookstore.

3. Have you taken any networking concepts or technologies classes? [Yes or No]

If Yes, you will probably be able to handle Microsoft's networking terminology, concepts, and technologies (brace yourself for frequent departures from normal usage). If you're rusty, brush up on basic networking concepts and terminology, especially networking media, transmission types, the OSI Reference model, and networking technologies such as Ethernet, token ring, FDDI, and WAN links.

If No, you might want to read one or two books in this topic area. The two best books that we know of are *Computer Networks, 3rd Edition*, by Andrew S. Tanenbaum (Prentice-Hall, 1996, ISBN 0-13-349945-6) and *Computer Networks and Internets*, by Douglas E. Comer (Prentice-Hall, 1997, ISBN 0-13-239070-1).

Skip to the next section, "Hands-On Experience."

4. Have you done any reading on operating systems or networks? [Yes or No]

If Yes, review the requirements stated in the first paragraphs after questions 2 and 3. If you meet those requirements, move on to the next section. If No, consult the recommended reading for both topics. A strong background will help you prepare for the Microsoft exams better than just about anything else.

Hands-On Experience

The most important key to success on all of the Microsoft tests is hands-on experience, especially with Windows NT Server and Workstation, plus the many add-on services and BackOffice components around which so many of the Microsoft certification exams revolve. If we leave you with only one realization after taking this self-assessment, it should be that there's no substitute for time spent installing, configuring, and using the various Microsoft products upon which you'll be tested repeatedly and in depth.

5. Have you installed, configured, and worked with:

   ➤ Windows NT Server? [Yes or No]

   If Yes, make sure you understand basic concepts as covered in Exam 70067 and advanced concepts as covered in Exam 70-068. You should also study the TCP/IP interfaces, utilities, and services for Exam 70-059, plus Internet Information Server capabilities for Exam 70-087.

You can download objectives, practice exams, and other information about Microsoft exams from the company's Training and Certification page on the Web at **www.microsoft.com/train_cert/**. Use the "Find an Exam" link to get specific exam info.

The MCSE Exam Cram Self-Assessment xxxiii

If you haven't worked with Windows NT Server, TCP/IP, and IIS (or whatever product you choose for your final elective), you must obtain one or two machines and a copy of Windows NT Server. Then, learn the operating system, and do the same for TCP/IP and whatever other software components on which you'll also be tested.

In fact, we recommend that you obtain two computers, each with a network interface, and set up a two-node network on which to practice. With decent Windows NT-capable computers selling for about $500 to $600 apiece these days, this shouldn't be too much of a financial hardship. You can order a BackOffice Trial Kit from Microsoft, which includes evaluation copies of both Workstation and Server, for under $50 from **www.backoffice.microsoft.com/downtrial/**.

➤ Windows NT Workstation? [Yes or No]

If Yes, make sure you understand the concepts covered in Exam 70-073.

If No, you will want to obtain a copy of Windows NT Workstation and learn how to install, configure, and maintain it. You can use *MCSE NT Workstation 4 Exam Cram* to guide your activities and studies, or work straight from Microsoft's test objectives if you prefer.

For any and all of these Microsoft exams, the Resource Kits for the topics involved are a good study resource. You can purchase softcover Resource Kits from Microsoft Press (search for them at **http://mspress.microsoft.com/**), but they're also included on the TechNet CD subscription (**www.microsoft.com/technet**). We believe that Resource Kits are among the best preparation tools available, along with the *Exam Crams* and *Exam Preps*, that you can use to get ready for Microsoft exams.

You have the option of taking the Window 95 (70-064) exam or the Windows 98 (70-098) exam, instead of Exam 70-073, to fulfill your desktop operating system requirement for the MCSE. Although we don't recommend these others (because studying for Workstation helps you prepare for the Server exams), we do recommend that you obtain Resource Kits and other tools to help you prepare for those exams if you decide to take one or both of them for your own reasons.

6. For any specific Microsoft product that is not itself an operating system (for example, FrontPage 98, SQL Server, and so on), have you installed, configured, used, and upgraded this software? [Yes or No]

If the answer is Yes, skip to the next section. If it's No, you must get some experience. Read on for suggestions on how to do this.

Experience is a must with any Microsoft product exam, be it something as simple as FrontPage 98 or as challenging as Exchange 5.5 or SQL Server 7.0. You can grab a download of BackOffice at **www.backoffice.microsoft.com/downtrial/**; for trial copies of other software, search Microsoft's Web site using the name of the product as your search term.

 If you have the funds, or your employer will pay your way, consider taking a class at a Certified Training and Education Center (CTEC) or at an Authorized Academic Training Partner (AATP). In addition to classroom exposure to the topic of your choice, you get a copy of the software that is the focus of your course, along with a trial version of whatever operating system it needs (usually, NT Server), with the training materials for that class.

Before you even think about taking any Microsoft exam, make sure you've spent enough time with the related software to understand how it may be installed and configured, how to maintain such an installation, and how to troubleshoot that software when things go wrong. This will help you in the exam, and in real life!

Testing Your Exam-Readiness

Whether you attend a formal class on a specific topic to get ready for an exam or use written materials to study on your own, some preparation for the Microsoft certification exams is essential. At $100 a try, pass or fail, you want to do everything you can to pass on your first try. That's where studying comes in.

We have included two practice exams in this book, so if you don't score that well on the first test, you can study more and then tackle the second test. We also have built three adaptive exams that you can take online through the Coriolis Web site at **www.coriolis.com/cip/core4rev/** (password: NEPTOL61982). If you still don't hit a score of at least 70 percent after these tests, you'll want to investigate the other practice test resources we mention in this section.

For any given subject, consider taking a class if you've tackled self-study materials, taken the test, and failed anyway. The opportunity to interact with an instructor and fellow students can make all the difference in the world, if you can afford that privilege. For information about Microsoft classes, visit the Training and Certification page at **www.microsoft.com/train_cert/** (use the "Find a Course" link).

If you can't afford to take a class, visit the Training and Certification page anyway, because it also includes pointers to free practice exams. And even if you can't afford to spend much at all, you should still invest in some low-cost practice exams from commercial vendors, because they can help you assess your readiness to pass a test better than any other tool. All of the following Web sites offer practice exams online for less than $100 apiece (some for significantly less than that):

➤ Beachfront Quizzer at **www.bfq.com/**

➤ Hardcore MCSE at **www.hardcoremcse.com/**

➤ LANWrights at **www.lanw.com/books/examcram/order.htm**

➤ MeasureUp at **www.measureup.com/**

7. Have you taken a practice exam on your chosen test subject? [Yes or No]

If Yes, and you scored 70 percent or better, you're probably ready to tackle the real thing. If your score isn't above that crucial threshold, keep at it until you break that barrier.

If No, obtain all the free and low-budget practice tests you can find (see the list above) and get to work. Keep at it until you can break the passing threshold comfortably.

When it comes to assessing your test readiness, there is no better way than to take a good-quality practice exam and pass with a score of 70 percent or better. When we're preparing ourselves, we shoot for 80-plus percent, just to leave room for the "weirdness factor" that sometimes shows up on Microsoft exams.

Assessing Readiness For Exam 70-058

In addition to the general exam-readiness information in the previous section, there are several things you can do to prepare for the Networking Essentials exam. As you're getting ready for Exam 70-058, visit the MCSE mailing list. Sign up at **www.sunbelt-software.com** (look for the "Subscribe to..." button). This is a great place to ask questions and get good answers, or simply to watch the questions that others ask (along with the answers, of course).

You should also cruise the Web looking for "braindumps" (recollections of test topics and experiences recorded by others) to help you anticipate topics you're likely to encounter on the test. The MCSE mailing list is a good place to ask where the useful braindumps are, or you can check Shawn Gamble's list at **www.commandcentral.com** or Herb Martin's Braindump Heaven at **http://209.207.167.177/**.

 **TIP** When using any braindump, it's OK to pay attention to information about questions. But you can't always be sure that a braindump's author will also be able to provide correct answers. Thus, use the questions to guide your studies, but don't rely on the answers in a braindump to lead you to the truth. Double-check everything you find in any braindump.

Microsoft exam mavens also recommend checking the Microsoft Knowledge Base (available on its own CD as part of the TechNet collection, or on the Microsoft Web site at **http://support.microsoft.com/support/**) for "meaningful technical support issues" that relate to your exam's topics. Although we're not sure exactly what the quoted phrase means, we have also noticed some overlap between technical support questions on particular products and troubleshooting questions on the exams for those products.

One last note: It might seem counterintuitive to talk about hands-on experience in the context of the Networking Essentials exam. But as you review the material for that exam, you'll realize that hands-on experience with networking media and technologies will be invaluable. Surprisingly, you'll also benefit from hands-on experience with Windows NT Server, particularly when it comes to configuring protocols, using Performance Monitor and Network Monitor, working with users, groups, and trust relationships, and so forth. This helps explain why some people believe that unless you have a strong general background in networking, you might be better off taking Networking Essentials last when pursuing an MCSE. The other, more technical exams will help prepare you for the most general, all-embracing exam—namely, the Networking Essentials exam itself.

Onward, Through The Fog!

Once you've assessed your readiness, undertaken the right background studies, obtained the hands-on experience that will help you understand the products and technologies at work, and reviewed the many sources of information to help you prepare for a test, you'll be ready to take a round of practice tests. When your scores come back positive enough to get you through the exam, you're ready to go after the real thing. If you follow our assessment regime, you'll not only know what you need to study, but when you're ready to make a test date at Sylvan or VUE. Good luck!

Microsoft Certification Exams

Terms you'll need to understand:

- √ Radio button
- √ Checkbox
- √ Exhibit
- √ Multiple-choice question formats
- √ Careful reading
- √ Process of elimination
- √ Adaptive tests
- √ Fixed-length tests
- √ Simulations

Techniques you'll need to master:

- √ Assessing your exam-readiness
- √ Preparing to take a certification exam
- √ Practicing (to make perfect)
- √ Making the best use of the testing software
- √ Budgeting your time
- √ Saving the hardest questions until last
- √ Guessing (as a last resort)

Exam taking is not something that most people anticipate eagerly, no matter how well prepared they may be. In most cases, familiarity helps offset test anxiety. In plain English, this means you probably won't be as nervous when you take your fourth or fifth Microsoft certification exam as you'll be when you take your first one.

Whether it's your first exam or your tenth, understanding the details of exam taking (how much time to spend on questions, the environment you'll be in, and so on) and the exam software will help you concentrate on the material rather than on the setting. Likewise, mastering a few basic exam-taking skills should help you recognize—and perhaps even outfox—some of the tricks and snares you're bound to find in some of the exam questions.

This chapter, besides explaining the exam environment and software, describes some proven exam-taking strategies that you should be able to use to your advantage.

Assessing Exam-Readiness

Before you take any more Microsoft exams, we strongly recommend that you read through and take the MCSE Exam Cram Self-Assessment included with this book (it appears just before this chapter, in fact). This will help you compare your knowledge base to the requirements for obtaining an MCSE, and it will also help you identify parts of your background or experience that may be in need of improvement, enhancement, or further learning. If you get the right set of basics under your belt, obtaining Microsoft certification will be that much easier.

Once you've gone through the Self-Assessment, you can remedy those topical areas where your background or experience may not measure up to an ideal certification candidate. But you can also tackle subject matter for individual tests at the same time, so you can continue making progress while you're catching up in some areas.

Once you've worked through an *Exam Cram* and have read the supplementary materials and taken the practice tests, you'll have a pretty clear idea of when you should be ready to take the real exam. We strongly recommend that you keep practicing until your scores top the 70 percent mark; 75 percent would be a good goal to give yourself some margin for error in a real exam situation (where stress will play more of a role than when you practice). Once you hit that point, you should be ready to go. But if you get through both practice exams in this book, and also the sample adaptive exams online (discussed in the Self-Assessment, the Introduction, and later in this chapter) without attaining that score, you should keep taking practice tests and studying the materials until you get there. You'll find more information about other practice test vendors in the Self-Assessment, along with even more pointers on how to study and prepare. But now, on to the exam!

The Exam Situation

When you arrive at the testing center where you scheduled your exam, you'll need to sign in with an exam coordinator. He or she will ask you to show two forms of identification, one of which must be a photo ID. After you've signed in and your time slot arrives, you'll be asked to deposit any books, bags, or other items you brought with you. Then, you'll be escorted into a closed room. Typically, the room will be furnished with anywhere from one to half a dozen computers, and each workstation will be separated from the others by dividers designed to keep you from seeing what's happening on someone else's computer.

You'll be furnished with a pen or pencil and a blank sheet of paper, or, in some cases, an erasable plastic sheet and an erasable pen. You're allowed to write down anything you want on both sides of this sheet. Before the exam, you should memorize as much of the material that appears on The Cram Sheet (in the front of this book) as you can, so you can write that information on the blank sheet as soon as you are seated in front of the computer. You can refer to your rendition of The Cram Sheet anytime you like during the test, but you'll have to surrender the sheet when you leave the room.

Most test rooms feature a wall with a large picture window. This permits the exam coordinator to monitor the room, to prevent exam-takers from talking to one another, and to observe anything out of the ordinary that might go on. The exam coordinator will have preloaded the appropriate Microsoft certification exam—for this book, that's Exam 70-058—and you'll be permitted to start as soon as you're seated in front of the computer.

All Microsoft certification exams allow a certain maximum amount of time in which to complete your work (this time is indicated on the exam by an on-screen counter/clock, so you can check the time remaining whenever you like). The adaptive Networking Essentials exam consists of anywhere from 15 to 50 questions. You can take up to 90 minutes to complete this exam.

All Microsoft certification exams are computer generated and use a multiple-choice format. Although this may sound quite simple, the questions are constructed not only to check your mastery of basic facts and figures about Networking Essentials, but they also require you to evaluate one or more sets of circumstances or requirements. Often, you'll be asked to give more than one answer to a question. Likewise, you might be asked to select the best or most effective solution to a problem from a range of choices, all of which technically are correct. Taking the exam is quite an adventure, and it involves real thinking. This book shows you what to expect and how to deal with the potential problems, puzzles, and predicaments.

Some Microsoft exams, including Networking Essentials, employ more advanced testing capabilities than might immediately meet the eye. Although the questions that appear are still multiple choice, the logic that drives them is more complex than older Microsoft tests, which use a fixed sequence of questions, called a *fixed-length test*. Other exams employ a sophisticated user interface, which Microsoft calls a *simulation*, to test your knowledge of the software and systems under consideration in a more or less "live" environment that behaves just like the original.

For all upcoming exams, and for Networking Essentials already, Microsoft is turning to a well-known technique, called *adaptive testing*, to establish a test-taker's level of knowledge and product competence. Adaptive exams look the same as fixed-length exams, but they discover the level of difficulty at which an individual test-taker can correctly answer questions. At the same time, Microsoft is in the process of converting all of its older fixed-length exams into adaptive exams as well.

On adaptive exams, test-takers with differing levels of knowledge or ability therefore see different sets of questions. Individuals with high levels of knowledge or ability are presented with a smaller set of more difficult questions, whereas individuals with lower levels of knowledge are presented with a larger set of easier questions. Two individuals may answer the same percentage of questions correctly, but the test-taker with a higher knowledge or ability level will score higher because his or her questions are worth more.

Also, the lower-level test-taker will probably answer more questions than his or her more knowledgeable colleague. This explains why adaptive tests, including Networking Essentials, use ranges of values to define the number of questions and the amount of time it takes to complete the test.

Adaptive tests work by evaluating the test-taker's most recent answer. A correct answer leads to a more difficult question (and the test software's estimate of the test-taker's knowledge and ability level is raised). An incorrect answer leads to a less difficult question (and the test software's estimate of the test-taker's knowledge and ability level is lowered). This process continues until the test targets the test-taker's true ability level. The exam ends when the test-taker's level of accuracy meets a statistically acceptable value (in other words, when his or her performance demonstrates an acceptable level of knowledge and ability) or when the maximum number of items has been presented (in which case, the test-taker is almost certain to fail).

Microsoft tests come in one form or the other—either they're fixed-length or they're adaptive. Thus, you must take the test in whichever form it appears;

there's no choosing one form over another. But if anything, it pays off even more to prepare thoroughly for an adaptive exam than for a fixed-length one: The penalties for answering incorrectly are built into the test itself on an adaptive exam, whereas the layout remains the same for a fixed-length test, no matter how many questions you answer incorrectly.

 **The biggest difference between an adaptive test and a fixed-length test is that on a fixed-length test, you can revisit questions after you've read them over one or more times. On an adaptive test, you must answer the question when it's presented and will have no opportunities to revisit that question thereafter. That's why careful preparation for the Networking Essentials exam is so important!**

In the section that follows, you'll learn more about how Microsoft test questions look and how they must be answered.

Exam Layout And Design

Some exam questions require you to select a single answer, whereas others ask you to select multiple correct answers. The following multiple-choice question requires you to select a single correct answer. Following the question is a brief summary of each potential answer and why it is either right or wrong.

Question 1

> Of the following cable types, which can span distances greater than 100 meters, but no more than 185 meters?
>
> ○ a. 10Base2
>
> ○ b. 10Base5
>
> ○ c. 10BaseT
>
> ○ d. 10BaseF

The correct answer is a. Maximum segment length for 10Base2 is limited to 185 meters, less insertion loss from attached devices. Answer b is incorrect because 10Base5 supports a maximum cable length of 500 meters, which exceeds the 185 meter limit in the question. Answer c is incorrect because 10BaseT is limited to a maximum of 100 meters and therefore cannot support segments longer than that. Answer d is incorrect because 10BaseF cable can be up to 2 km long, which is considerably longer than 185 meters.

This sample question format corresponds closely to the Microsoft certification exam format—the only difference on the exam is that questions are not followed by answer keys. To select an answer, you would position the cursor over the radio button next to the answer. Then, click the mouse button to select the answer.

Let's examine a question that requires choosing multiple answers. This type of question provides checkboxes rather than radio buttons for marking all appropriate selections.

Question 2

> Which of the following devices segment network traffic? [Check all correct answers]
>
> ❑ a. Gateway
>
> ❑ b. Bridge
>
> ❑ c. Multiplexer
>
> ❑ d. Router

The correct answers are b and d. Both bridges and routers segment network traffic. The difference between the two is that a bridge can see only MAC layer addresses, whereas a router can see network addresses at the network layer. Routers don't work with nonroutable protocols such as NetBEUI, but bridges can. Either device can segment networks based on the kinds of addresses it can handle. A gateway translates between incompatible protocols or applications but cannot segment a network; thus, answer a is incorrect. A multiplexer can aggregate multiple data streams through a single transmission link but cannot segment a network either; therefore, answer c is also incorrect.

For this type of question, more than one answer is required. As far as the authors can tell (and Microsoft won't comment), such questions are scored as wrong unless all the required selections are chosen. In other words, a partially correct answer does not result in partial credit when the test is scored. For Question 2, you have to check the boxes next to items b and d to obtain credit for a correct answer. Notice that picking the right answers also means knowing why the other answers are wrong!

Although these two basic types of questions can appear in many forms, they constitute the foundation on which all the Microsoft certification exam questions rest. More complex questions include so-called exhibits, which are usually screenshots of some kind of network diagram or topology. For some of these questions, you'll be asked to make a selection by clicking on a checkbox or radio button on the screenshot itself. For others, you'll be expected to use the information displayed therein to guide your answer to the question. If software is involved, familiarity with the underlying utility is your key to choosing the correct answer(s).

Other questions involving exhibits use charts or network diagrams to help document a workplace scenario that you'll be asked to troubleshoot or configure. Careful attention to such exhibits is the key to success. Be prepared to toggle frequently between the exhibit and the question as you work.

Recognizing Your Exam Type: Fixed-Length Or Adaptive

When you begin your exam, the software will tell you the test is adaptive, if in fact the version you're taking is presented as an adaptive test. If your introductory materials fail to mention this, you're probably taking a fixed-length test.

> You'll be able to tell for sure if you are taking an adaptive or fixed-length test by the first question. If it includes a checkbox that lets you mark the question for later review, you're taking a fixed-length test. Adaptive test questions can be visited (and answered) only once, and include no such checkbox.

The Fixed-Length Exam Strategy

A well-known principle when taking fixed-length exams is to first read over the entire exam from start to finish while answering only those questions you feel absolutely sure of. On subsequent passes, you can dive into more complex questions more deeply, knowing how many such questions you have left.

Fortunately, the Microsoft exam software for fixed-length tests makes the multiple-visit approach easy to implement. At the top-left corner of each question is a checkbox that permits you to mark that question for a later visit.

> *Note: Marking questions makes review easier, but you can return to any question by clicking the Forward or Back button repeatedly.*

As you read each question, if you answer only those you're sure of and mark for review those that you're not sure of, you can keep working through a decreasing list of questions as you answer the trickier ones in order.

> There's at least one potential benefit to reading the exam over completely before answering the trickier questions: Sometimes, information supplied in later questions will shed more light on earlier questions. Other times, information you read in later

> questions might jog your memory about Networking Essentials facts, figures, or behavior that also will help with earlier questions. Either way, you'll come out ahead if you defer those questions about which you're not absolutely sure.

Here are some question-handling strategies that apply to fixed-length tests. Use them if you have the chance:

▶ When returning to a question after your initial read-through, read every word again—otherwise, your mind can fall quickly into a rut. Sometimes, revisiting a question after turning your attention elsewhere lets you see something you missed, but the strong tendency is to see what you've seen before. Try to avoid that tendency at all costs.

▶ If you return to a question more than twice, try to articulate to yourself what you don't understand about the question, why the answers don't appear to make sense, or what appears to be missing. If you chew on the subject for awhile, your subconscious might provide the details that are lacking or you might notice a "trick" that will point to the right answer.

As you work your way through the exam, another counter that Microsoft provides will come in handy—the number of questions completed and questions outstanding. For fixed-length tests, it's wise to budget your time by making sure that you've completed one-quarter of the questions one-quarter of the way through the exam period (or the first 14 questions in the first 23 minutes) and three-quarters of them three-quarters of the way through (42 questions in the first 58 minutes).

If you're not finished when 85 minutes have elapsed, use the last 5 minutes to guess your way through the remaining questions. Remember, guessing is potentially more valuable than not answering, because blank answers are always wrong, but a guess may turn out to be right. If you don't have a clue about any of the remaining questions, pick answers at random, or choose all a's, b's, and so on. The important thing is to submit an exam for scoring that has an answer for every question.

At the very end of your exam period, you're better off guessing than leaving questions unanswered.

The Adaptive Exam Strategy

If there's one principle that applies to taking an adaptive test, it could be summed up as "Get it right the first time." You cannot elect to skip a question and move on to the next one when taking an adaptive test, because the testing software uses your answer to the current question to select whatever question it plans to present next. Nor can you return to a question once you've moved on, because the software gives you only one chance to answer the question.

Also, when you answer a question correctly, you are presented with a more difficult question next, to help the software gauge your level of skill and ability. When you answer a question incorrectly, you are presented with a less difficult question, and the software lowers its current estimate of your skill and ability. This continues until the program settles into a reasonably accurate estimate of what you know and can do, and takes you on average through somewhere between 15 and 35 questions as you complete the test.

The good news is that if you know your stuff, you'll probably finish most adaptive tests in 20 to 30 minutes. The bad news is that you must really, really know your stuff to do your best on an adaptive test. That's because some questions are so convoluted, complex, or hard to follow that you're bound to miss one or two, at a minimum, even if you do know your stuff. So the more you know, the better you'll do on an adaptive test, even accounting for the occasionally weird or unfathomable questions that appear on these exams.

If you encounter a question on an adaptive test that you can't answer, you must guess an answer immediately. Because of the way the software works, you may have to suffer for your guess on the next question if you guess right, because you'll get a more difficult question next!

Exam-Taking Basics

The most important advice about taking any exam is this: *Read each question carefully!* Some questions are deliberately ambiguous, some use double negatives, and others use terminology in incredibly precise ways. The authors have taken numerous exams—both practice and live—and in nearly every one have missed at least one question because they didn't read it closely or carefully enough.

Here are some suggestions on how to deal with the tendency to jump to an answer too quickly:

➤ Make sure you read every word in the question. If you find yourself jumping ahead impatiently, go back and start over.

➤ As you read, try to restate the question in your own terms. If you can do this, you should be able to pick the correct answer(s) much more easily.

Above all, try to deal with each question by thinking through what you know about networking technologies, topologies, WAN links, protocols, and so forth—the characteristics, behaviors, facts, and figures involved. By reviewing what you know (and what you've written down on your information sheet), you'll often recall or understand things sufficiently to determine the answer to the question.

Question-Handling Strategies

Based on exams we have taken, some interesting trends have become apparent. For those questions that take only a single answer, usually two or three of the answers will be obviously incorrect, and two of the answers will be plausible—of course, only one can be correct. Unless the answer leaps out at you (if it does, reread the question to look for a trick; sometimes those are the ones you're most likely to get wrong), begin the process of answering by eliminating those answers that are most obviously wrong.

Things to look for in obviously wrong answers include spurious menu choices or utility names, nonexistent software options, and terminology you've never seen. If you've done your homework for an exam, no valid information should be completely new to you. In that case, unfamiliar or bizarre terminology probably indicates a totally bogus answer.

Numerous questions assume that the default behavior of a particular utility is in effect. If you know the defaults and understand what they mean, this knowledge will help you cut through many Gordian knots.

Mastering The Inner Game

In the final analysis, knowledge breeds confidence, and confidence breeds success. If you study the materials in this book carefully and review all the practice questions at the end of each chapter, you should become aware of those areas where additional learning and study are required.

Next, follow up by reading some or all of the materials recommended in the "Need To Know More?" section at the end of each chapter. The idea is to become familiar enough with the concepts and situations you find in the sample questions that you can reason your way through similar situations on a real exam. If you know the material, you have every right to be confident that you can pass the exam.

After you've worked your way through the book, take the practice exams in Chapters 12 and 14. This will provide a reality check and help you identify areas to study further. Make sure you follow up and review materials related to

Microsoft Certification Exams 11

the questions you miss on a practice exam before scheduling a real exam. Only when you've covered all the ground and feel comfortable with the whole scope of the practice exam should you take a real one.

If you take the practice exam and don't score at least 75 percent correct, you'll want to practice further. Microsoft provides free Personal Exam Prep (PEP) exams. The self-assessment exams from the Microsoft Certified Professional Web site's download page (**www.microsoft.com/train_cert/download/downld.htm**) include a practice Networking Essentials exam. If you're more ambitious or better funded, you might want to purchase a practice exam from a third-party vendor.

As a special bonus to readers of this book, your authors have created three adaptive practice exams on Networking Essentials. Coriolis offers these practice exams on its Web site at **www.coriolis.com/cip/core4rev** (the password is NEPTOL61982; consult the Introduction for more information about how to find and take these practice exams).

Armed with the information in this book and with the determination to augment your knowledge, you should be able to pass the Networking Essentials exam. However, you need to work at it, or you'll spend the exam fee more than once before you finally pass. If you prepare seriously, you should do well. Good luck!

Additional Resources

A good source of information about Microsoft certification exams comes from Microsoft itself. Because its products and technologies—and the exams that go with them—change frequently, the best place to go for exam-related information is online.

If you haven't already visited the Microsoft Certified Professional site, do so right now. The MCP home page resides at **www.microsoft.com/mcp** (see Figure 1.1).

The menu options in the left column of the home page point to the most important sources of information in the MCP pages. Here's what to check out:

- ➤ **Certifications** Use this menu entry to read about the various certification programs that Microsoft offers.

- ➤ **Find Exam** Use this menu entry to pull up a search tool that lets you list all Microsoft exams and locate all exams relevant to any Microsoft certification (MCP, MCSE, MCSD, and so on) or those exams that cover a particular product. This tool is quite useful not only to examine the options but also to obtain specific exam preparation information,

12   Chapter 1

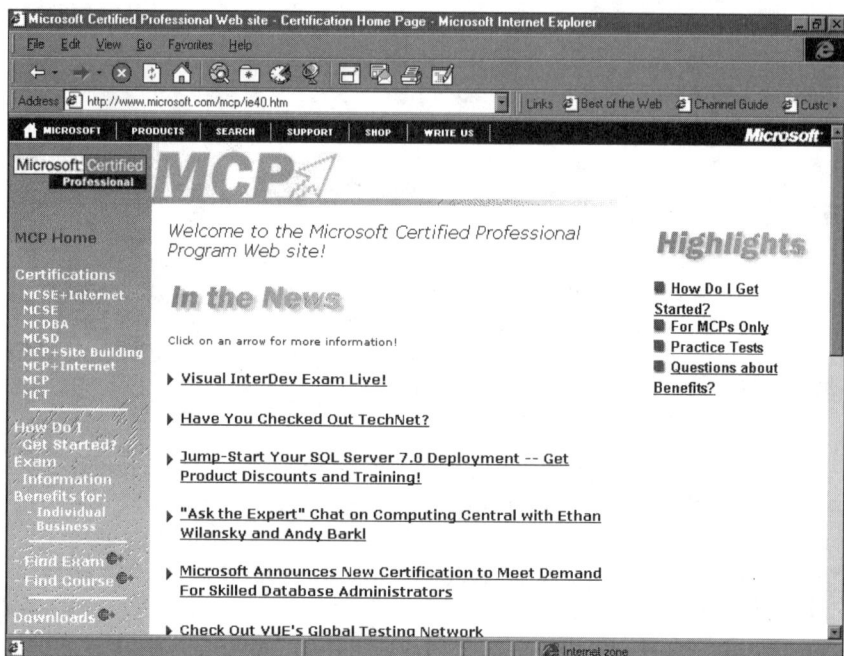

Figure 1.1   The Microsoft Certified Professional home page.

because each exam has its own associated preparation guide. This is Exam 70-058.

➤ **Downloads** Use this menu entry to find a list of the files and practice exams that Microsoft makes available to the public. These include several items worth downloading, especially the Certification Update, the Personal Exam Prep (PEP) exams, various assessment exams, and a general exam study guide. Try to make time to peruse these materials before taking your first exam.

These are just the high points of what's available in the Microsoft Certified Professional pages. As you browse through them—and we strongly recommend that you do—you'll probably find other informational tidbits mentioned that are every bit as interesting and compelling.

Networking Concepts And Terms

Terms you'll need to understand:

- ✓ Local area network (LAN)
- ✓ Wide area network (WAN)
- ✓ Metropolitan area network (MAN)
- ✓ Peer-to-peer network
- ✓ Client/server network

Techniques you'll need to master:

- ✓ Understanding the features, advantages, and disadvantages of peer-to-peer and client/server networks
- ✓ Choosing a network technology that meets your needs
- ✓ Knowing when to implement what kind of network

To have a general understanding of networking, you must have a firm grasp of what a network is, as well as the terms used to describe it. In this chapter, we introduce you to some networking basics, including network components, network design, the types of networks, how communication takes place over a network, and how to set up network resources for users to share. Along the way, we point out some important items that you'll need to know. In addition, we provide additional resources for further study on the topics that we cover throughout this chapter.

Basic Terminology

Here are some basic networking terms and their definitions:

- **Account** Information about a user, which can include the user's account name, the user's password, and the access permissions assigned to the user for network resources.

- **Application server** A specialized server—located on the network—that provides access to client/server applications and to the data belonging to those applications.

- **Central processing unit (CPU)** The collection of circuitry—usually a single chip on most PCs—that supplies the "intelligence" for most computers.

- **Centralized administration** A method for controlling network resource access and managing network setup and configuration data from a single point of access.

- **Client** A networked computer that requests resources or services from another computer, usually a server of some kind.

- **Client/server** A computing model in which certain computers (clients) request services and other computers (called servers) respond to these client requests. Microsoft generally refers to this type of network as a server-based network.

- **Dedicated server** A network computer that acts only as a server and is not intended for regular use as a client machine.

- **Device sharing** The capability to permit users to share access to devices of all kinds, including servers and peripherals such as printers or plotters. This is the principal reason for having a network.

Networking Concepts And Terms   15

- **Directory server** A specialized server that responds to client requests for specific resources and services. In Windows NT parlance, this kind of server is commonly called a "domain controller."

- **Disk space** The amount of space available on a disk drive, generally measured in megabytes (MB).

- **Domain controller** On a Windows NT Server-based network, a directory server that provides access controls over users, accounts, groups, computers, and other network resources.

- **Email** A networked application that permits users to send electronic messages to individual or multiple users, or to named groups of users.

- **Ethernet** A networking technology developed in the early 1970s that is governed by the IEEE 802.3 specifications. It is one of the most popular types of networking technology in use today.

- **File and print server** The most common type of network server. It provides networked file storage and retrieval services and handles print jobs for clients.

- **Group** A named collection of user accounts treated as a single entity, usually created for a specific purpose. (For example, the Production group might be the only named entity permitted to use a design application. By adding or removing users from the Production group, the network administrator controls who may access the application.)

- **Hybrid network** A network that combines the principles of client/server and peer-to-peer networking.

- **IEEE 802 specification** A series of standards created by the Institute of Electrical and Electronics Engineers that standardized network communications.

- **Industry Standard Architecture (ISA)** The bus architecture that supports the 16-bit PC adapter interface that is included in most PCs available on the market today.

- **Internetwork** Literally a network of networks. This term describes a logical network that consists of two or more physical networks. Unlike a WAN, an internetwork may reside in a single location, but because it includes too many computers or spans too much distance, it cannot fit within the scope of a single LAN.

- **Local area network (LAN)** A collection of computers and other connected devices that fits within the scope of a single physical network. LANs provide the building blocks for internetworks and WANs.

- **Locally attached device** A device that is attached directly to a single computer, rather than a device that's available only over the network (called network-attached or server-attached, depending on whether it has a built-in network interface or whether it must be attached directly to a server).

- **Metropolitan area network (MAN)** A network that makes use of WAN technologies to interconnect LANs within a specific geographical region, such as a city.

- **Network administrator** The person responsible for the installation, configuration, and maintenance of a network.

- **Network interface card (NIC)** A PC adapter board that permits a computer to be attached to some sort of network medium. It translates digital information into electrical signals for outgoing network communications and translates incoming signals into their digital equivalents for delivery to the machine.

- **Network medium** The cable, whether metallic or fiber optic, that links computers on a network. This term is also used to describe frequencies used in wireless network communications.

- **Network model/type** The type of networking capabilities available on a network, such as peer-to-peer, server-based, or a combination of the two.

- **Network operating system (NOS)** The specialized software that allows a computer to take part in networked communications and to employ a broad range of networking services. Windows NT is a network operating system available in Workstation and Server versions; Windows 95 and Windows For Workgroups also include built-in network client and peer-to-peer capabilities.

- **Network protocol** The set of rules used for communicating across a network. A common protocol is required for any two networked devices to be able to communicate successfully.

- **Network resources** Devices, information, and services that are available across a network.

- **Operating system (OS)** The basic program running on any computer that controls the underlying system and hardware. It is required for any computer to work.

- **Password** A privately selected string of letters, numbers, and other characters (which should be hard to guess) used to identify a particular user and to control access to protected resources.

- **Peer-to-peer network** A type of network in which all connected computers can be a client and/or a server to other computers on the network.

- **Peripheral device** In networking context, a device, such as a printer or a modem, that can be shared across a network.

- **Peripheral Component Interconnect (PCI)** A 32-bit PC bus that offers higher performance and more sophisticated capabilities than the 16-bit ISA bus.

- **Random access memory (RAM)** The memory cards or chips installed in a PC that provide working space for the CPU to use when running applications, providing network services, and so on. As far as network servers go, the more RAM you have, the better.

- **Request-response** How the client/server relationship works. A request from a client leads to some kind of response from a server (usually, the service or data requested, but sometimes an error message or a denial of service based on access permissions).

- **Security** The set of access controls and permissions that are used to determine if a server can grant a service or resource request from a client.

- **Server** The computer that responds to service or resource requests from network clients.

- **Server-based network** A type or model of network in which a networked server provides services and resources to client computers and manages and controls access to those services and resources.

- **Sharing** The way resources are made available to the network. The main reason for establishing a network is to share resources.

- **Specialized server** A type of special-function server. It can be an application server, a communications server, a directory server or domain controller, a fax server, a mail server, or a Web server, among other roles.

- **Standalone** Describes a computer, device, or application that's not attached to a network.

- **User** The person who uses a computer, whether standalone or networked.

- **Wide area network (WAN)** A collection of interconnected networks in which a third-party communications carrier is used to transmit communications between networks. WAN links can be expensive because they are charged on the basis of bandwidth, so few WAN links support the same bandwidth as that available on most LANs.

- **Workgroup model** How Microsoft refers to a peer-to-peer network that includes one or more Windows-based computers.

With these terms in mind, let's move on to discuss some networking fundamentals.

What Is A Network?

Put simply, a network is a connection between at least two computers so that they can share resources. Although most networks are more complex than this two-computer scenario, all networks are based on the concept of sharing. There's actually a great deal of technology involved when one computer connects to and communicates with another. In addition, there are many types of physical connections and related software to consider. In the following sections, we discuss some fundamental concepts behind all networks and explain what kinds of network models are appropriate for various business environments.

LAN, WAN, And MAN

There are three types of networks: local area networks (LANs), wide area networks (WANs), and metropolitan area networks (MANs). A LAN is a collection of networked computers that reside within a small physical region, such as an office building. A WAN can connect networks across the globe; a third-party communications carrier is generally used to transmit communications between networks. MANs use WAN technologies to interconnect LANs within a specific geographical region, such as a city.

In addition to these distinctions, a LAN, WAN, or MAN can be peer-to-peer networks, client/server networks, or hybrid networks (networks that make use of both client/server and peer-to-peer technologies). The following sections discuss these topics in detail.

Peer-To-Peer Networks

Computers on a peer-to-peer network can act as both a client and a server. Because all computers on this type of network are peers, peer-to-peer networks have no centralized control over shared resources. Any individual machine can share its resources with any computer on the same network, however and whenever it chooses to do so. The peer relationship also means that no one computer has higher access priority, nor heightened responsibility to provide shared resources.

Every user on a peer-to-peer network is also a network administrator. That is, each user controls access to the resources that reside on his or her machine. It is possible to give all others unlimited access to local resources, or to grant only restricted (or no) access to others. Likewise, each user decides whether other users can access resources simply by requesting them, or whether the resources are password-protected.

Due to the flexibility and individual discretion regarding network resources on a peer-to-peer network, institutionalized chaos is the norm for peer-to-peer networks. For these reasons, security should be a major concern. You can set up a peer-to-peer network where resources are collected into workgroups, but without network-wide security. In a workgroup setting, users who know the right passwords can access resources; those who do not, can't.

This setup may be workable on small networks, but it might also require that users know—and remember—a different password for every shared resource on a network. In a peer-to-peer environment, as the number of users and resources grows, the network can become unworkable. This is not because the network can't function properly, but because users can't cope with the complexity involved.

In addition, most peer-to-peer networks consist of collections of typical end-user PCs that are linked by a common network medium. These types of machines are not designed to act as network servers; therefore, the network can easily bog down as more users try to access resources on any particular machine. Additionally, a user whose machine is being accessed across the network has to put up with reduced performance while that machine services network information requests. For example, if a user's machine has a network-accessible printer attached to it, that machine will slow down every time other users send a job to that printer. Although this doesn't affect the other users, it may bother the user working at the slowed machine.

It is also difficult to organize data on a peer-to-peer network. When every network computer can be a server, it is difficult for users to keep track of what information is on which machine. If each of 10 users is responsible for a collection of documents, any user might have to search through files on all 10 machines to find a particular file. As networks grow, the decentralized nature of this type of network makes locating resources increasingly difficult, as the number of peers to be checked increases. Also, decentralization makes backing up data tricky, because instead of backing up a centralized data repository, you must back up each network computer to protect shared data.

At first glance, it may seem that all of these issues and added complexity make peer-to-peer networks unworthy of consideration. Keep in mind, however, that peer-to-peer networks offer some powerful inducements, particularly for smaller organizations and networks. Peer-to-peer networks are the easiest and cheapest kind of network to install. Most peer-to-peer networks require only an operating system, such as Windows 98 or Windows For Workgroups, on the machines, along with NICs and a common network medium. Once the computers are connected, users can immediately begin sharing information and resources.

Here are some benefits of peer-to-peer networks:

➤ They are easy to install and configure.

➤ Individual machines do not depend on a dedicated server.

➤ Users are able to control their own shared resources.

➤ This type of network is inexpensive to purchase and operate.

➤ You don't need any equipment or software other than an operating system, NICs, and cables.

➤ It is not necessary to have an employee act as a dedicated administrator to run the network.

➤ This type of network is well suited for networks with 10 or fewer users.

As with anything, peer-to-peer networks have their drawbacks as well:

➤ You can only apply network security to one resource at a time.

Networking Concepts And Terms

- Users might have to remember as many passwords as there are shared resources.
- You must perform individual backups on each machine to protect all shared data.
- When someone accesses shared resources, the machine where the resource resides suffers a performance hit.
- There is no centralized organizational scheme to locate or control access to data.

Client/Server Networks

Although the term "client/server" commonly describes network servers, Microsoft prefers the term "server-based" to describe them. In simple terms, a server is a machine whose only function is to respond to client requests. Servers are seldom operated directly by someone—and then usually only to install, configure, or manage its services. In general, a server is a combination of specialized software and hardware that provides services on a network to other computers (workstations) or to other processes.

Server-based networks rely on special-purpose computers called servers that provide centralized repositories for network resources and incorporate centralized security and access controls. In comparison, peer-to-peer networks have no centralized security or maintenance functions.

There are a number of reasons to implement a server-based network, including centralized control over network resources through the use of network security and control through the server's configuration and setup. From a hardware standpoint, server computers typically have faster CPUs, more memory, larger disk drives, and extra peripherals—such as tape drives and CD-ROM jukeboxes—compared to client machines. Servers are also built to quickly and efficiently handle multiple requests for shared resources. Servers are usually dedicated to servicing network client requests. In addition, physical security—access to the machine itself—is a key component of network security. Therefore, it's important for servers to be located in special, controlled-access rooms that are separate from general-access office areas.

Server-based networks also provide centralized verification of user accounts and passwords. Windows NT, for example, uses the domain model concept for management of users, groups, and machines, and for control of network resource access. Before a user can access network resources, he must provide his name and password to a domain controller, a server that checks account names and passwords against a database of such information. The domain controller will only allow valid account and password combinations to access certain resources. Also, only network administrators can modify the security information in the domain controller's database. This approach provides centralized security, and it permits you to manage resources with varying degrees of control, depending on their importance, sensitivity, or location.

Unlike the peer-to-peer model, server-based networks typically require only a single login to the network itself, which reduces the number of passwords users must remember. In addition, network resources like files and printers are easier to find because they are generally located on specific servers, not on individual user machines across the network. The concentration of network resources on a smaller number of servers also makes data resources easier to back up and maintain.

Unlike peer-to-peer networks, server-based networks are much more scaleable. As the network population grows, peer-to-peer networks bog down seriously and can become sluggish and unmanageable. In comparison, server-based networks can handle anywhere from a handful of users and resources to tens of thousands of users and geographically dispersed resources. In other words, a server-based network can grow as a company grows, and not hold it back.

Like the peer-to-peer network model, server-based networks also have disadvantages. Foremost on the list are the additional costs involved in operating such a network. Server-based networks need one or more high-powered—and therefore more expensive—computers to run special-purpose (also expensive) server software. In addition, server-based networks require someone knowledgeable to run them. Training employees to acquire the necessary skills to manage a server-based network, or hiring an already-trained network administrator, also adds to the costs of operating such networks.

There are other negative aspects of server-based networks. Centralization of resources and control does simplify access, control, and aggregation of resources, but it also introduces a single point of failure on networks. If the server is not operational, a server-based network is not a network at all. On networks with more than one server, loss of any single server means loss of all resources associated with that server. Also, if the server that goes down is the only source of access control information for a certain set of users, those users can't access the network, either.

Networking Concepts And Terms

Here are some benefits of server-based networks:

➤ They provide centralized user accounts, security, and access controls, which simplifies network administration.

➤ More powerful equipment means more efficient access to network resources as well.

➤ Users only have to remember a single password for network login, which allows them to access all resources that they have permission to access.

➤ Server-based networks are scalable.

Now, let's take a look at some server-based networking cons:

➤ A server failure can render a network unusable; at best, it results in loss of network resources.

➤ Such networks require an expert staff to manage the complex, special-purpose server software, which adds to the overall cost.

➤ Costs also increase due to the requirements of dedicated hardware and specialized software.

Choosing A Network

Choosing a network depends on the circumstances. You should select a peer-to-peer network only when all of the following conditions apply:

➤ There are no more than 10 network users (preferably, no more than 5).

➤ All machines on the network are in close enough proximity to fit within a single LAN.

➤ Budget considerations require an inexpensive solution.

➤ You don't need any specialized servers (for example, fax servers, communication servers, or application servers).

On the other hand, a server-based network makes sense when one or more of the following conditions are true:

➤ More than 10 users must share network access.

➤ You require centralized control, security, resource management, or backup.

▶ You require access to specialized servers, or there is a heavy demand for network resources.

▶ You are using an internetwork or you require WAN access.

When a network has more than 5 but less than 10 users, budget limitations often incline organizations toward peer-to-peer. But if the organization is expecting to grow, or specialized network servers sound appealing, it's best to begin with a server-based network.

Practice Questions

Question 1

> Which of the following are true about a server-based network? [Check all correct answers]
> - a. There is centralized control of network resources.
> - b. All networked computers act as both clients and servers.
> - c. You can implement centralized security to protect network resources.
> - d. It can grow as an organization grows.

Answers a, c, and d are all correct. Server-based networks do provide centralized control and security for network resources; therefore, answers a and c are correct. Answer d is also correct; server-based networks are quite scalable. Answer b is incorrect because this describes behavior of a peer-to-peer network.

Question 2

> Which of the following are advantages of a large-scale server-based network? [Check all correct answers]
> - a. Ease of administration
> - b. Centralized backups of network data
> - c. Inexpensive to implement
> - d. Increased performance

Answers a, b, and d are all correct. Server-based networks are easier to administer than peer-to-peer implementations, centralized backups are allowed, and there is increased network performance due to the power of the hardware involved. Answer c is incorrect; server-based networks can be very expensive, especially in a large-scale setting.

Question 3

> Which of the following is a drawback of peer-to-peer networking?
>
> ○ a. A server failure can render a network unusable; at best, it results in loss of network resources.
>
> ○ b. Costs increase due to the requirements of dedicated hardware and specialized software.
>
> ○ c. When you access shared resources, the machine where the resource resides suffers a performance hit.
>
> ○ d. An expert staff is needed to manage the complex, special-purpose server software, which adds to the overall cost.

Answer c is the correct choice; machines that house network resources do take a performance hit when that resource is accessed. Answer a is incorrect; if a machine in a peer-to-peer environment goes down, only the resources on that particular machine are unavailable and the rest of the network continues to work. Answer b is incorrect; this is a drawback of a server-based network. Answer d is incorrect; peer-to-peer networks are easy to implement and no specialized staff is needed for full-time support.

Question 4

> Which of the following describes a local area network?
>
> ○ a. Connects networks across the globe
>
> ○ b. A collection of networked computers that reside within a small physical region
>
> ○ c. Requires the use of a third-party communications carrier to handle connections
>
> ○ d. Uses WAN technologies to interconnect networks within a specific geographical region

Answer b is correct; LANs are limited to a small physical region. Answer a is incorrect; LANs are generally limited to a single building. Answers c and d are incorrect; they discuss requirements of WANs and MANs, respectively.

Question 5

> Which of the following terms describes the specialized software that gives a computer the ability to take part in networked communications?
>
> ○ a. Ethernet
> ○ b. NOS
> ○ c. CPU
> ○ d. ISA

Answer b is correct; the NOS is what enables a computer to communicate across a network. Answer a is incorrect; Ethernet is a network architecture, not an application. Answer c is incorrect; the CPU is hardware, not software. Answer d is incorrect; ISA is a bus architecture that supports the 16-bit adapter interface cards in many PCs.

Need To Know More?

 Chellis, James, Charles Perkins, and Matthew Strebe: *MCSE: Networking Essentials Study Guide, 2nd Edition*. Sybex Network Press, San Francisco, CA, 1998. ISBN 0-7821-2220-5. Chapter 1, "An Introduction to Networks," discusses network types at length.

 Microsoft Press: *Networking Essentials, 2nd Edition*. Redmond, WA, 1997. ISBN 1-57231-527-X. Unit 1, Lesson 2, "The Two Major Types of Networks," discusses all of the topics in this chapter in great detail.

 Search the TechNet CD-ROM (or its online version through **www.microsoft.com**) using the keywords "client/server," "peer-to-peer," and "network design."

Network Protocols

Terms you'll need to understand:

- √ OSI Reference Model
- √ Application layer
- √ Presentation layer
- √ Session layer
- √ Transport layer
- √ Network layer
- √ Data Link layer
- √ Physical layer
- √ Media Access Control sublayer
- √ Logical Link Control sublayer
- √ IEEE 802 specifications
- √ Redirectors
- √ Protocols: NetBEUI, TCP/IP, XNS, AppleTalk, APPC, X.25, and HDLC

Techniques you'll need to master:

- √ Interpreting the OSI Reference Model and how it relates to protocol suites
- √ Exploring the IEEE's 802 network specifications
- √ Understanding and using redirectors
- √ Comprehending and implementing protocols

To enable networked communications, computers must be able to transmit data among one another. Protocols, agreed-upon methods of communication, make this possible. In this chapter, we discuss the various network protocols and how they make networked communications possible.

In addition, we introduce you to the standards upon which network protocols are based: the Open Systems Interconnection (OSI) Reference Model and the IEEE 802 standards. The OSI Reference Model was developed by the International Standards Organization (ISO) to provide a standardized method for computers to communicate; the Institute of Electrical and Electronic Engineers (IEEE) 802 standards further expanded this model. As always, we provide pointers along the way that will assist you in preparing for the Networking Essentials exam and give you additional resources should you need more details on the topics we discuss in this chapter.

The OSI Reference Model

As the concept of networking became more widespread in the business world, the idea of being able to connect networks and disparate systems became a necessity. For this type of communication to take place, however, there needed to be a standard design. The solution came in 1978 when the ISO released an architecture that would achieve this goal. These specifications were revised in 1984 and became international standards for networked communication. It is important for network administrators to know the history and understand the function of this specification, which is called the OSI Reference Model.

The OSI model presents a layered approach to networking. Each layer of the model handles a different portion of the communications process. By separating such communications into layers, the OSI model simplified how network hardware and software work together. It also eased troubleshooting woes by providing a specific method for how components should function. Now that we know why the model was implemented, let's move on to explore just how it works.

Keep in mind that the OSI model is a completely conceptual reference. Later in the chapter, we'll discuss how protocol suites map to the model to provide network communications.

Learning The Layers

The OSI Reference Model divides networking into seven layers, as shown in Figure 3.1. These layers are described as follows:

- **Application layer** Provides a set of interfaces for applications to use to gain access to networked services.

- **Presentation layer** Converts data into a generic format for network transmission; for incoming messages, it converts data from this format into a format that the receiving application can understand.

- **Session layer** Enables two parties to hold ongoing communications—called sessions—across a network.

- **Transport layer** Manages the transmission of data across a network.

- **Network layer** Handles addressing messages for delivery, as well as translates logical network addresses and names into their physical counterparts.

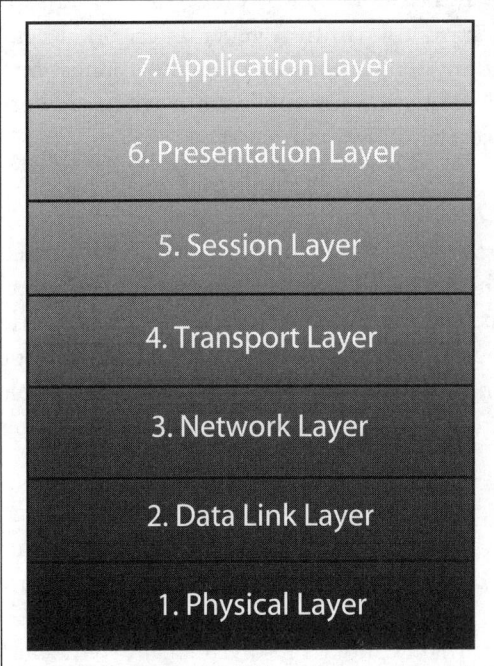

Figure 3.1 The OSI model separates networking functions into seven layers.

- **Data Link layer** Handles special data frames between the Network layer and the Physical layer.
- **Physical layer** Converts bits into signals for outgoing messages and converts signals into bits for incoming messages.

> It is essential that you know the layers of the OSI model. A great instructor once provided the following mnemonic, which helps you remember the order of these layers: From the bottom up, take the first letter of each layer (PDNTSPA) and assign a more approachable phrase such as "Please Do Not Throw Sausage Pizza Away."

In the following sections, we'll examine each layer of the OSI Reference Model in more detail.

Layer 7: The Application Layer

The Application layer is referred to as the top layer of the OSI Reference Model. This layer allows access to network services—such as networked file transfer, message handling, and database query processing—that support applications directly. This layer also controls general network access, transmission of data from sending applications to receiving applications, and provides error and status information for applications when network errors interfere with service access or delivery.

Layer 6: The Presentation Layer

The Presentation layer manages data-format information for networked communications. Also called the network's translator, it converts outgoing messages into a generic format that can be transmitted across a network. Then, it converts incoming messages from that generic format into one that makes sense to the receiving application. This layer is also responsible for protocol conversion, data encryption and decryption, and graphics commands.

Information sent by the Presentation layer may sometimes be compressed to reduce the amount of data to be transferred (this also requires decompression on the receiving end). It is at this layer that a special software facility known as a redirector operates. The redirector intercepts requests for service and redirects requests that cannot be resolved locally to the networked resource that can handle them.

Layer 5: The Session Layer

The Session layer allows two networked resources to hold ongoing communications, called a session, across a network. In other words, applications on each end of the session are able to exchange data for the duration of the session. This layer manages session setup, information or message exchanges, and tear-down when the session ends. It is also responsible for identification that allows only designated parties to participate in the session, and handles security services to control access to session information.

The Session layer provides synchronization services between tasks at each end of the session. This layer places checkpoints in the data stream, so if communications fail, only data after the most recent checkpoint will need to be retransmitted. The Session layer also manages issues such as who may transmit data at a certain time and for how long, and maintains a connection through transmission of messages that keep the connection active. These messages are designed to keep the connection from being closed down due to inactivity.

Layer 4: The Transport Layer

The Transport layer manages the flow control of data between parties across a network. It does this by segmenting long streams of data into chunks that adhere to the maximum packet size for the networking medium in use. The layer also provides error checks to guarantee error-free data delivery and resequences chunks back into the original data when it is received. In addition, the Transport layer provides acknowledgment of successful transmissions and is responsible for requesting retransmission if some packets arrive with errors.

Layer 3: The Network Layer

The Network layer addresses messages for delivery and translates logical network addresses and names into their physical equivalents. This layer also decides how to route transmissions between computers. To decide how to get data from one point to the next, the Network layer considers other factors, such as quality of service information, alternative routes, and delivery priorities. This layer also handles packet switching, data routing, and network congestion control.

Layer 2: The Data Link Layer

The Data Link layer handles special data frames between the Network and Physical layers. At the receiving end, this layer packages raw data from the

Physical layer into data frames for delivery to the Network layer. A data frame is the basic unit for network traffic as data is sent across the network medium. It is a highly structured format in which data from the upper layers is placed for transmission and from which data is extracted upon receipt and passed on to the upper layers.

Layer 1: The Physical Layer

The Physical layer converts bits into signals for outgoing messages and converts signals into bits for incoming ones. This layer arranges the transmission of a data frame's bits when they are dispatched across the network. The Physical layer manages the interface between a computer and the network medium and tells the driver software and the network interface what needs to be sent across the medium.

That concludes the layer-by-layer discussion of the OSI Reference Model. Now, let's take a look at how the IEEE 802 specifications further standardized network communication.

IEEE 802 Specifications

At roughly the same time the OSI model was developed, the IEEE published the 802 specifications, which defined standards for the physical components of a network. These components, namely network interface cards (NICs) and network media, are also accounted for in the Physical and Data Link layers of the OSI model. The 802 specs defined how network adapters access and transmit information over the network cable.

The 802 specifications fall into 12 distinct categories, each of which has its own number, as described in the following:

- **802.1** Internetworking
- **802.2** Logical Link Control (LLC)
- **802.3** Carrier-Sense Multiple Access with Collision Detection (CSMA/CD) LANs (Ethernet)
- **802.4** Token Bus LAN
- **802.5** Token Ring LAN
- **802.6** Metropolitan Area Network (MAN)
- **802.7** Broadband Technical Advisory Group
- **802.8** Fiber Optic Technical Advisory Group

Network Protocols 35

- **802.9** Integrated Voice and Data Networks
- **802.10** Network Security Technical Advisory Group
- **802.11** Wireless Networks
- **802.12** Demand Priority Access LAN, 100VG-AnyLAN

As previously mentioned, the 802 specification actually expanded the OSI Reference Model. This expansion is at the Physical and Data Link layers, which define how more than one computer can access the network without causing interference with other computers on the network. The 802 standards provide more detail at these layers by breaking the Data Link layer into the following sublayers (see Figure 3.2):

- **Logical Link Control (LLC)** For error correction and flow control
- **Media Access Control (MAC)** For access control

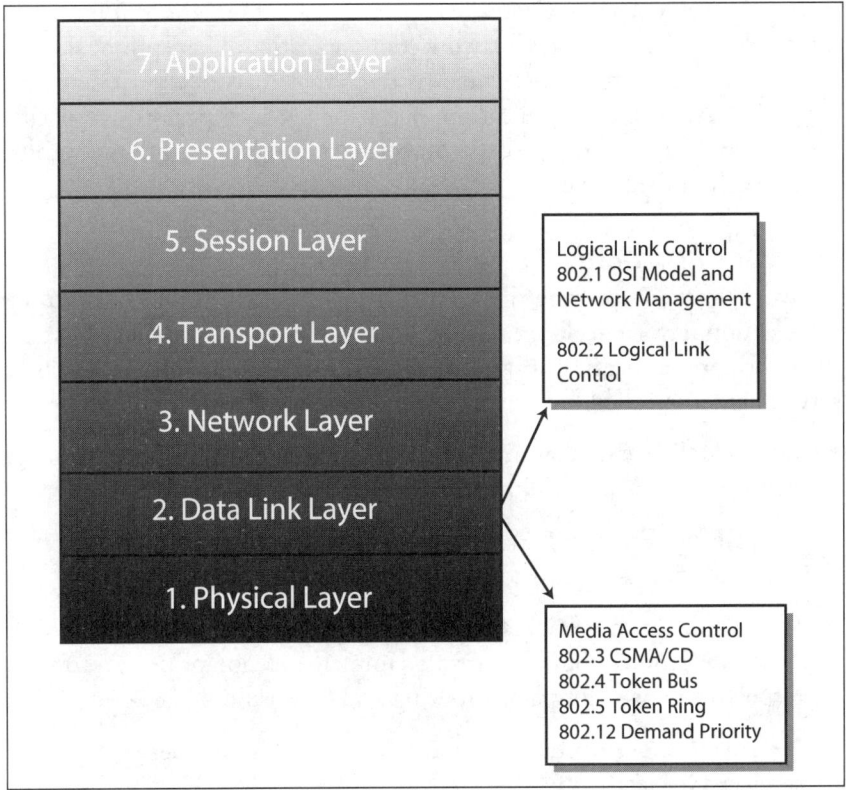

Figure 3.2 The 802 specs within the OSI model.

The Logical Link sublayer (as defined by 802.2) controls data-link communication, and defines the use of logical interface points, called Service Access Points (SAPs), that other computers can use to transfer information from the LLC sublayer to the upper OSI layers.

The Media Access Control sublayer provides shared access for multiple NICs with the Physical layer. The MAC has direct communication with a computer's NIC and is responsible for ensuring error-free data transmission between computers on a network.

This concludes the theoretical discussion of network models. In the following section, we'll discuss how protocol suites are mapped to this model to provide networked communications.

Up And Down The Protocol Stack

In general, most protocols follow the guidelines established by the OSI model. A protocol suite, also called a stack, is a combination of protocols that work together to achieve network communication. These protocol suites are generally broken up into three sections that map to the OSI model: network, transport, and application. Because each layer performs a specific function and has its own rules, a protocol stack often has a different protocol for each of these layers.

Network Protocols

Network protocols provide the following services: addressing and routing information, error checking, requesting retransmissions, and establishing rules for communicating in a particular networking environment. These services are also called link services. Some popular network protocols are:

➤ **DDP (Delivery Datagram Protocol)** Apple's data transport protocol that is used in AppleTalk

➤ **IP (Internet Protocol)** Part of the TCP/IP protocol suite that provides addressing and routing information

➤ **IPX (Internetwork Packet Exchange) and NWLink** Novell's NetWare protocol (and Microsoft's implementation of this protocol, respectively) used for packet routing and forwarding

➤ **NetBEUI** Developed by IBM and Microsoft, it provides transport services for NetBIOS

Transport Protocols

In addition, protocol suites also contain transport protocols, which are responsible for ensuring reliable data delivery between computers. Some popular transport protocols are:

- **ATP (AppleTalk Transaction Protocol) and NBP (Name Binding Protocol)** AppleTalk's session and data transport protocols

- **NetBIOS/NetBEUI** NetBIOS establishes and manages communications between computers; NetBEUI provides data transport services for that communication

- **SPX (Sequenced Packet Exchange) and NWLink** Novell's connection-oriented protocol that is used to guarantee data delivery (and Microsoft's implementation of this protocol)

- **TCP (Transmission Control Protocol)** The portion of the TCP/IP protocol suite that is responsible for reliable delivery of data

Application Protocols

Finally, there are application protocols, which are responsible for application-to-application services. Some popular application protocols are:

- **AFP (AppleTalk File Protocol)** Apple's remote file management protocol

- **FTP (File Transfer Protocol)** Another member of the TCP/IP protocol suite that is used to provide file transfer services

- **NCP (NetWare Core Protocol)** Novell's client shells and redirectors

- **NFS (Network File System)** A client/server file system protocol primarily used to share directories with Unix systems

- **SMB (Server Message Block)** A protocol that sits above NetBEUI and NetBIOS that defines and formats commands for information passing between networked computers

- **SMTP (Simple Mail Transport Protocol)** A member of the TCP/IP protocol suite that is responsible for transferring email

- **SNMP (Simple Network Management Protocol)** A TCP/IP protocol that is used to manage and monitor network devices

That's it for our discussion of how protocol suites map to the established network standards. We now provide a more detailed look at the protocol suites.

Protocols

As already mentioned, computers must agree on a protocol to be used for any type of communication to take place. The following sections provide more detail on the more common protocols in use today.

NetBEUI

NetBEUI is a simple Network layer transport protocol that was developed to support NetBIOS networks. Like NetBIOS, NetBEUI is not routable, so it really has no place on an enterprise network. NetBEUI is the fastest transport protocol available to Windows NT. It's great for fast transmission, but is not usable across routed networks. Benefits of NetBEUI include: speed, good error protection, ease of implementation, and low memory overhead. Some disadvantages are: It's not routable, it has very little support for cross-platform applications, and it has very few troubleshooting tools available.

TCP/IP

TCP/IP is the most widely used protocol suite in networking today. This is due in part to the vast growth of the global Internet. TCP/IP is able to span wide areas and is very flexible. In addition, it provides cross-platform support, routing capabilities, as well as support for the Simple Network Management Protocol (SNMP), the Dynamic Host Configuration Protocol (DHCP), the Windows Internet Name Service (WINS), the Domain Name Service (DNS), and a host of other useful protocols. However, TCP/IP's rich set of features are provided at the expense of additional overhead, which may make it too cumbersome for some networks or applications.

AppleTalk

It should come as no surprise that the AppleTalk protocol is used for communication with Macintosh computers. By enabling AppleTalk, you allow Mac clients to store and access files located on a Windows NT Server, print to Windows NT printers, and vice versa. An item of note: You must first install the Windows NT Services For Macintosh before you can install AppleTalk. Also, Mac support is only available from an NTFS partition.

APPC

The Advanced Program-to-Program Communication (APPC) protocol, developed by IBM, is a peer-to-peer protocol used in IBM's Systems Network Architecture (SNA) for use on AS/400-series computers.

X.25

X.25 is a set of wide-area protocols that are used in packet-switching networks. It was created to connect remote terminals to mainframes. Although many other wide-area communications types are available in the United States, X.25 is still widely used in Europe.

HDLC

High-level Data Link Control (HDLC) is a flexible, bit-oriented data link protocol that is based on IBM's Synchronous Data Link Control (SDLC). It has been standardized by the ISO. HDLC can support half- or full-duplex transmission, circuit- or packet-switched networks, peer-to-peer or client/server networks, and transmission over cable or wireless media.

XNS

The Xerox Network System (XNS) was created by Xerox for use in Ethernet networks. XNS is the basis for Novell's IPX/SPX, but it is seldom found in today's networks.

Practice Questions

Question 1

> Which of the following IEEE 802 specifications provides details on network security?
>
> ○ a. 802.8
>
> ○ b. 802.9
>
> ○ c. 802.10
>
> ○ d. 802.11

Answer c is correct because the 802.10 provides information on network security. The 802.8 spec details fiber optic networks. Therefore, answer a is incorrect. Answer b is incorrect because 802.9 details integrated voice and data networks. The 802.11 specification details wireless networks. Therefore, answer d is incorrect.

Question 2

> Which layer of the OSI model converts data into a generic format for network transmission?
>
> ○ a. Transport layer
>
> ○ b. Session layer
>
> ○ c. Presentation layer
>
> ○ d. Application layer

Answer c is the correct choice; the Presentation layer is responsible for data conversion. Answer a is incorrect because the Transport layer manages the transmission of data across a network. The Session layer maintains a session between computers. Therefore, answer b is also incorrect. The Application layer provides an interface for applications to use to gain access to networked services, so answer d is incorrect.

Question 3

> Which layer of the OSI model manages flow control and error correction?
>
> ○ a. Transport layer
> ○ b. Session layer
> ○ c. Network layer
> ○ d. Physical layer

Answer a is the correct choice. The Transport layer is responsible for error-handling information and flow control. The Session layer maintains a session between computers. Therefore, answer b is incorrect. The Network layer handles packet addressing and sequencing. Therefore, answer c is incorrect. The Physical layer is responsible for communication with the network media. Therefore, answer d is incorrect.

Question 4

> Which layer of the OSI model establishes the route between the sending and receiving computer?
>
> ○ a. Transport layer
> ○ b. Session layer
> ○ c. Network layer
> ○ d. Physical layer

Answer c is the correct choice. The Network layer is responsible for determining the route from the source to destination computer. The Transport layer is responsible for error-handling information and flow control. Therefore, answer a is incorrect. The Session layer maintains a session between computers. Therefore, answer b is also incorrect. The Physical layer is responsible for communication with the network media. Therefore, answer d is incorrect.

Question 5

> In which OSI model layer does the Media Access Control sublayer reside?
>
> ○ a. Transport layer
> ○ b. Network layer
> ○ c. Data Link layer
> ○ d. Physical layer

The only correct answer to this question is answer c. Only the Data Link layer was given sublayers by the IEEE 802 specifications, which defined the Media Access Control and Logical Link Control sublayers. None of the other choices was given sublayers. Therefore, a, b, and d are incorrect.

Question 6

> Which of the following protocols is considered a network protocol?
>
> ○ a. IPX
> ○ b. Telnet
> ○ c. FTP
> ○ d. SPX

Answer a is the correct choice; IPX is a network protocol. Telnet and FTP are both application protocols. Therefore answers b and c are incorrect. SPX is a transport protocol. Therefore, answer d is also incorrect.

Question 7

> Which of the following protocols is considered a transport protocol?
>
> ○ a. SNMP
> ○ b. SMTP
> ○ c. FTP
> ○ d. IPX
> ○ e. TCP

Answer e is correct; TCP is a transport protocol. SNMP, SMTP, and FTP are application protocols. Therefore, answers a, b, and c are incorrect. IPX is a network protocol. Therefore, answer d is also incorrect.

Question 8

> Which of the following protocols are considered application protocols? [Check all correct answers]
>
> ❏ a. TCP
> ❏ b. SNMP
> ❏ c. FTP
> ❏ d. SPX
> ❏ e. NetBEUI

Answers b and c are both correct because SNMP and FTP are both application protocols. TCP and SPX are transport protocols. Therefore answers a and d are incorrect. NetBEUI is a transport protocol. Therefore, answer e is incorrect.

Question 9

> Which of the following 802 specifications provide details on how an Ethernet network operates?
>
> ○ a. 802.2
> ○ b. 802.3
> ○ c. 802.4
> ○ d. 802.5

Answer b is correct because the 802.3 specification defines standards for Ethernet networks. 802.2 defines Logical Link Control. Therefore, answer a is incorrect. 802.4 defines Token Bus LANs. Therefore, answer c is incorrect. 802.5 defines Token Ring LANs; therefore, answer d is also incorrect.

Need To Know More?

 Chellis, James, Charles Perkins, and Matthew Strebe: *MCSE: Networking Essentials Study Guide, 2nd Edition*. Sybex Network Press, San Francisco, CA, 1998. ISBN 0-7821-2220-5. Chapter 3, "The Theoretical Network," discusses the OSI Reference Model at length.

 Microsoft Press: *Networking Essentials, 2nd Edition*. Redmond, WA, 1997. ISBN 1-57231-527-X. Unit 3, Lesson 7, "The OSI and 802 Networking Models," and Unit 3, Lesson 10, "Protocols," both discuss the topics covered in this chapter in great detail.

Cabling And Interfaces

Terms you'll need to understand:

- ✓ Network media
- ✓ Unshielded twisted-pair
- ✓ Shielded twisted-pair
- ✓ Coaxial cable
- ✓ Thinnet cable
- ✓ Thicknet cable
- ✓ Wireless media
- ✓ Broadband
- ✓ ARCNet
- ✓ Plenum
- ✓ Fiber optic cable
- ✓ Network Device Interface Specification (NDIS)
- ✓ Open Data-link Interface (ODI)
- ✓ Media Access Control (MAC)

Techniques you'll need to master:

- ✓ Understanding cable types, their advantages, and their disadvantages
- ✓ Knowing which cable type to use with network technologies
- ✓ Understanding NDIS and ODI

At the most basic level of any network communications lies the medium by which data is transmitted. For the purposes of data transmission, the term "media" can include both cabling and wireless technologies. Although physical cables are the most commonly used media for network connectivity, wireless technologies are becoming increasingly popular for their ability to link wide area networks (WANs). The type of media you use in your network is a key consideration. Media vary in several ways, including data transmission speed, ease of installation, and expense. When planning your network, you should consider these and other factors carefully.

Cable Types

There are several different cable types that are used in modern networks. Size, cost, data transfer rates, minimum/maximum lengths, and ease of installation vary for all of them. Various networking situations and requirements may require distinctly different cable types. This section describes the uses and limitations of each type of cable.

Twisted-Pair Cable

Twisted-pair cable is a media type used in many network topologies, including Ethernet, ARCNet, and IBM Token Ring. Twisted-pair cabling comes in two types: shielded and unshielded.

Probably the most commonly used type of networking cable in America, twisted-pair cabling was originally developed for use in telephone lines. A familiar example would be the cabling used to connect the telephone to the wall jack—CAT1, two-pair, unshielded twisted-pair (UTP) cabling, also known as "silver satin" cable. This is one type of twisted-pair cabling that typically consists of two pairs of insulated copper wires, twisted around each other, then enclosed within a plastic sheath. The twisting of the wires around each other provides a degree of protection from crosstalk (we'll cover this shortly) and other types of outside interference.

Unshielded Twisted-Pair Cabling

The Electronics Industries Association and the Telecommunications Industries Association (EIA/TIA) have created standards (EIA/TIA 568 Commercial Building Wiring Standard) that define UTP cable categories. Five types of UTP are available. They are referred to, in ascending quality order, as CAT1 through CAT5. The higher category cables usually contain more wire pairs, and these wires contain a higher number of twists per foot.

Cabling And Interfaces   47

The CAT1 telephone cabling that we have already mentioned, although adequate for voice communications, does not support digital data transfer, and, therefore, should not be used in this capacity. CAT2 cabling is an older type of UTP that is rarely used. It supports data transfer rates of up to 4 Mbps. CAT3 cable, with a data transfer rate of up to 10 Mbps, is the realistic minimum grade of UTP required for today's data networks. In fact, CAT3 cable is the lowest category of UTP that meets the IEEE 802.3 (explained in the next chapter) standards for a 10BaseT Ethernet network.

CAT4 cable is an intermediate UTP cable specification that supports data transfer rates of up to 16 Mbps. For new network installations, UTP CAT2 through 4 have been largely abandoned in favor of the newer CAT5 UTP, which can handle data transfer rates up to 100 Mbps.

Unshielded twisted-pair cabling is connected from each host computer's NIC to the network patch panel, which is then connected to a network hub, using RJ-45 connectors at each connection point. An RJ-45 connector is an eight-wire (four-pair) media connector. It is slightly larger than (but similar in appearance to) the RJ-11 connector used to attach a phone line from a wall jack to your telephone or modem.

> **Note:** *It is possible, though unusual, to use an RJ-11 connector for data networking because RJ-11 is usually used to attach lower grades of cable.*

A good example of this configuration is the Ethernet 10BaseT standard network, which is characterized by UTP (CAT3 through 5) cable that uses RJ-45 connectors. Shielded twisted-pair (STP) cable can also be used, but it is less common. This cable type supports a data transmission rate of 10 through 100 Mbps and can transmit data up to 100 meters without a repeater. 10BaseT networks are a popular all-around choice because they are supported on most platforms, use inexpensive media, and are easier to troubleshoot than other network types. It is also possible in many cases to run UTP through already-existing telephone line conduits, thus adding to its ease of installation.

Although it is inexpensive and easier to install, UTP cabling is not without its drawbacks: namely, interference from outside electromagnetic sources, and signal crossing between adjacent wires, called *crosstalk*. To some degree, the wire's design—the twisting of one wire around the other—cancels out much of the natural signal overflow and interference that exist from one wire to the other. Although electromagnetic interference and crosstalk can occur on other media types, UTP is particularly susceptible because it lacks the shielding present in other cable types. This lack of shielding also makes UTP particularly vulnerable to wiretapping—a point you should examine carefully if data security is a priority.

UTP is also subject to a greater degree of attenuation, or lessening of signal strength over distance, than other cable types. This means that cable segments using UTP have the most stringent distance limitations—no segment may exceed 100 meters in length. Cable length maximums exist because signals weaken over distance, as they are partly absorbed by the media on which they travel. This attenuation causes the signals to become unreadable after the specified distances, unless a repeater (a device that cleans up and retransmits the signal) is used.

Shielded Twisted-Pair Cabling

Shielded twisted-pair (STP) cabling has traditionally been used in several network types, including AppleTalk and Token Ring. STP, which is of similar internal construction, is subject to the same 100-meter restriction as UTP. In addition, shielded twisted-pair cable usually contains, at its core, four or more pairs of twisted copper wires. STP differs from UTP in that it contains shielding—an electrically grounded woven copper mesh or aluminum foil that surrounds the cable's internal wires. This shielding separates them from the cable's outer sheath and provides resistance to external electromagnetic interference (EMI). Some types of STP also use shielding internally around each wire pair to keep the pair separated from the others, which further reduces crosstalk. Additionally, STP is considered to be more secure than UTP, because its shielding makes it somewhat less vulnerable to wiretapping.

STP cabling data transmission rates and distance restrictions are identical to those of UTP. Although STP provides more protection from EMI than UTP, it is not often used in newer network installations because it is more difficult to install and maintain. One reason for this is that the shielding makes the cable less flexible; another consideration is that STP usually requires electrical grounding.

Coaxial Cable

Coaxial cable was the first cable type used to connect computers to a network, and it helped form the basis of the original Ethernet standard. This cable type consists of a copper conductive center wire that is thicker than the wires found in twisted-pair cable, thus enabling higher data transmission rates over longer distances. The center conductor is covered by a layer of

Cabling And Interfaces

plastic foam insulating material, which, in turn, is surrounded by a second conductor, usually woven copper mesh or aluminum foil. This outer conductor is not used to transfer data, but it provides an electrical ground and shields the center conductor from internal and external interference.

Although not used as much as UTP in newer network installations, coaxial cabling is still common in much of the already-installed computer network base. It is also the type of cabling used for cable television hookups. Coaxial cabling can transmit data at 10 Mbps, for maximum distances of 185 to 500 meters. Coaxial cable manufacturers have created specifications that separate coaxial cables into categories (see Table 4.1) depending on characteristics such as impedance (current resistance, measured in ohms) and cable thickness. Coaxial cabling schemes usually require terminators, the impedance of which must be properly matched to the cable type. The two main coaxial cable types used in local area networks are Thin Ethernet (also known as "Thinnet") and Thick Ethernet (also known as "Thicknet"). In coaxial configurations, Thinnet and Thicknet are often combined within the same network, with Thicknet cabling used for the backbones and Thinnet used for the branch segments.

Thinnet

Thinnet cable, also referred to as RG-58 cable, is the most commonly used coaxial media in computer networks. Second in popularity only to UTP, it is the most flexible of the coaxial cable types, about one-quarter inch in diameter. Thinnet cable can be used to connect each computer

Table 4.1 Coaxial cable types.

Type	Name
RG-8 and RG-11	Thicknet (50 ohms)
RG-58 Family:	Thinnet (50 ohms)
RG-58/U	Thinnet, solid copper center conductor
RG-58 A/U	Thinnet, wire-strand center conductor
RG-58 C/U	Thinnet, military grade
RG-59	Broadband/Cable television (75 ohms)
RG-59 /U	Broadband/Cable television (50 ohms)
RG-62	ARCNet (93 ohms)

directly to the others on the LAN, using British Naval Connector (BNC) T-connectors and 50-ohms terminators. Because Thinnet configurations require no special equipment or external transceivers and can be used without hubs, Thinnet cabling schemes are an easy and relatively inexpensive way to set up a small network quickly.

According to the IEEE specification for 10Base2 Ethernet networks, the BNC T-connectors (shown in Figure 4.1) and BNC barrel connectors are used to attach RG-58 A/U or RG-58 C/U cable segments to each other. They also link the network cable to the transceiver on each computer's NIC. The BNC barrel connector is similar to the T-connector except that the barrel does not have the bottom part of the "T." Terminators (shown in Figure 4.2), which are resistors that prevent signal echo, are required at both ends of each segment. This configuration supports data transmission speeds of up to 10 Mbps, with maximum cable lengths of 185 meters between repeaters.

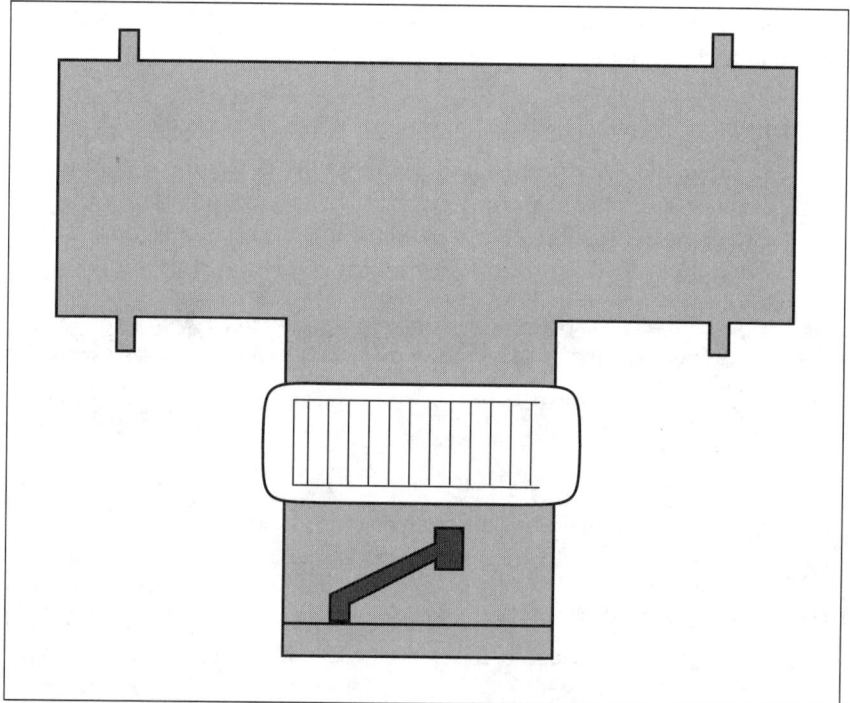

Figure 4.1 An illustration of a BNC T-connector.

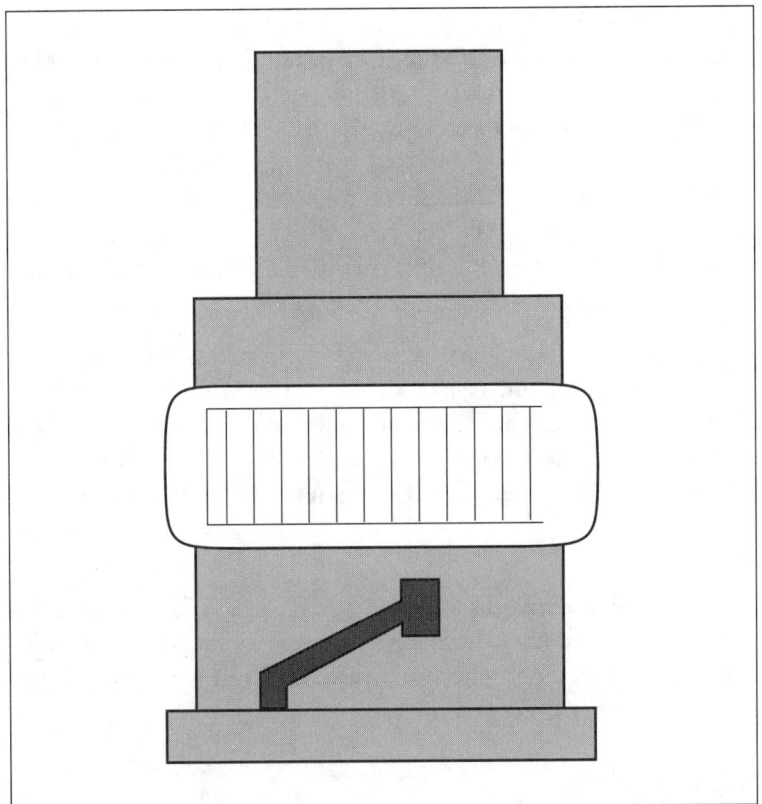

Figure 4.2 An example of a BNC terminator.

Thinnet's greater transmission distance and shielding (which provides better security than twisted-pair cabling), make it a good choice in cases where these qualities are critical. However, because it is less flexible, it is somewhat more difficult to work with. It is also not the best choice in a situation where the network cabling must be installed in existing telephone wiring conduits—if this is an issue, UTP is preferable.

Thicknet

Thicknet, which was used for the original Ethernet specification, is a thicker and more expensive cable than Thinnet. It is similar in construction to Thinnet, but is a great deal less flexible. Thicknet cabling is used as the basis for a standard Ethernet (10Base5) network. The IEEE Thick Ethernet specification for 10Base5 networks uses either RG-8 or RG-11 cable (approximately one-half inch in diameter) as a linear bus. The difference is that it uses attachment unit interface (AUI) external transceivers connected to each NIC by means of a "vampire," or tap that pierces the cable's sheath to access the wire. Each AUI is connected to a compatible AUI (called a DB15) connector on its computer's NIC. Thicknet cabling has a thick center conductor core, which allows it to transmit reliably at a distance of up to 500 meters per cable segment—a significant distance advantage over Thinnet. For this reason, it is often used to create backbones that link Thinnet networks. Thicknet media can transmit data at a rate of up to 10 Mbps.

Although the thickness of Thicknet cabling allows for longer transmission distances, greater security, and resistance to interference, its rigidity and bulkiness make it very difficult to install. It is also quite expensive. For these reasons, Thicknet networks are rare today. Thicknet is not a good choice for a new network installation if you can use another solution.

ARCNet
ARCNet token-passing networks generally use RG-62 A/U coaxial cable. RG-62 cabling is not used for Ethernet networks. ARCNet cable is similar to cable television cable and at one time was popular in networks. Today, support for ARCNet networks is minimal.

Plenum Cabling
The plenum is the crawl space in a building that lies between the ceiling and the roof. The special grades of fire-resistant cables used in this area are called plenum cables. This area is commonly used for telephone and network wiring. Fire codes require that cabling installed in the plenum area be fire resistant and have casing material that will not give off hazardous fumes if it does burn.

Fiber Optic Cable
At the cutting edge of network cabling technology, fiber optic cable provides superior data transmission speed over longer distances. It is also immune to interference and eavesdropping. Fiber optic cable consists of a glass or plastic center conductor, surrounded by another layer of glass or plastic cladding, and a protective outer jacket (see Figure 4.3). Data is transmitted across the cable by a laser or light-emitting diode (LED) transmitter that sends one-way light pulses through the center glass fiber. The glass cladding helps to keep the light focused into the inner core. The signal is received at the other end by a photodiode receiver that converts the light pulses to an electrical signal that the receiving computer can use.

Cabling And Interfaces 53

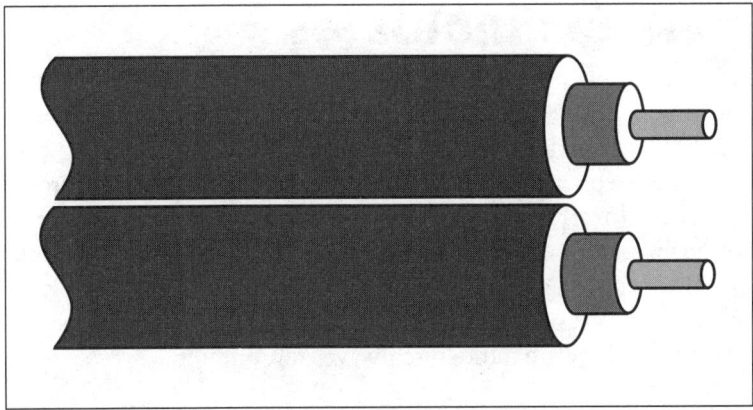

Figure 4.3 A drawing of fiber optic cable.

 Be ready to identify drawings of fiber cabling, twisted-pair cabling, T-connectors, and terminators.

Data transmission speeds for fiber optic networks range from 100 Mbps to 2 Gbps (Gigabits per second), and data can be sent reliably up to a distance of 2 kilometers without a repeater. A fiber optic cable can support video and voice, as well as data transmission. Because the light pulses are completely closed within the outer sheath, fiber media are virtually impervious to outside interference or eavesdropping. These qualities make fiber optic cabling an attractive option for networks that must be very secure or require extremely fast transmission over long distances.

Because light pulses can only travel in one direction, fiber optic cabling systems must contain an incoming cable and an outgoing cable for each segment that will be transmitting and receiving data. Fiber cabling is also rigid and difficult to install, making it the most expensive of all network media types. You should probably consider alternate cabling types first, when they are adequate for the situation. Fiber media require special connectors and highly skilled installers, factors that further contribute to the high implementation expense. One way to minimize the expense is to limit use of fiber cabling to network backbones, or in areas where EMI, flammability, or other environmental issues are of concern. You must carefully analyze cost factors versus requirements before deciding on fiber optic cable for a network installation.

Wireless Technologies

In addition to traditional physical media, wireless data transmission methods can provide a convenient, and sometimes necessary, alternative to network cabling connections. Wireless technologies vary in signal type, frequency (higher frequencies mean higher transmission rates), and transmission distance. Interference and cost are significant considerations. Because of the increasing numbers of WANs, and the need for mobile computing solutions, wireless network technologies comprise an ever-growing segment of the network population. The three main types of wireless data transmission technology are radio, microwave, and infrared.

Radio Waves

Radio technologies transmit data via radio frequencies and have practically nonexistent distance limitations. They are used to link LANs over great geographical distances. Radio transmission is generally expensive, subject to government regulation, and is quite susceptible to electronic and atmospheric interference. They are highly susceptible to eavesdropping, and thus, require encryption or other transmission modifications to attain a reasonable level of security.

Microwaves

Microwave transmission uses higher frequencies for both short distance and global transmissions; its main limitation is that the transmitter and receiver must be within the line of sight of each other. Microwave transmission is commonly used to connect LANs in separate buildings, where using physical media is impossible or impractical. A good example of this would be two adjacent skyscrapers, where using cables would be impossible. Microwave is also used in global transmissions, which use geosynchronous satellites and ground-based dishes to adhere to the line-of-sight requirement. Microwave transmission can be extremely expensive, but microwaves are less susceptible to interference and eavesdropping than radio waves and provide higher bandwidth.

Infrared Transmissions

Infrared technologies, which operate at very high frequencies approaching those of visible light, can be used to establish close-range point-to-point or broadcast transmissions. They typically use LEDs to transmit infrared waves to the receiver. Because they can be physically blocked, and can experience interference from bright light, infrared transmissions are limited to short-distance, line-of-sight applications. Infrared transmission is commonly used within stores or office buildings, or sometimes to link two buildings. Another popular use of infrared is for wireless data transfer in portable computers. Infrared technologies range from inexpensive to very expensive.

Cabling Considerations

When planning a network or adding to an existing network, you must consider several points concerning the cabling: cost, distance, transfer rate, ease of installation, number of nodes supported, and resistance to interference. We have discussed several types of cabling in this chapter, so let's compare the cable types using each of these considerations (see Table 4.2).

When designing or adding to a network, you should take each of the factors in Table 4.2 into consideration. Also, you should know how many computers you will have on the network and on each segment. Table 4.3 illustrates the different types of networking specifications and the number of computers (nodes) that you can have on each.

Table 4.2 Cable type comparisons.

Type	Speed	Distance	Installation	Interference	Cost
10BaseT	10 Mbps	100 M	Easy	Highly susceptible	Least expensive
100BaseT	100 Mbps	100 M	Easy	Highly susceptible	More expensive than 10BaseT
STP	16 Mbps to 155 Mbps	100 M	Moderately easy	Somewhat resistant	More expensive than Thinnet or UTP
10Base2	10 Mbps	185 M	Medium difficulty	Somewhat resistant	Inexpensive
10Base5	10 Mbps	500 M	More difficult than Thinnet	More resistant than most cable	More expensive than most cable
Fiber Optic	100 Mbps to 2 Gbps	2 K	Most difficult	Not susceptible to electronic interference	Most expensive type of cable

Understanding NDIS And ODI

Network software architectures contain several distinct layers. Based loosely on the seven layers of the OSI Reference Model of network protocols, from the bottom layer, which deals with the hardware that makes up the physical connection, to the top layer, which is comprised of the network applications. At one time, the code for all functions of the OSI model was entirely rewritten for each new combination of NIC, protocol, and redirector. This provided for an overly large number of combinations, required a great deal of reworking the code, and was inflexible; each NIC driver could only be bound to a single protocol stack, and vice versa.

To solve this problem, a more modular approach for each layer's function was required. This was addressed by creating device interfaces—blocks of program code that act as a standard communication interface between the functional layers. These device interfaces act as interpreters: One layer does not have to understand the way an adjacent layer performs a certain task for the two layers to communicate and cooperate in getting a task done.

The main benefit of interfaces is that, once written, they provide the same services to, and understand the communications of, drivers and protocols written by any vendor that has adhered to the interface specification. Vendor driver developers do not have to understand the application programming interfaces (APIs) of other vendors in order to develop compatible software. This means that proprietary layers of code can be removed and

Table 4.3 Nodes per network type.

Network Type	Nodes Per Segment	Nodes Per Network
10BaseT	2	1,024
10BaseF*	2	1,024
100BaseT	2	1,024
10Base2 (5 segments, 3 populated)	30	900**
10Base5 (5 segments, 3 populated)	100	1,024

*The 10BaseF specification is similar to 10BaseT except fiber optic cabling is used. The fiber cable can be run at much higher speeds, but if the computers only transfer at 10 Mbps, then the specification is 10BaseF.

**Although the theoretical maximum for a single 10Base2 network is 1,024 nodes, practical limitations on devices per segment result in an effective maximum of 900, or 30 devices for each of 60 segments that may have nodes attached.

replaced to allow for changes and upgrades. The OSI Reference Model also allows for multiple pieces of proprietary software to reside together at the same functional layer, thus enabling the binding of multiple NIC drivers to multiple network protocols, using the same intermediary device interface.

Microsoft, in combination with IBM, developed the Network Device Interface Specification (NDIS) as its implementation of the device interface concept, specifically to reside between the NIC (also called MAC or Media Access Control) driver and the protocol stack in the Data Link layer of the OSI Reference Model. NDIS allows for the binding of multiple NDIS-compliant network cards to one protocol stack or multiple protocols to a single NIC, or binds multiple protocols to multiple NICs.

Novell and Apple developed Open Datalink Interface (ODI), Novell's implementation of NDIS. It is used in Novell's NetWare networks, and provides functionality comparable to NDIS. It allows Novell's IPX/SPX protocol (and Microsoft's IPX implementation, NWLINK) to be bound to multiple NIC drivers. It also provides support for NetBIOS names.

Practice Questions

Question 1

> 10BaseT topologies have which of the following characteristics? [Check all correct answers]
>
> ❑ a. Use of 50-ohm BNC terminators and T-connectors
> ❑ b. RJ-11 connectors
> ❑ c. UTP cabling
> ❑ d. STP cabling

The answers for this question are c and d. 10BaseT networks typically use some type of twisted-pair cabling (either STP or UTP). Also, BNC terminators and T-connectors are used with Thinnet (10Base2) networks. Although many hubs support 10Base2 and 10BaseT connectors, you should not assume that 10Base2 components will be used on a 10BaseT network. Therefore, answer a is incorrect. RJ-11 connectors are used with regular phone cable or modems and are not normally associated directly with 10BaseT networking. Therefore, answer b is incorrect.

Question 2

> If a 10BaseT network has been installed and one of the segments exceeds 100 meters, which type of device can help to prevent signal attenuation?
>
> ○ a. Tuner
> ○ b. Receiver
> ○ c. Amplifier
> ○ d. Repeater

The correct answer is d. When signal attenuation (the degradation of an electric signal over distance) is a problem, a repeater can be used to duplicate and boost the signal. The trick in this question was the word "amplifier," which acts in a similar manner as a repeater.

Question 3

You have been asked to review XYZ Company's network configuration (see graphic). The network is a 10BaseT network using (CAT5) twisted-pair cabling. Which of the following are problems with this network?

○ a. All of the cables are too long.

○ b. Segments to computers A, D, and F are too long.

○ c. Segments to computers A and F are too long.

○ d. Segment to computer F is too long.

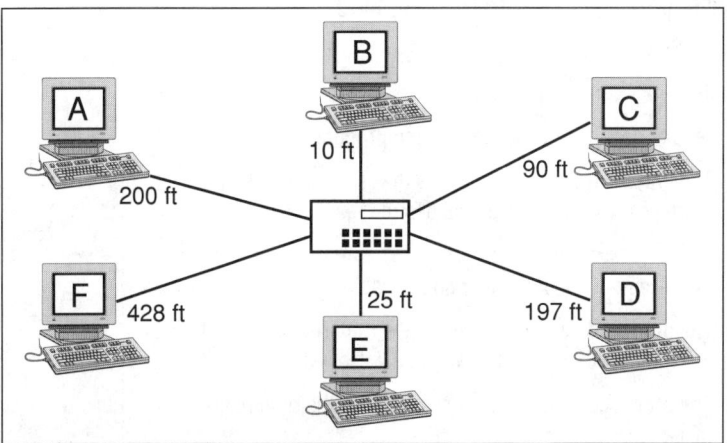

If you know that 10BaseT cable can be 100 meters in length (which is equivalent to about 328 feet), the answer to the question is obviously d. The only segment that is longer than 328 feet is the one going to computer F.

Chapter 4

Question 4

> Your network consulting firm has been asked to implement a network for a small company. It wants to connect its 25 computers to a small LAN.
>
> Required Result:
>
> - The company needs a network that must be able to support transfer rates up to 10 Mbps.
>
> Optional Desired Results:
>
> - The company would like to minimize costs.
> - The company would like to use the existing cabling with RJ-45 connectors currently installed in the building.
>
> Proposed Solution:
>
> - Implement a Thinnet network.
>
> Which results does the proposed solution produce?
>
> ○ a. The proposed solution produces the required result and produces both of the optional desired results.
>
> ○ b. The proposed solution produces the required result and produces only one of the optional results.
>
> ○ c. The proposed solution produces the required result, but does not produce any of the optional desired results.
>
> ○ d. The proposed solution does not produce the required result.

Because the proposed solution is 10Base2 or Thinnet, only answer c is correct. 10Base2 allows for a 10 Mbps transfer rate, but it is not the least expensive solution in this case and it cannot utilize the existing cabling with RJ-45 connectors. To successfully answer this question, you should know that cable with RJ-45 connectors is used in 10BaseT networks and that it can handle transmission speeds of up to 10 Mbps. Because cable with RJ-45 connectors is already preinstalled, a 10BaseT network would meet required and optionally desired results.

Question 5

> You are assembling a five-host 10Base2 network as shown in the graphic. Which locations on the network cable will require both a T-connector and a terminator? [Check all correct answers]
>
> ❑ a. Location 1
> ❑ b. Location 2
> ❑ c. Location 3
> ❑ d. Location 4
> ❑ e. Location 5

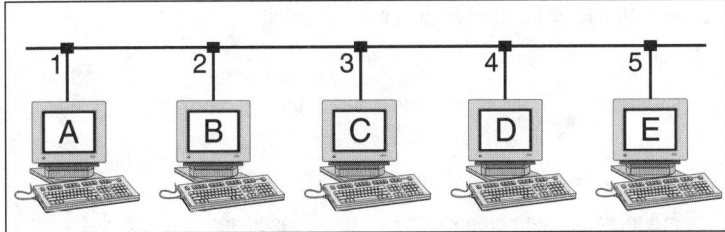

The correct answers are a and e. Thinnet (10Base2) cable must be terminated at both ends. According to the graphic, one end is at location 1 (computer A) and the other end is at location 5 (computer E). The other locations only require a T-connector to attach the two sides of the coaxial cable.

Question 6

You are installing a network between two buildings for a graphics publishing company. The company is going to connect its small network between the two buildings, which are approximately 900 meters apart. Each building already has a small 10BaseT LAN.

Required Result:

- Connect the LANs in each building with the appropriate type of cabling.

Optional Desired Results:

- The segment attaching the two buildings should be immune to electronic interference.
- The cabling should be inexpensive and easy to install.

Proposed Solution:

- Install a 10BaseFL (fiber optic) line connecting the two buildings.

Which results does the proposed solution produce?

- ○ a. The proposed solution produces the required result and produces both of the optional desired results.
- ○ b. The proposed solution produces the required result and produces only one of the optional results.
- ○ c. The proposed solution produces the required result, but does not produce any of the optional desired results.
- ○ d. The proposed solution does not produce the required result.

The correct answer to the question is b. The proposed solution is the only appropriate choice because only a fiber optic cable could traverse the 900 meters between the two buildings. Fiber optic cable is not vulnerable to electronic interference; however, it isn't easy to install. Fiber optic cable is also expensive.

Question 7

Of the following cable types, which is the most susceptible to crosstalk?

○ a. STP

○ b. CAT5 UTP

○ c. Coaxial

○ d. Fiber optic

Answer b is correct. Unshielded twisted-pair is the most susceptible to crosstalk (communication bleed-over from one wire to another). Coaxial and STP are also susceptible to crosstalk, but they have shielding to reduce the chance of it.

Question 8

Which of the following cable types is used for ARCNet (Attached Resource Computer Networks)? [Check the best answer]

○ a. CAT5 UTP

○ b. RG-62

○ c. RJ-45

○ d. RG-58

For ARCNet, always choose RG-62 cabling, which makes answer b correct. The standard cable for ARCNet is RG-62. ARCNet can use fiber optic and twisted-pair cabling; however, this question is asking you to choose a single "best" answer, therefore, it's kind of tricky.

Question 9

Which type of connectors are characteristic of a Thinnet network? [Check all correct answers]

- ❏ a. BNC barrel connectors
- ❏ b. Vampire tap
- ❏ c. T-connector
- ❏ d. AUI connector
- ❏ e. Terminators

Answers a, c, and e are correct. Thicknet (10Base5) uses vampire taps and AUI connectors. Thinnet (10Base2) uses BNC barrel and T-connectors, and terminators should be placed at the end of each segment of the network.

Question 10

On a 10Base2 network (as depicted in the graphic), client B cannot connect to any other computers. All other machines are communicating correctly on the network. Which of the following is the most likely cause of the network problem?

- ○ a. Faulty terminator
- ○ b. High rate of collisions
- ○ c. Faulty cabling between clients A and B
- ○ d. Faulty cabling between clients B and C
- ○ e. Faulty network card on client B

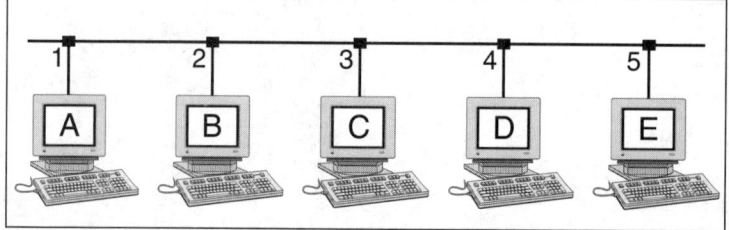

Answer e is correct. The most likely cause of networking problems that affects only client B is a faulty network card. The other situations listed would most likely cause network connectivity problems for all computers on the network.

Question 11

> What do the NDIS and ODI interfaces allow you to do?
>
> ○ a. Bind multiple protocols to a single network adapter
>
> ○ b. Bind multiple network cards to a single computer
>
> ○ c. Resolve IP addresses to NetBIOS computer names
>
> ○ d. Separate the Application layer from the Session layer of the OSI Reference Model

The only correct answer is a. NDIS and ODI are interfaces that were designed to allow you to bind multiple protocols to a single network adapter. They do not perform any of the other functions listed above.

Need To Know More?

Chellis, James, Charles Perkins, and Matthew Strebe: *MCSE: Networking Essentials Study Guide, 2nd Edition*. Sybex Network Press, San Francisco, CA, 1998. ISBN 0-7821-2220-5. Chapter 2, "Network Components," discusses all cable types at length.

Microsoft Press: *Networking Essentials, 2nd Edition*. Redmond, WA, 1997. ISBN 1-57231-527-X. Unit 2, Lesson 4, "Network Cabling—the Physical Media," discusses all of the topics in this chapter in great detail.

Search the TechNet CD (or its online version through **www.microsoft.com**) using the keywords "cabling," "NDIS," "Thicknet," and related cable, connector, and interface names.

Network Hardware And Topologies

5

Terms you'll need to understand:

- √ Network interface card (NIC)
- √ Interrupt request line (IRQ)
- √ Base memory address
- √ Transceiver
- √ Repeater
- √ Amplifier
- √ Hub
- √ Bridge
- √ Router
- √ Brouter
- √ Gateway
- √ Bus
- √ Ring
- √ Star
- √ Mesh

Techniques you'll need to master:

- √ Installing and configuring a network interface card
- √ Understanding and configuring IRQs
- √ Understanding hubs, bridges, routers, brouters, and gateways and their uses
- √ Knowing the features, advantages, and disadvantages of the bus, ring, star, and mesh topologies

In the previous chapter, you learned about network cables and connectors. This chapter continues the discussion of the physical network by explaining network adapter configuration. We also cover the various methods and standards related to configuring a network and the devices used to connect separate networks.

Networking Components

There are many networking devices that you can use to create, segment, and enhance networks. In this section, we discuss several networking devices, such as network adapter cards, repeaters, amplifiers, bridges, routers, and gateways.

Adapters

The network adapter, or NIC (network interface card), is the piece of hardware that physically connects a computer to the network. Before you make this connection, you must successfully install and configure this card. The simplicity or complexity of this installation and configuration depends on the type of network adapter you decide to use. For some configurations, you may not have to do anything other than install the network card in the appropriate slot in your computer. Self-configuring and Plug and Play adapters automatically configure themselves appropriately. If you don't have a Plug and Play adapter, or are using an OS that doesn't support Plug and Play, you must configure the interrupt request line (IRQ, or interrupt) and the Input/Output (I/O) address. The IRQ is the logical communication line that the device uses to communicate with the processor. The I/O address is a three-digit hexadecimal number that identifies a communication channel between hardware devices and the CPU. Both the IRQ and I/O address must be appropriately configured for the network card to function correctly.

You should know the common interrupts and I/O addresses so that you can configure the network card to operate without conflict. Usually, if two devices have the same resources (I/O address or IRQ) assigned, there will be a conflict. Therefore, your goal is to find and set a unique IRQ and I/O address for the network card to use. The interrupts, I/O addresses, and related devices that you should know are described in Table 5.1.

Network Hardware And Topologies

Table 5.1 Vital statistics for common interrupts and I/O addresses.

Common Use	IRQ	I/O Addresses
System timer	0	N/A
Keyboard	1	N/A
Secondary IRQ controller or video adapter	2	N/A
COM 2 or COM 4	3	2F0 to 2FF
COM 1 or COM 3	4	3F0 to 3FF
Usually unassigned (may be used by LPT 2 or sound card)	5	N/A
Floppy disk controller	6	N/A
LPT 1	7	N/A
Realtime clock	8	N/A
Usually unassigned (may cascade from IRQ 2)	9	370 to 37F
Usually unassigned (may be a primary SCSI controller)	10	N/A
Usually unassigned (may be a secondary SCSI controller)	11	N/A
PS/2 Mouse	12	N/A
Math coprocessor	13	N/A
Primary hard disk controller	14	N/A
Unassigned (may be a secondary hard disk controller)	15	N/A

IRQ 2 cascades to IRQ 9 because there were only eight IRQ options originally. To create 15 IRQ options, IRQ 2 was used to create a second set of IRQs starting at IRQ 9. This means that IRQ 2 is actually an indicator between the first set of IRQs (0 through 8) and the second set (9 through 15).

Base Memory Address

Some NICs have the capability to use the computer's memory (RAM) as a buffer to store incoming and outgoing data frames. The base memory address is a hexadecimal value that represents a location in RAM where this buffer resides. Because other devices also use base memory addresses in RAM, it's important to remember to select a base memory address that does not conflict with other devices. The Windows 95 or 98 Device Manager reports the settings for individual devices and determines if there are any conflicts in the system (see Figure 5.1). If you have Windows NT, use Windows NT Diagnostics (WINMSD.EXE) to determine which system resources are being utilized.

Transceiver Settings

Network cards support various types of network connections. On a NIC, the physical interface between itself and the network is called a transceiver—a term used to refer to a device that both transmits and receives data. Transceivers on network cards can receive and transmit digital or analog signals. The type of interface that the network adapter uses can often be defined on the physical network adapter. Jumpers (small connectors that create a circuit between two pins on the physical card) can usually be set to specify the type of transceiver the adapter should use, according to the networking scheme. For example, a jumper set in one position may enable the RJ-45 connector to support a twisted-pair network; in another position, the same jumper might enable an external transceiver to be used in a 10Base5 (Thicknet) network. (This option may be selected by setup software in newer NICs.)

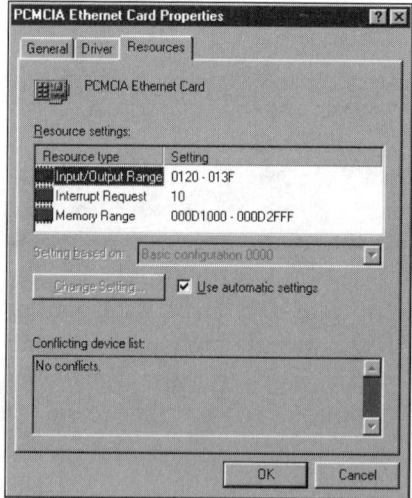

Figure 5.1 Windows 95 Device Manager PCMCIA Ethernet Card Properties dialog box.

Configuration Scenario

Suppose you want to install a network adapter in your computer, which is already using COM 1, COM 2, LPT 1, and LPT 2 (all using their common default settings). You have a network card that is configured for IRQ 7 and I/O port 0x300. Which device will be in conflict with the network adapter? If you take a look at the interrupt lines listed in Table 5.1, you will see that LPT 1 uses interrupt 7 for its communications. This means that either LPT 1 or the network card will have to use a different interrupt to resolve the conflict. If you decide to reset the interrupt on the network card, what interrupts can you use based on the information given? Again, from Table 5.1, you should see that IRQ 5 is taken by LPT 2, and IRQs 4 and 3 are being used by COM 1 and 2, respectively. This means that the normally available interrupts 9, 10, 11, and 15 would most likely be open.

If you are using Windows 95, you can view a list of interrupts in use by selecting the Computer Properties dialog box in the Device Manager, shown in Figure 5.2. This would give you a quick view of the resources in use on your computer. To see the resources in use on a Windows NT system, you would use the Windows NT Diagnostics program.

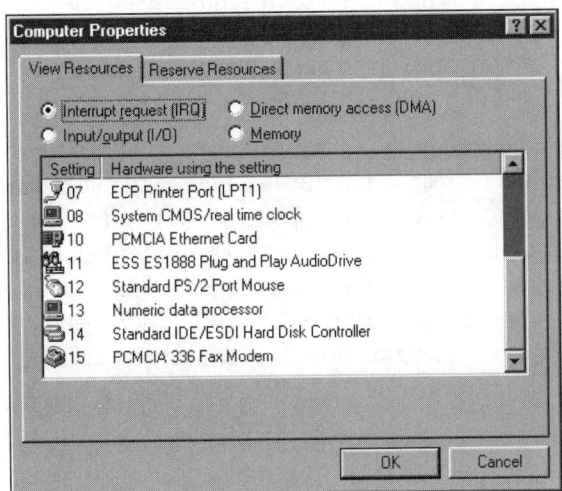

Figure 5.2 Windows 95 Device Manager Computer Properties dialog box.

Repeaters And Amplifiers

As mentioned in Chapter 4, signal strength degrades, or attenuates, over distance. To counteract signal degradation, you can use repeaters and/or amplifiers, which boost the signals that pass through them on the network.

Repeaters are used in networks with digital signaling schemes to combat attenuation. Also known as baseband transmission, digital signals consist of data bits that are either on or off, represented by a series of ones and zeros. Repeaters allow for reliable transmission at greater distances than the media type would normally allow. When a repeater receives an attenuated incoming baseband transmission, it cleans up the signal, increases its strength, and passes it on to the next segment.

Amplifiers, although similar in purpose, are used to increase transmission distances on networks that use analog signaling, referred to as broadband transmission. Analog signals can transfer both voice and data simultaneously—the wire is divided into multiple channels so different frequencies can be transferred at the same time.

> Repeaters (and amplifiers) operate at the Physical layer of the OSI model. They can be used to connect cable segments—even those using different media types—as long as both segments to be joined use the same media-access method. In fact, most hubs (excluding passive hubs) function as repeaters.

Usually, network architectures specify the maximum number of repeaters allowed on a single network. The reason for this is a phenomenon called *propagation delay*. In cases where there are multiple repeaters on the same network, the brief period of time each repeater takes to clean up and amplify the signal, multiplied by the number of repeaters/amplifiers, can cause a noticeable delay of transmissions on the network. When deciding whether to choose repeaters as a connection option, you must also consider that they have no addressing or translation capability, and thus, cannot be used to ease network congestion.

Hubs

A hub is a hardware device, operating at the OSI Physical layer, that acts as a central connecting point and joins lines in a star network configuration (star configuration is covered in the next section). There are three main types of hubs: passive, active, and intelligent. Passive hubs, which don't require power, act merely as a physical connection point, adding nothing to the signals that pass through. Active hubs, on the other hand, require power, which they use to regenerate and strengthen signals passing through them. Intelligent hubs can provide services such as packet switching and traffic routing.

Bridges

The bridge is another device used to connect network segments. Bridges can be an improvement over repeaters because bridges ease congestion on busy networks. Bridges read the target destination's MAC address from each incoming data packet, then examine the "bridging" tables to determine what to do with the packet.

 Bridges operate at the Data Link layer of the OSI model.

Because it functions basically as a repeater, a bridge can receive transmissions from any segment; however, it is more discriminating than a repeater in retransmitting these signals. If the packet's destination address is on the same segment the packet was received on, the bridge will not forward the packet. But, if the packet's destination lies on a different segment, the bridge knows to pass it along. By only fowarding packets destined for other network segments, the bridge reduces network congestion. However, bridges do forward all broadcast transmissions they receive, and therefore, are unable to reduce broadcast traffic.

Bridges can connect segments that use different media types; for example, a connection of 10BaseT media to 10Base2. Bridges can also connect networks using different media-accessing schemes, such as an Ethernet network and a Token Ring network. An example of such a device is a translation bridge, which is a bridge that translates between different media-access methods, allowing the translation bridge to link various network types. Another special type of bridge, a transparent bridge (or learning bridge), "learns" over time where to direct packets it receives. It does this by continually building bridging tables, adding new entries when they become necessary.

Possible disadvantages of bridges are the fact that they take longer than repeaters to pass data through because they examine the MAC address of each packet. They are also more expensive and difficult to operate.

Routers

A router is a networking connectivity device that works at the OSI Network layer and can link two or more network segments (or subnets). It functions in a similar manner to a bridge; but, instead of using the machine's MAC address to filter traffic, it uses the network address information found in the Network layer area of the data packet. After obtaining this address information, the router uses a routing table of network addresses to determine where to forward the packet. It does this by comparing the packet's network address to the entries in the routing table. If a match is found, the packet is sent to the determined route. If a match is not found, however, the data packet is usually discarded.

Routers work at the Network layer of the OSI model.

There are two types of routing devices: static and dynamic. Static routers use routing tables that a network administrator must create and update manually. In contrast, dynamic routers build and update their own routing tables. They use information found on both their own segments and data obtained from other dynamic routers. Dynamic routers contain constantly updated information on possible routes through the network, as well as information on bottlenecks and link outages. This information lets them determine the most efficient path available at a given moment to forward a data packet to its destination.

As routers can make intelligent path choices—and filter out packets they do not need to receive—they help lessen network congestion, conserve resources, and boost data throughput. Additionally, they make data delivery more reliable because routers can select an alternate path for the packet if the default route is down.

The term "router" can refer to a piece of electronic hardware designed specifically for routing. Router can also mean a computer (equipped with a routing table) that is attached to different network segments through multiple NICs, and hence, can fulfill a routing function between the linked segments.

Routers are superior to bridges in their ability to filter and direct data packets across the network. In addition, unlike bridges, they can be set to not forward broadcast packets, which reduces network broadcast traffic. Another major advantage of the router as a connectivity device is that, because it works at the Network layer, it can connect networks that use different network architectures and media-access methods. Routers cannot translate across protocols. A router can, for example, connect an Ethernet subnet to a Token Ring segment.

Routable protocols, like TCP/IP and IPX/SPX, are those that have Network layer addressing information. A non-routable protocol, such as NetBEUI, does not contain network address information. Because the router operates at this layer, it is only able to process protocols that include network address information.

There are several factors you need to consider when deciding on a router as a connectivity device. Routers are more expensive and difficult to operate than repeaters. They have slower throughput than bridges because they must perform additional processing on the data packet. Also, dynamic routers can add excessive traffic to the network because of the constant messages they send to each other when updating their routing tables.

Brouters

The term *brouter* is a combination of the words "bridge" and "router." As its name would suggest, a brouter combines the functions of a bridge and a router. When a brouter receives a data packet, it checks to see if the packet was sent in either a routable or non-routable protocol. If it is a routable protocol packet, the brouter will perform a routing function, sending the packet to its destination outside the local segment, if necessary.

In contrast, if the packet contains a non-routable protocol, the brouter performs a bridging function, using the MAC address to find the proper recipient on the local segment. Brouters must maintain both bridging and routing tables to perform these two functions; therefore, they operate at both the Data Link and Network layers of the OSI model.

Gateways

A gateway is a method of enabling communications between two or more network segments. A gateway is usually a dedicated computer that runs gateway software and provides a translation service, which allows for communications between dissimilar systems on the network. For example, using a gateway, an Intel-based PC on one segment can both communicate and share resources with a Macintosh computer or a mainframe.

Another function of gateways is to translate protocols. A gateway can receive an IPX/SPX message that is bound for a client running another protocol, such as TCP/IP, on a remote network segment. After it determines that the message packet's destination is a TCP/IP station, the gateway will actually convert the message data to the TCP/IP protocol. (This is in contrast with a bridge, which merely "tunnels" a message using one protocol inside the data format of another protocol—if translation is to occur, the receiving end does it.) Mail gateways perform similar translation operations. They convert emails and other mail transmissions from your native mail application's format to a more universal mail protocol, such as SMTP, which can then be used to route the message across the Internet.

 Gateways primarily operate at the Application layer of the OSI model, although they often fulfill certain functions at the Session layer and occasionally as low as the Network layer. However, for most purposes, consider the gateway to operate only at or above the Transport layer.

Although gateways have many advantages, you need to consider a few things when deciding whether to use them on your network. Gateways are difficult to install and configure. They are also more expensive than other connectivity devices. One other issue: Due to the extra processing cycle that the translation process requires, gateways can be slower than routers and related devices.

Network Topologies

A network's topology is a description of its physical layout. How computers are connected to each other on the network and the devices that connect them are included in the physical topology. There are four basic topologies: bus, ring, star, and mesh. Other topologies are usually hybrids of two or more of the main types. Choosing the physical topology type for your network is one of the first steps in planning. The choice of a topology will depend on a variety of factors, such as cost, distances, security needs, which network operating system you intend to run, and whether the new network will use existing hardware, conduits, and so on.

Bus

A physical bus topology, also called a linear bus, consists of a single cable to which all the computers in the segment are attached (see Figure 5.3). Messages are sent down the line to all attached stations, regardless of which one is the recipient. Each computer examines every packet on the wire to determine whom the packet is for; if it is for another station, the computer discards it. Likewise, a computer will receive and process any packets on the bus that are addressed to it.

Network Hardware And Topologies   77

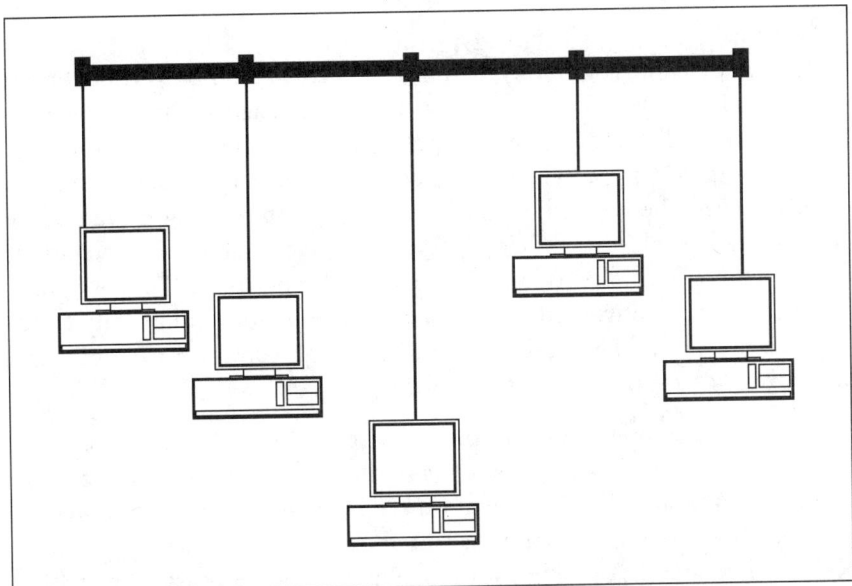

Figure 5.3 The bus topology connects computers to a linear segment.

The bus' main cable, known as the backbone, is terminated at each end to prevent message transmissions from bouncing back and forth between the two ends of the bus. Two media types commonly used in bus networks, Thicknet and Thinnet (refer back to Chapter 4 for discussion of these terms), require 50-ohm terminators. Without proper termination, communications on the bus will be unreliable, or will fail altogether.

The bus topology is the fastest and simplest way to set up a network. It requires less hardware and cabling than other topologies, and it is easier to configure. It is good way to quickly set up a temporary network. It is also usually the best choice for small networks (that is, those with 10 computers or less).

There are a couple of drawbacks you should be aware of when considering whether to implement a bus topology for your network. A malfunction of a station or other component on the network can be difficult to isolate. Furthermore, a malfunction in the bus backbone can bring down the entire network.

 All things considered, if your goal is to set up a small or temporary network, a linear bus topology is the best way to go.

Ring

Ring topologies are commonly seen in Token Ring and FDDI (fiber optic) networks. In a physical ring topology, the data line actually forms a logical ring to which all computers on the network are attached (see Figure 5.4). Unlike a bus topology, which uses a contention scheme to allow the stations to access the network media, media access on the ring is granted by means of a logical "token" that is passed around the circle to each station, giving it an opportunity to transmit a packet if it needs to. This configuration allows each networked computer a more equitable opportunity to access the media, and hence, to transmit its data. A computer can only send data when it has possession of the token.

Because each computer on the ring is part of the circle, it is capable of retransmitting any data packets it has received that are addressed to other stations on the ring. This regeneration keeps the signal strong, eliminating the need for repeaters. Because the ring forms a continuous loop, termination is not required. A ring network topology is relatively easy to install and configure, requiring minimal hardware.

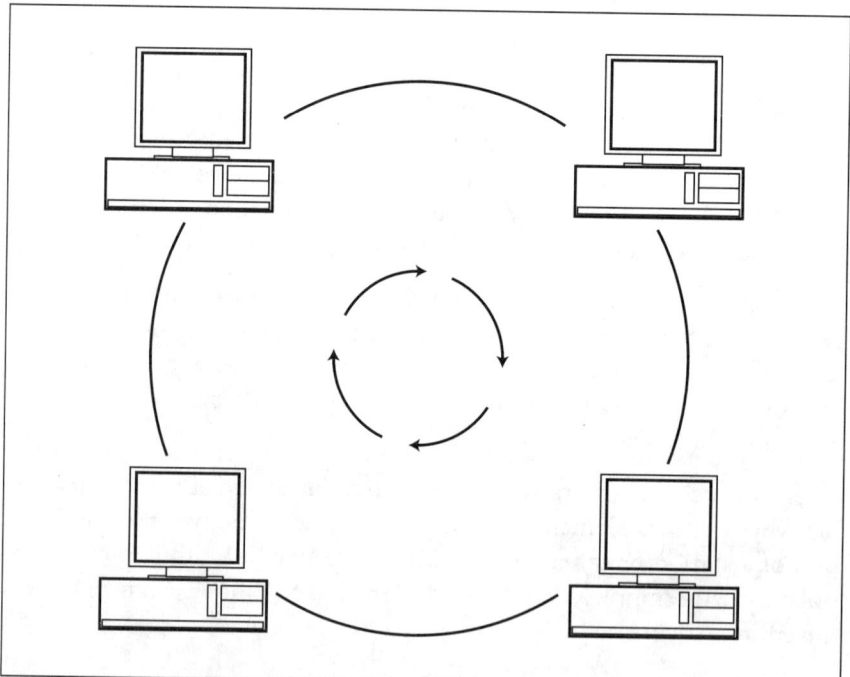

Figure 5.4 The ring topology creates a physical and logical loop.

Network Hardware And Topologies 79

A physical ring topology has several disadvantages. As with a linear bus, a malfunction on one station can bring down the entire network. It is also difficult, especially in larger networks, to maintain a logical ring. Finally, if adjustments or reconfigurations are necessary on any part of the network, you must temporarily bring down the entire network.

 The ring topology provides equal access to the network media for all computers.

Star

In a star topology, all computers on the network are connected to one another using a central hub (see Figure 5.5). Each data transmission that the station sends goes directly to the hub, which then sends the packet on toward its destination. Like in the bus topology, a computer on a star network can attempt to send data at any time; however, only one may actually transmit at a time. If two stations send signals out to the hub at exactly the same time, neither transmission will be successful, and each computer will

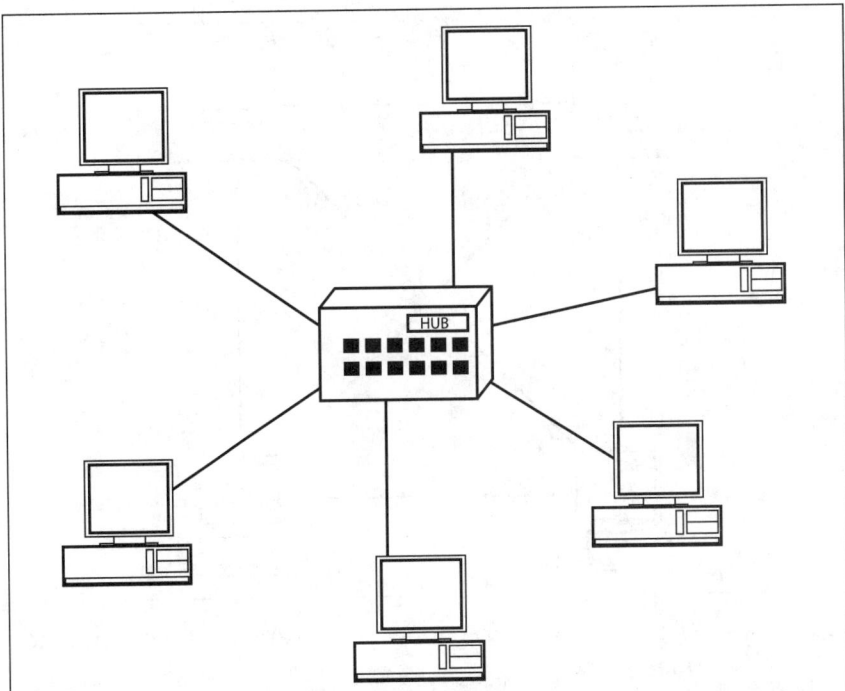

Figure 5.5 In the star topology, computers are connected to one another via a central hub.

have to wait a random period of time before reattempting to access the media. Star topologies are generally more scalable than other types.

A major advantage of implementing a star topology is that, unlike on a linear bus, a malfunction of one station will not disable the entire network. It is easier to locate cable breaks and other malfunctions in a star topology. This capability facilitates the location of cable breaks and other malfunctions. Additionally, the star topology's centralized hub makes it is easier to add new computers or reconfigure the network.

There are a couple of drawbacks inherent in the implementation of a star topology. For one, this type of configuration uses more cabling than most other networks because of the separate lines required to attach each computer to the hub. Also, the central hub handles most functions, so failure of this one piece of hardware will shut down the entire network.

 The star topology is the easiest topology to reconfigure.

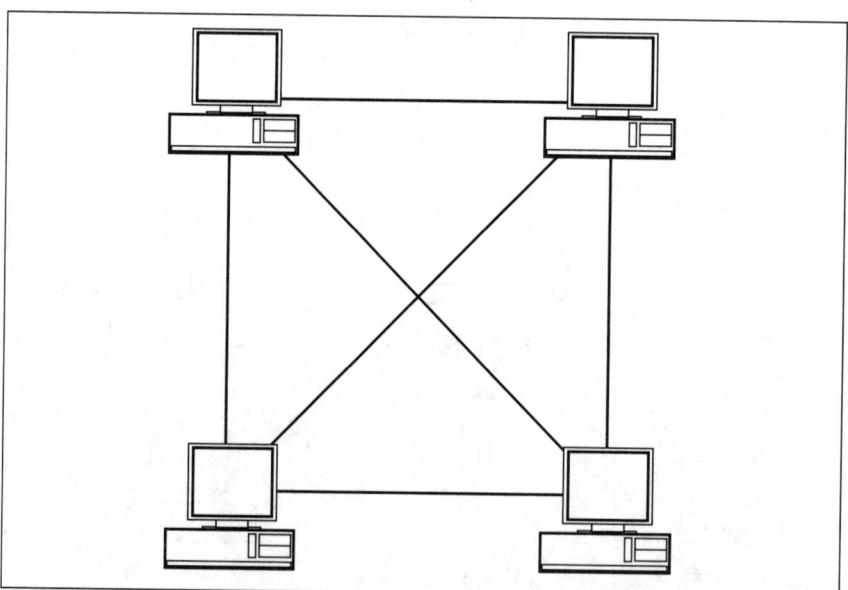

Figure 5.6 The mesh topology connects each and every computer to one another.

Mesh

The mesh topology connects each computer on the network to the others (see Figure 5.6). Meshes use a significantly larger amount of network cabling than do the other network topologies, which makes it more expensive. Additionally, these networks are much more difficult to install than the other topologies. So why would someone use a mesh? The answer is fault tolerance. Fault tolerance is the ability of a system to work around a failure. On a network with a broken segment, that means going around it. Every computer has multiple possible connection paths to the other computers on the network, so a single cable break will not stop network communications between any two computers.

 The mesh topology is highly fault tolerant.

Hybrids

Many organizations choose to use a combination of the main network topologies. We will discuss three such hybrids: star bus, star ring, and hybrid mesh.

Star Bus

As its name implies, the star bus hybrid topology brings together the star and bus topologies (see Figure 5.7). The advantages of using a star bus are that no single computer or segment failure can bring down the entire network. Also, if a single hub fails, only the computers connected to that hub cannot communicate on the network, whereas the other computers are not affected and can continue normal communications.

Star Ring

The star ring topology is also known as a star-wired ring because the hub itself is wired as a ring. As you can see in Figure 5.8, the star ring looks identical to the star topology on the surface, but the hub is actually wired as a logical ring. This topology is popular for Token Ring networks because it is easier to implement than a physical ring, but it still provides the token-passing capabilities of a physical ring inside the hub. Just like in the ring topology, computers are given equal access to the network media through the passing of the token. A single computer failure cannot stop the entire network, but if the hub fails, the ring that the hub controls also fails.

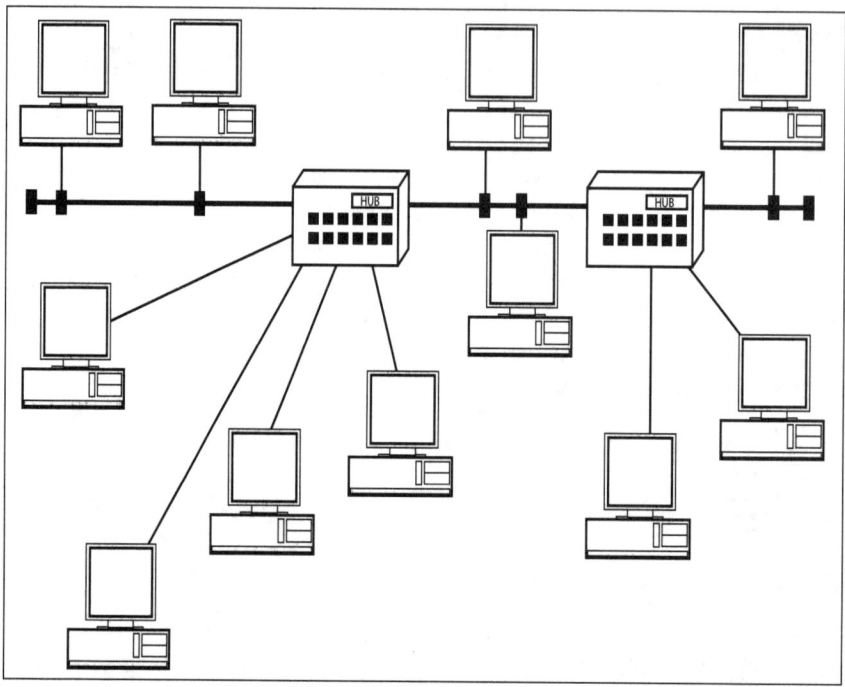

Figure 5.7 A star bus topology.

Hybrid Mesh

Implementing a true mesh on a large network would be expensive, time consuming, and difficult. A hybrid mesh network can provide some of the essential benefits of a true mesh network without using as much cable. Most large organizations do not have mission-critical data stored on all the computers in the network; rather, they store it on the network's servers. Companies that would like to provide their networks with fault tolerance at the network-cabling level may want to limit their mesh to only the mission-critical computers on the network. This means that the mesh exists on only part of the network (see Figure 5.9). This type of mesh still provides fault tolerance among the mission-critical servers, but does not add extra protection for individual network clients. A hybrid mesh would cost less than a complete mesh network, but it would not be as fault tolerant.

Networking Standards And Technologies

In an effort to standardize networking technologies, two groups defined networking standards: the International Standards Organization (ISO) and

Network Hardware And Topologies 83

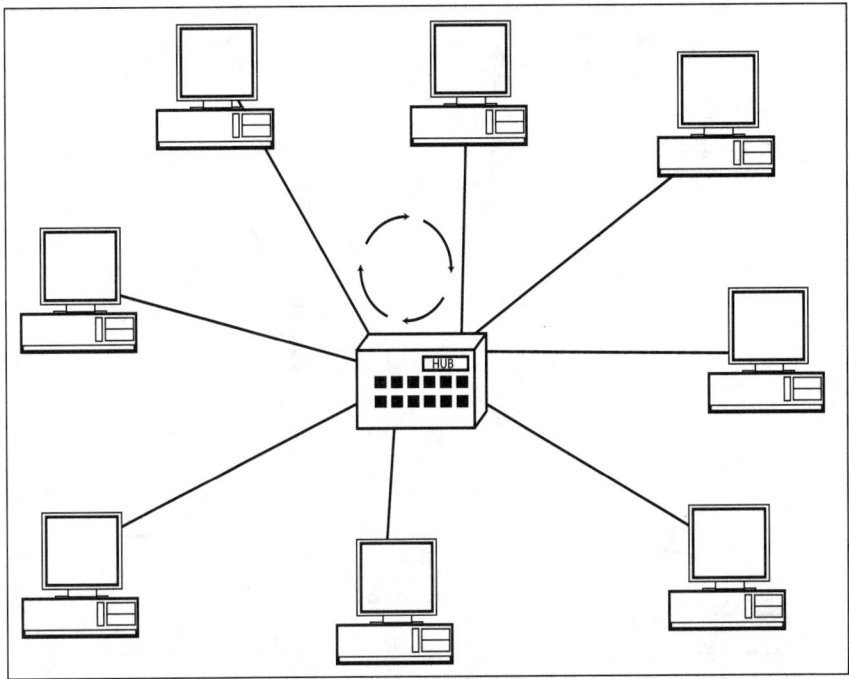

Figure 5.8 The star ring looks identical to the star topology on the surface, but the hub is actually wired as a logical ring.

the Institute of Electrical and Electronic Engineers (IEEE). The ISO created the OSI Reference Model and the IEEE further defined the lower layers of the OSI model.

IEEE 802

The IEEE started its project to further define the Physical and Data Link layers of networking in February of 1980. It named the project 802 after the year and month of the project's beginning. The 802 Project resulted in 12 different specifications that defined network topologies, interface cards, and connections. The specifications that you should be concerned with for the Networking Essentials exam are:

- ▶ **802.2** Divided the OSI model's Data Link layer into the Logical Link Control (LLC) and Media Access Control (MAC) sublayers (see Figure 5.10)

- ▶ **802.3** Defined Ethernet Carrier Sense Multiple Access with Collision Detection (CSMA/CD)

- ▶ **802.5** Defined standards for Token Ring networks

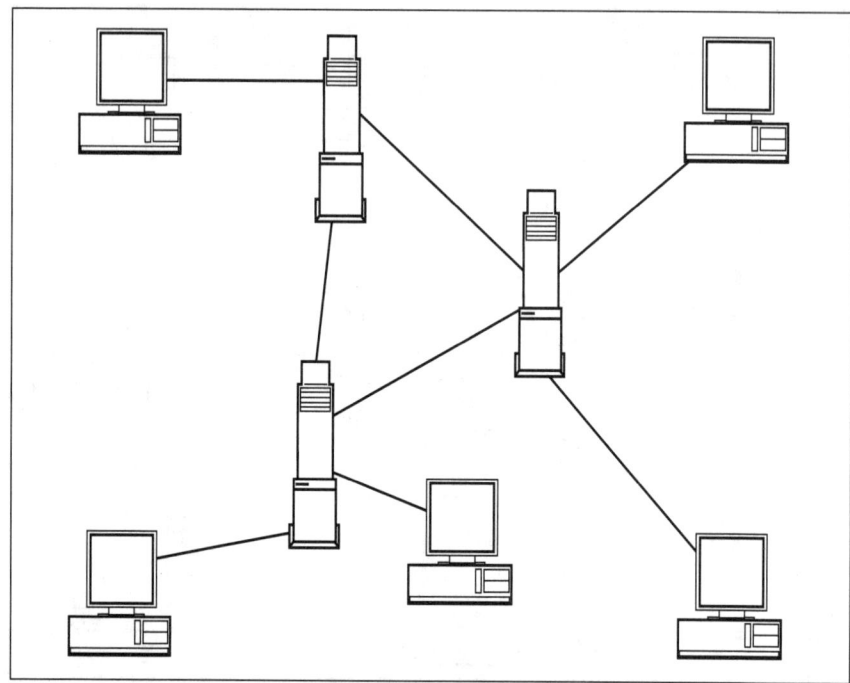

Figure 5.9 The hybrid mesh provides partial fault tolerance at a lower cost than a true mesh.

802.2—Division Of The Data Link Layer

The IEEE decided to further divide the OSI Reference Model's Data Link layer to separate its responsibilities into a Logical Link Control (LLC) sublayer and a Media Access Control (MAC) sublayer (see Figure 5.10). The LLC sublayer is responsible for maintaining a link when two computers are sending data across the network. The LLC exposes Service Access Points (SAPs), which allow computers to communicate with the upper layers of network stack.

802.3—Ethernet CSMA/CD

The 802.3 standard essentially describes how computers communicate on an Ethernet network using CSMA/CD. There are three basic parts to this description:

- **Carrier Sense** A computer checks to see if the network is being used before it attempts to transmit. This is called carrier sense because the computer actually listens to the network to see if a carrier signal is present. If there is no carrier signal, the computer sends its data

Network Hardware And Topologies   85

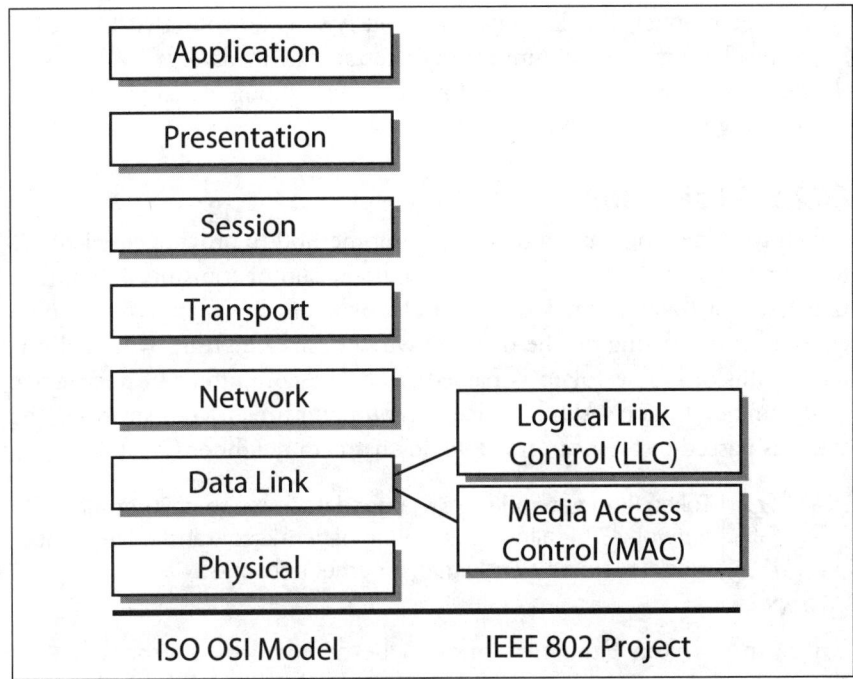

Figure 5.10 The IEEE 802.2 specification subdivided the OSI Reference Model's Data Link layer.

transmission. If there is a carrier signal (meaning another computer is transmitting), the computer does not transmit data until the carrier wave has terminated.

➤ **Multiple Access** All computers connected to the wire can transmit when they have data to send. They do not have to take turns transmitting data, meaning multiple computers can access the wire at a given time.

➤ **Collision Detection** If two computers do transmit data at the same time, their transmission signals can collide; the computers that sent the data have the ability to detect the collision. If the computers detect a collision or multiple carrier signals, they will resend their data. Each computer waits a random interval before transmitting again. Because each computer resends the data after separate random wait periods, the chance of both computers retransmitting at the same time is minimal.

A large number of collisions can seriously slow down network performance because each computer must retransmit its data. If collisions are affecting your network performance, you should consider segmenting your network with a router.

802.5—Token Ring

Token Ring networks use a token-passing method to provide equal access to the network for all computers. Computers cannot transmit data unless they have the token (a small data frame). Token passing keeps two computers from transmitting on the network wire at the same time, which eliminates collisions. The token is passed from one computer's nearest active upstream neighbor (NAUN). Once the computer finishes transmitting, the token is passed to the nearest active downstream neighbor (NADN).

> Token Ring networks use a larger data frame than Ethernet networks. This allows Token Ring networks to transfer large data blocks more efficiently than Ethernet networks.

Errors in a Token Ring network can be detected by a process called "beaconing." The first computer that is powered on in a Token Ring network becomes the Active Monitor (the other computers on the network are Standby Monitors). The Active Monitor is responsible for ensuring that the data successfully travels around the ring. The Active Monitor does this by sending out a data packet to its NADN every seven seconds. The data packet travels around the ring and is eventually returned to the Active Monitor. If a computer does not receive a packet from its NAUN every seven seconds, it creates a packet that announces its address, its NAUN's address, and its beacon type (Active or Standby). The packet travels the network to its farthest point, which indicates where the break or error is located. The computers on the ring can use that information to automatically reconfigure the ring to avoid the cable break. Token Ring's ability to function in spite of a single failure means that it is fault tolerant.

> A physical ring structure is different from the logical Token Ring network. Token Ring and CSMA/CD describe how computers communicate on the network. The physical topology looks different than the logical method the computers use to communicate on the network.

In a Token Ring network, computers are typically connected to a multistation access unit (usually referred to as an MAU or MSAU) and a smart multistation access unit (SMAU). These devices are essentially Token Ring hubs that are wired as logical rings. Each hub has connections for computers and a ring in (RI) and ring out (RO) connection so that multiple MAUs can be connected. An IBM MSAU has 10 connection ports that can host up to 8 computers. There can be up to 33 MSAUs on a Token Ring network.

AppleTalk

AppleTalk is the name of the networking method used by Apple Macintosh computers. The cabling system for an AppleTalk network is called LocalTalk. LocalTalk uses a network media-access method called Carrier Sense Multiple Access with Collision Avoidance (CSMA/CA), which is similar to the Ethernet CSMA/CD method. The major difference between the two methods is that in CSMA/CA, the computer actually broadcasts a warning packet before it begins transmitting on the wire. This packet eliminates almost all collisions on the network because each computer on the network does not attempt to broadcast when another computer sends the warning packet. The major drawback of trying to avoid network collisions is that broadcasting the intent to send a message increases network traffic.

AppleTalk also differs from other networking implementations in that it has a dynamic network addressing scheme. During bootup, the AppleTalk card broadcasts a random number on the network as its card address. If no other computer has claimed that address, the broadcasting computer configures the address as its own. If there is a conflict with another computer, the computer will try to use different combinations until it finds a working configuration.

ARCNet

The Attached Resource Computer Network (ARCNet) was created in 1977 by Datapoint Corporation. ARCNet uses a token-passing method in a logical ring similar to Token Ring networks. However, the computers in an ARCNet network do not have to be connected in any particular fashion. ARCNet can utilize a star, bus, or star bus topology. Data transmissions are broadcast throughout the entire network, which is similar to Ethernet. However, a token is used to allow computers to speak in turn. The token is not passed in a logical ring order because ARCNet does not use the ring topology; instead, the token is passed to the next-highest numerical station number. Station numbers are set on the ARCNet network adapters via dual in-line package (DIP) switches on the card. You can set the station identifier on the card yourself. When setting this identifier, it is best to make the numbers increase based on proximity of one adapter to another. For instance, you wouldn't want stations five and six to be on the opposite ends of the network because the token would have to cross the entire network to go from station five to six.

 ARCNet is no longer a popular networking method because you must manually configure ARCNet cards, and ARCNet speeds are a mere 2.5 Mbps. However, you should know that ARCNet uses RG-62 (93 ohms) cabling; it can be wired as a star, bus, or star bus; and it uses a logical-ring media-access method.

FDDI

The Fiber Distributed Data Interface (FDDI) is another networking standard to consider. FDDI uses fiber cable and a token-passing media-access mechanism to create a fast and reliable network. Speeds of FDDI rings can be up to 100 Mbps and include 500 nodes over a distance of 100 kilometers (62 miles).

FDDI rings have the ability to implement priority levels in token passing. For instance, a mission-critical server may be given a higher priority than other computers on the network, which would allow it to pass more data frames on the network than the other machines.

FDDI rings can be implemented with two rings: a primary and a secondary ring. All data is transmitted on the primary ring, while the secondary ring provides fault tolerance. If there is a break in the primary ring, the secondary ring can be used to compensate for the cable break. Data is actually passed in the opposite direction on the secondary ring so that the cable break does not stop the ring's communications (see Figure 5.11).

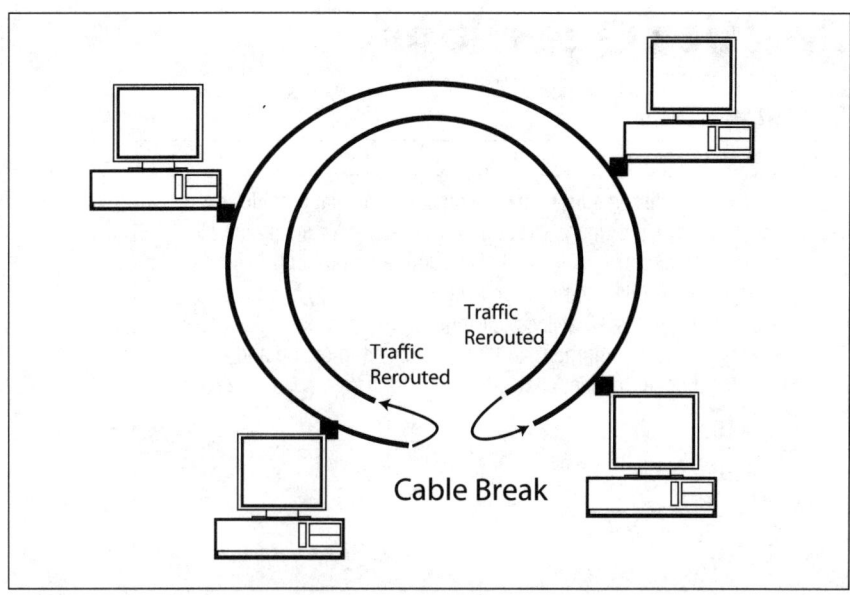

Figure 5.11 The FDDI network can recover from cable breaks using its secondary ring.

Practice Questions

Question 1

> You are considering starting a training company that provides on-site classroom instruction to various businesses. Your service will include a temporary networked classroom environment. Assuming that the facilities do not have pre-installed wiring and that the classroom will use 10 or less computers, which topology would require the least equipment and be the easiest to set up and tear down? [Choose the best answer]
>
> ○ a. Star
> ○ b. Bus
> ○ c. Ring
> ○ d. Mesh

The best answer to this question is b. The bus is the easiest topology to use for temporary networks. The bus topology does not require hubs and minimizes the amount of cable that you will need. The ring topology would be slightly more difficult than a bus because you would have to hook up a physical ring or use a hub that was wired as a ring. Star would be easy to set up, but would require at least one hub. Additionally, the star topology would probably require more wire because every computer would have to be connected to the hub. Mesh would require the most cabling and would be difficult to configure.

Question 2

> If you must configure a network for three mission-critical servers and want to provide a highly fault-tolerant cabling scheme, which topology would you implement? [Choose the best answer]
>
> ○ a. Star
> ○ b. Bus
> ○ c. Ring
> ○ d. Mesh

The best answer is d. The mesh is a highly fault-tolerant architecture that gives computers multiple access routes to one another. The other topologies provide only one connection path between each computer. Warning: Do not read FDDI ring into the question set. If the question wanted you to consider an FDDI ring topology, it would have specifically stated "FDDI ring."

Question 3

Which of the following network access methods sends a signal indicating its intent to transmit data on the wire? [Choose the best answer]

○ a. CSMA/CD

○ b. Token passing

○ c. CSMA/CA

○ d. Beaconing

The correct answer is c. Only Carrier Sense Multiple Access with Collision Avoidance broadcasts its intent to send data on the wire. Token passing uses a token to avoid collisions and Carrier Sense Multiple Access with Collision Detection causes the computer to retransmit frames if a collision is detected. Beaconing is the method that Token Ring networks use to identify and route network communications around a network error.

Question 4

Which type of network media-access method do IBM LANs with multistation access units employ?

○ a. Beaconing

○ b. Token passing

○ c. CSMA/CD

○ d. CSMA/CA

The answer here is b. IBM networks that employ MAUs are Token Ring networks. Token Ring networks use token passing to allow a single station to transmit on the network at a time.

Chapter 5

Question 5

Your network is experiencing heavy traffic and signal attenuation due to long cable distances between computers.

Required Result:

- Correct the signal attenuation problem.

Optional Desired Results:

- Reduce the broadcast traffic that is present on your network.
- Filter the network traffic to reduce the number of frames transferred across the network.

Proposed Solution:

- Install repeaters between distant segments.

Which results does the proposed solution produce?

○ a. The proposed solution produces the required result and produces both of the optional desired results.

○ b. The proposed solution produces the required result and produces only one of the optional desired results.

○ c. The proposed solution produces the required result but does not produce any of the optional desired results.

○ d. The proposed solution does not produce the required result.

The answer to this question is c. The repeaters will stop the signal attenuation by regenerating the signal, but they do not have the ability to reduce traffic in any way.

Question 6

> Your network is experiencing heavy traffic and signal attenuation due to long cable distances between computers.
>
> Required Result:
>
> - Correct the signal attenuation problem.
>
> Optional Desired Results:
>
> - Reduce the broadcast traffic that is present on your network.
> - Filter the network traffic to reduce the number of frames transferred across the network.
>
> Proposed Solution:
>
> - Install repeaters between distant segments. Install routers and configure them to filter broadcast traffic.
>
> Which results does the proposed solution produce?
>
> - a. The proposed solution produces the required result and produces both of the optional desired results.
> - b. The proposed solution produces the required result and produces only one of the optional desired results.
> - c. The proposed solution produces the required result but does not produce any of the optional desired results.
> - d. The proposed solution does not produce the required result.

The correct answer to this question is a. The routers have the ability to filter the broadcast traffic and route packets to the correct computers. Routers are usually used to segment the network and reduce the traffic on the wire. The repeaters will correct the signal attenuation problem.

Question 7

> Which of the following network devices functions at the Network layer of the OSI model?
>
> ○ a. Bridge
>
> ○ b. Repeater
>
> ○ c. Router
>
> ○ d. Gateway

The answer here is c. Routers function at the Network layer; bridges function at the Data Link layer; and gateways function at the Transport layer of the OSI model and higher.

Question 8

> You are installing a network card in a computer that has several devices configured. There is a printer on LPT 1, a mouse on COM 1, a modem on COM 2, and a SCSI host adapter occupying IRQ 10. The computer also has a sound card using IRQ 5. If your network card supports IRQs 3 through 5 and 9 through 11, which of the following IRQs could you set it for in this computer? [Check all correct answers]
>
> ❑ a. IRQ 3
>
> ❑ b. IRQ 4
>
> ❑ c. IRQ 10
>
> ❑ d. IRQ 11

The correct answer is d, IRQ 11. COM 1 is using IRQ 4, COM 2 is using IRQ 3, and LPT1 is using IRQ 5, so the only remaining open IRQ is 11.

Network Hardware And Topologies

Question 9

> Which of the following is most likely the problem if the operating system is unable to detect the network card? [Choose the best answer]
>
> ○ a. Wrong frame type is set on the network card
> ○ b. Wrong IRQ is set on the network card
> ○ c. Wrong IRQ is set on the IDE controller card
> ○ d. Wrong protocol is bound to the network adapter

Only answer b is correct. The only situation that would cause the operating system to miss the network card is an incorrect IRQ setting. The wrong protocol and/or frame type would only disable the network communications. An incorrect setting on an IDE controller would probably keep the computer from booting. To answer this type of question, it is best that you memorize the common IRQs and their related devices (see Table 5.1 earlier in this chapter).

Question 10

> Your network uses only the NetBEUI protocol. You would like to segment the network to reduce traffic. Which of the following devices could you use for this network?
>
> ○ a. Router
> ○ b. Bridge
> ○ c. Gateway
> ○ d. Multiplexer

The correct answer is b. Routers have the ability to segment the network, but NetBEUI is a non-routable protocol, so you cannot use a router on this particular network (unless you decide to choose a different protocol). Bridges can work with any protocol because they only look at the MAC address of the packet.

Question 11

> Your company has two LANs that use different protocols. You need to connect the two LANs, but you do not want to configure additional protocols on either network. Which device could you use to perform this task?
>
> ○ a. Bridge
>
> ○ b. Router
>
> ○ c. Brouter
>
> ○ d. Gateway

The correct answer is d. Only the gateway has the ability to translate from one protocol to another. The simple answer of "router" for b does not include a multiprotocol router.

Question 12

> At which location(s) should there be terminators on the pictured Thinnet (bus topology) network (see graphic)? [Check all correct answers]
>
> ❏ a. Location 1
>
> ❏ b. Location 2
>
> ❏ c. Location 3
>
> ❏ d. Location 4
>
> ❏ e. Location 5

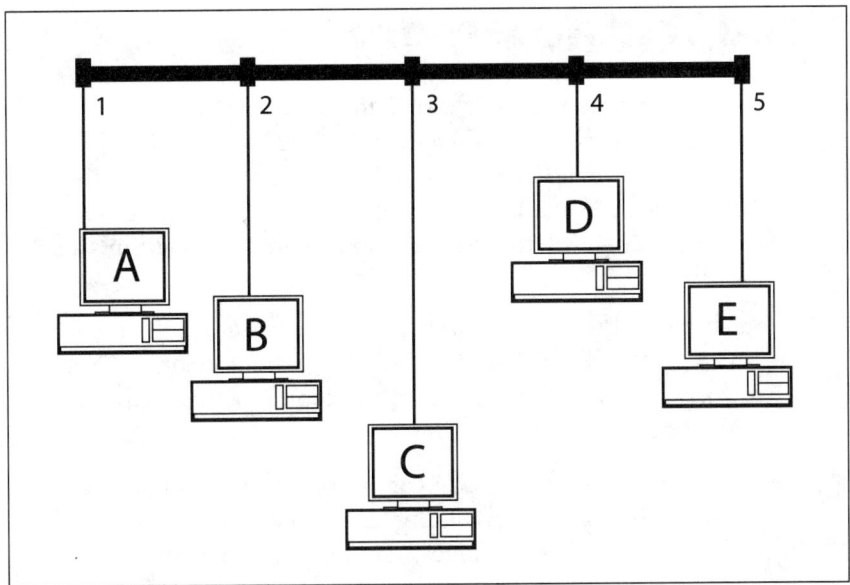

The answers to this question are a and e, locations 1 and 5, respectively. Remember that the bus topology requires a terminator at each end of the network.

Need To Know More?

Chellis, James, Charles Perkins, and Matthew Strebe: *MCSE: Networking Essentials Study Guide, 2nd Edition*. Sybex Network Press, San Francisco, CA, 1998. ISBN 0-7821-2220-5. Chapter 1, "An Introduction to Networks," contains excellent coverage of the various topics contained within this chapter.

Microsoft Press: *Networking Essentials, 2nd Edition*. Redmond, WA, 1997. ISBN 1-57231-527-X. Unit 1, Lesson 3, "Network Design," discusses all of the topics in this chapter in great detail.

Search the TechNet CD (or its online version through **www.microsoft.com**) using the keywords "topology," "Ethernet," "hubs," "bridges," "routers," and "brouters."

Network Planning And Design

Terms you'll need to understand:

- √ Security
- √ Disaster recovery
- √ 10Base2
- √ 10Base5
- √ Coaxial cable
- √ Twisted-pair cable
- √ Fiber optic cable
- √ Ethernet
- √ Token Ring
- √ ARCNet
- √ Fault tolerance
- √ Repeaters
- √ Bridges
- √ Routers
- √ Brouters
- √ Gateways

Techniques you'll need to master:

- √ Understanding the concepts behind a successful network deployment
- √ Implementing fault tolerant features for network security

LAN communication functions are primarily performed by a combination of hardware and the firmware specifically designed to support it; therefore, the physical and logical implementations are essential to every network. Hardware can typically be defined as the network interface card (NIC), the cabling plant, and the hub or concentrator unit. To implement LANs successfully and logically, you must take into consideration user requirements, protocols, and a variety of architectures, which have strengths and weaknesses. We examine these topics throughout this chapter.

First, we cover what considerations must be taken into account when choosing a particular topology or network protocol. Next, we discuss topology requirements, including Ethernet and Token Ring—which we introduced in Chapter 5—and the restrictions of each media type. Then, we take a look at selecting an appropriate network architecture and network design principles. Finally, we review the guidelines for planning a successful deployment.

Network Layout Principles

There are several factors to consider when designing a network. Layout will be influenced by such elements as the following:

- Cost
- Distance limitations
- Potential growth
- Location
- Security
- Disaster recovery
- Capacity

Although you want the network to be as cheap, fast, unlimited, and secure as possible, the reality is that such a thing does not exist; you must achieve a balance among all the components. A matrix that takes design into consideration can be constructed. In this design, all factors can be numbered with the higher numbers taking priority over lower numbers. For example, if you are a designer for a small engineering firm that both expects little to no growth and has great capacity requirements due to bandwidth-intensive

Network Planning And Design 101

applications, you would probably give greater weight to cost and capacity at the expense of disaster recovery and growth potential.

Cabling Considerations

The most basic networking component is the cabling plant. You should know how to select an appropriate cabling scheme, which we covered in detail in Chapter 4. You must take into consideration cost as well as distance limitations and restrictions. In the case of the engineering firm in the earlier example, a bus topology is appropriate because it is cheaper to implement than a star or ring topology. The trade-off is disaster recovery, because a single cable break affects all other workstations on the bus. Another consideration is media type. Your choices are twisted-pair, coaxial, or fiber optic cable—or wireless technology.

Here's what you need to know:

➤ Thinnet or 10Base2 networks use coaxial cable. The type is 50-ohm RG-58 A/U. Don't confuse it with RG-59A/U or RG-62A/U cables, used for cable television and ACRNet, respectively.

➤ Thinnet is used for relatively short-distance communication and is fairly flexible to facilitate routing between workstations. Thinnet connects directly to a workstation's network adapter card using a BNC T-connector, and uses the NIC's internal transceiver.

➤ Coaxial cable is also used for Thicknet or standard Ethernet cabling. It is less flexible, because it's about half-an-inch in diameter. Thicknet was traditionally used to connect several smaller Thinnet segments, because Thicknet was more expensive and difficult to install, and makes for a better backbone cable.

➤ Coaxial cable has the following advantages: low maintenance costs; simple to install; better resistance to signal noise over longer distances; and electronic support components are less expensive.

➤ Disadvantages of coaxial cable include limited distance and topology, low security (easily tapped); and it is difficult to make major changes to the cabling topology.

➤ To link two coaxial segments together, use a barrel or T-connector.

- Twisted-pair cable has the following advantages: It's well understood; it's easy to add computers to existing networks; it may already be installed in many buildings; and it is the least expensive cable medium.

- Twisted-pair cable has the following disadvantages: It's susceptible to noise, distance, and bandwidth limitations; it's least secure (easiest to tap); and it requires more expensive electronic support components (that is, hubs).

- Fiber optic cable advantages include: most secure (hardest to tap); highest bit rates; lowest loss over great distances; not subject to interference; supports voice, video, and data; smallest in size; and greatest longevity.

- Disadvantages of fiber optic cable are: most expensive medium in terms of installation and maintenance; somewhat delicate cable (can't be sharply bent); mostly limited to point-to-point applications because support components are expensive and not readily available.

Topology Requirements

Now that we've discussed media and how it affects the network topology, let's examine what the requirements are for the two most common topologies in use today: twisted-pair Ethernet and Token Ring. Token Ring is commonly used in large companies that need to network PCs with IBM mainframes and is less common in small businesses. It can have higher transmission speeds and can support more computers on a single network segment (up to 260, depending on the media type) than Ethernet. It is more expensive than Ethernet and is harder to install and maintain. We usually see its network cables diagrammed as a ring; but in reality, workstation cables radiate from a central hub to the computers, like a rimless spoke.

The layout for twisted-pair Ethernet looks like that of Token Ring, with computers attached to cables radiating from a central hub. As with Token Ring, the workstation cable runs up to 100 meters from a port in the hub to the network interface. The greatest advantage of twisted-pair Ethernet is that it is somewhat fault tolerant: If a transceiver starts jabbering or causing broadcast storms, the concentrator will usually be intelligent enough to shut down that port.

Also, the hub minimizes network failures. If a twisted-pair cable breaks, only that cable's computer is affected. If a thin Ethernet cable breaks, the entire network stops functioning because 10Base2 is a bus topology. However, hubs complicate expansion: If you have an eight-port hub and want to add a ninth computer, you need a bigger hub (or another hub, with a maximum of four repeater levels). If you have eight computers on a thin Ethernet segment, you can add a ninth with an additional cable and T-connector. Again, a trade-off must be made between cost, distance limitations, potential growth, and capacity.

10BaseT Ethernet Restrictions

Here are some limitations of 10BaseT Ethernet:

- Workstations may be no more than 328 feet (100 meters) from the concentrator port.
- 1,024 stations are allowed on a segment without bridging.

10Base2 Ethernet Restrictions

Here are some limitations of 10Base2 Ethernet:

- The Ethernet 5-4-3 rule for connecting segments is 5 trunk segments can be connected, with 4 repeaters or concentrators, with no more than 3 populated segments (on coaxial cable).
- Length of trunk segment may be up to 607 feet (185 meters).
- A maximum of 30 workstations is allowed per trunk.
- There may be no more than 1,024 workstations per network.
- Entire network trunk length can't exceed 3,035 feet (925 meters).
- The minimum cable length between workstations is 20 inches.

10BaseFL Fiber Optic Inter-Repeater Link (FOIRL) Restrictions

10BaseFL is a standard defined by the IEEE 802.3 specification and is used over two fiber-optic links to transmit and receive data. It is highly resistant to noise and interference, and has a distance limitation of two kilometers.

Token Ring Restrictions

Here are some limitations of Token Ring:

- The maximum number of workstations is 260 on Type 1 or fiber optic cable at 16 Mbps.
- The maximum number of workstations is 72 on Type 3 cable at 4 Mbps.
- The distance between MSAUs (multistation access units) is 100 meters or 328 feet (Type 1 cabling) to 45 meters or 148 feet (Type 2 cabling).
- Each ring can have up to 33 MSAUs.
- Maximum distance of the ring is 4 kilometers with fiber optic cable.

ARCNet Restrictions

Here are some limitations of ARCNet:

- Bus segment length for coaxial cable is a maximum of 1,000 feet, with a limit of 8 workstations per coaxial segment.
- Bus segment length for twisted pair is a maximum of 400 feet.
- There is a maximum of 255 workstations per network.
- Workstations can be located up to 600 feet from the active hub.
- The maximum distance from passive hubs to active hubs is 100 feet; the maximum distance between two active hubs is 2,000 feet.
- The maximum distance allowed between workstations is 20,000 feet.
- There can be no more than 4 workstations on a passive hub, no more than 100 feet from a hub.
- Passive hubs cannot be connected to other passive hubs.

Selecting A Network Architecture

The network architect is guided first by the list of requirements, in order of priority, for the proposed network. When selecting a network architecture, you'll want to consider the following factors:

- Hardware requirements
- Software requirements

Network Planning And Design

- Telecommunication needs
- Disaster recovery needs
- Corporate culture and organization
- Information analysis
- Environmental conditions

The types of hardware you need to consider include workstations, servers, backup systems, peripherals such as printers and CD-ROM towers, uninterruptible power supplies (UPSs), routers, bridges, hubs, minicomputers, and/or mainframes. If your network includes legacy systems, you'll need to integrate that technology smoothly with newer, open systems. It would not make sense to install a 155 Mbps ATM network in a company that still uses 486-class machines with ISA buses. Consider not only configuration, but usage as well. If your network utilization is very high and performance is slow, but your organization is expecting a growth spurt, consider replacing your aging Ethernet concentrators with high-powered switches to relieve congestion and create room for expansion and growth.

Software Considerations

What software will reside on the network? Perhaps your organization uses dumb terminals connected to a mainframe that runs proprietary, mission-critical applications. Perhaps several database programmers are on staff and the use of SQL Servers in your company is quite high.

Maybe your company uses only standard office applications, such as Microsoft Office. You may belong to a graphical design firm that uses bandwidth-intensive design software. Or you may work for Mr. Scrooge, who doesn't believe in spending money for network management, monitoring, or administration software tools. The choice of architecture will be different in each of these cases.

Telecommunications Considerations

The telecommunications needs that you need to consider include such things as PBXs, data links to the WAN, and remote access for a traveling sales force or a work-at-home initiative. If your company plans to use the same data link for voice as well as video and data, you'll need a T1-class connection. If this link is mission critical, you need to either establish a second, fail-safe link or make arrangements with your carrier for a virtual redundant link.

For example, if you must communicate primarily with the corporate headquarters in Atlanta, and you are in New York City, NetBEUI would not be an appropriate protocol for your network because it is not routable. If your work-at-home users all have 19.2 Kbps modems, the dial-in access will be an information bottleneck and you wouldn't need to put your communications server on a high-speed backbone.

Disaster Recovery And Fault-Tolerance Considerations

How important is disaster recovery to your organization? Consider a medical facility. Its network must be available 24 hours a day and it must be secure, to protect the confidentiality of patients' medical records. The network equipment should be protected by UPSs, and all file servers should be kept in locked closets, away from unauthorized personnel. The facility would probably need redundant equipment such as file servers, hubs, and routers even though redundancy is very expensive.

A bus topology wouldn't be appropriate because a cable break affects all workstations behind the break. Token Ring probably wouldn't be very effective either, because damage to a portion of the ring can knock several workstations off the network if the design isn't right.

Corporate Culture And Organizational Considerations

An effective, efficient network must also take into account the culture and organization of the company. For instance, if you belong to a small office that can't support a full-time MIS staff, you would probably choose a simple protocol, such as NWLink, and a fool-proof topology, such as twisted-pair Ethernet, which doesn't require a great deal of maintenance or administrative overhead. On the other hand, if you are designing for a law firm, where security is paramount, you'll need a file server for user-level security. A peer-to-peer network, such as Windows 98, that supports only share-level security would not be a good choice even though it is inexpensive.

You must also consider the following:

➤ What types of users will the network support and how will they use it?

➤ Will vendors and subcontractors be allowed to access your network?

Network Planning And Design   **107**

▶ Will that access be local, through the Internet, or by way of dial-in access?

Share-level security, also called password-protected shares, assigns a password to each resource on the network. User-level security, also called access permissions, assigns rights to the network resources on a user-by-user basis. But, if your company requires high levels of security, encryption provides the best protection for user data.

If your network users are not computer-savvy, you would not want to choose an operating system such as NetWare or Unix, because they require a high level of understanding or ongoing, in-depth training. A simple, user-friendly network operating system (NOS) would be easier to understand and implement.

The best way to partition users is to identify how much latitude they need to successfully do their jobs. For example, someone who uses few applications and rarely upgrades software or hardware does not need a flexible and expandable environment. This is typical of task-oriented users. On the other hand, power or "knowledge-oriented" users—who need to use several different applications and upgrade hardware frequently—need more flexibility. Although it's obvious that centralized management leads to lower total cost of ownership and more security, the desire to centrally manage systems should not be more important than giving users the right tools for their jobs.

Information Analysis Considerations

Consider the informational needs of your network users. It may not be a matter of what they need to know, but *when* they need to know it. A bank or financial institution will probably use fast, dumb terminals that communicate with an off-site mainframe to access customers' records for loan processing. If the data is not immediately accessible during normal banking hours, the company stands to lose a substantial amount of money, as well as the goodwill of its customers.

In the case of a large governmental agency, on the other hand, data is usually updated through batch processing during the night, and information is not available in realtime. In most organizations of any size, there is such a substantial amount of data that sophisticated data warehousing and data mining tools are needed along with a cadre of analysts to extract the relevant information. In this case, the analysts would probably require faster machines and faster network access than the typical user, because information could be as old as 24 hours.

Environmental Considerations

Environmental conditions may include the obvious, such as space, electricity, cleanliness, and security, but these considerations may really be as simple as what's in place today. For instance, you would probably choose twisted-pair Ethernet if your building has CAT3 or better cabling already installed. However, if your manufacturing company plans to add another building to its campus and your existing buildings use a Token Ring network to access a mainframe, it wouldn't make sense to install Ethernet. Breaking that uniformity would result in higher installation costs, and a gateway would be required. Likewise, there's a higher cost of ownership for hybrid networks like this, which doubles the amount of hardware and knowledge you need to do your job.

Network Design Principles

Now that we've considered the elements of network design, let's consider the mechanisms involved. There is a truism in this business: Networks never shrink, they only grow. You must always design for growth whenever the budget allows. When a LAN has exceeded its limitations, you must start another LAN. For devices on one LAN to communicate with others on the second LAN, you must link the two. There are many ways to do this, depending on the architectures of the LANs, the cabling media, and the distance between the LANs.

Sometimes, your company may have merged with another. The two LANs to be interconnected may be dissimilar and geographically distinct. In this case, you might even be forced to link both LANs to a WAN. If your company has a large sales force always on the move, you should consider adding a communications server to provide dial-in access to the LAN/WAN.

Repeaters, Bridges, Routers, Brouters, And Gateways

In Chapter 5, you learned the difference between repeaters, bridges, routers, brouters, and gateways. It is important to remember their functions because it will affect which one you use to connect LANs to other LANs, to join LANs to WANs, to extend cable beyond its distance limitation, and to reduce network traffic.

 Repeaters work at the Physical layer of the OSI model, bridges work at the Data Link layer, and routers work at the Network layer. Gateways tend to work at the Application layer performing protocol conversion, but they may act at all seven layers.

The distance limitations of various media types are due to signal attenuation, which is dictated by the media composition. Repeaters are used to extend the distance that a signal can travel by regenerating the signal before sending it to the neighboring cable segment. They perform no segmentation or traffic arbitration, but rather regenerate and pass along everything that comes in. Segments that are joined by a repeater must be of the same media access scheme, protocol, and transmission type, but can be of dissimilar media type (for example, a repeater could connect 10BaseT to 10Base2).

Bridges are needed to connect networks and to provide network segmentation. Bridges can connect dissimilar media and they maintain tables of MAC addresses. Bridges will not pass data across a segment if the source and destination are on the same segment. When a bridge handles error correction, performance improves because the bridge (rather than end devices) checks for errors that might lead to a request for retransmission. Therefore, a bridge is a good choice to improve network performance because it improves performance and is less expensive than a router.

Routers are often confused with bridges, but they perform more functions more intelligently. Routers are able to accommodate multiple paths between network segments, allowing packets to take the best possible route between sender and receiver. Bridges can't take advantage of multiple paths simultaneously. Routers also provide flow control, filtering, and broadcast management, so they are sometimes used to decrease network traffic propagation or for additional firewalling in a TCP/IP network. But routers, which work at higher layers of the OSI model, distinguish protocols and are not suitable in a NetBEUI network.

Brouters combine the characteristics of a bridge and a router, so they are a good choice for complex networks with several protocols because they can provide bridging functions for one protocol and routing functions for another.

Gateways are typically used to translate between dissimilar protocols, data structures, languages, or architectures. A gateway may be software or strictly hardware. The most common example would be setting up a Windows NT Server to act as a gateway for a Novell NetWare network, so that the Microsoft clients can access the NetWare resources without adding software to the workstation. Another common example would be connecting email systems, such as Microsoft Mail and cc:Mail, so that users can send mail to other email users, regardless of what email package sender and receiver may use.

Finally, you would use a multiplexer to combine several data channels for transmission across a high-speed data link, such as a T1 or frame relay line. It is possible and sometimes cost effective to combine voice, data, and video on the same WAN link by using a multiplexer. The multiplexer will combine data streams from different sources into one feed for transmission over a WAN link.

Planning For Successful Deployment

Here are several factors to consider when planning for a network installation:

- Cabling
- Topology
- Network operating system
- Software and hardware
- Fault tolerance, disaster recovery, and security
- Protocols
- User requirements
- Administration

To plan for a successful network installation, you would:

1. **Conduct a survey of existing conditions.** This step is crucial to determining the parameters within which you must work. Remember each of the factors listed earlier. The existing conditions form the framework for any network design.

2. **Document the network requirements.** Again, using the already mentioned guidelines, be sure to document the following items:

    - How many computers are currently in use and how many are expected for the future?
    - What type of computers are involved?

Network Planning And Design 111

- What special peripherals are required?
- Will the LAN be tied to a mainframe or a WAN?
- What software is in use or expected to be used?
- What type of administrative control is necessary?
- What level of resource sharing will be required?

3. **Select the network operating system (NOS).** This is the next step because it dictates what types of file server hardware you will need and which transport protocols you will support. Make sure the NOS can serve your existing and future network requirements and will be supported for a long time to come. Also, consider the administrative burden that the network operating system may create.

4. **Plan the logical network.** This involves choosing a transport protocol and data link technologies, dividing the network into subnets if necessary, and choosing security domains.

5. **Determine the network technology.** This is often the most difficult step, because it involves planning for unknowns. Estimating client loads and determining what technologies will support those loads is tough when you must estimate capacities. For instance, although a Token Ring network delivers a faster bit rate than an Ethernet network, workstations must wait for the token to begin transmission, which may make the Ethernet appear more responsive. Token Ring networks load in a simple, deterministic manner when clients are added, whereas overloaded Ethernet networks can cease functioning altogether.

6. **Plan the physical plant.** The environment, as well as the chosen network architectures, dictate what cabling media and topology are required. User and corporate requirements necessitate how and where the file servers, hubs, routers, and switches are stored and maintained.

7. **Select a file server hardware platform.** Make sure that all hardware is listed on Microsoft's Hardware Compatibility List (HCL), which you can find on the Web, on the TechNet CD, or supplied by your local Microsoft dealer or VAR. This simple step will save you a lot of grief when it's time for technical support.

8. **Determine storage requirements.** Again, this is tough to do for a new installation because there is no background data. Use the guidelines given for the network operating system

you've chosen and the manufacturer's data supplied with your file server hardware. Then, plan to double your storage every year. Make sure you have adequate RAM to support your storage requirements.

9. **Plan client support.** Use this planning time to focus on completing migration from 16-bit to 32-bit Windows-based applications. Make sure your clients can support new technology. To productively run databases, browsers, and other common applications, the majority of the desktops today should be Intel 486 (or equivalent) or higher, with a minimum of 16 MB of RAM and compatible hardware and software. Make sure your routers support all the protocols your network will need.

Practice Questions

Question 1

> The Enormous Corporation is moving from NetWare 3.12 to Windows NT. Due to its terrible environmental record, the corporation is constantly involved in lengthy lawsuits. The company legal department is worried about confidential information placed on corporate file servers and would like to secure that information from everyone except itself. The company would also like to be able to use Internet email to share information, because it is a geographically diverse company, but it is afraid of hackers. What security measures should be implemented in this situation? [Check all correct answers]
>
> ❑ a. Gateway Service For NetWare
> ❑ b. Encryption
> ❑ c. User-level permissions
> ❑ d. File-level permissions

Both b and c are correct. User-level permissions imply that a file server has authenticated security based on a predefined set of criteria. Also, they are more secure than file-level permissions, answer d. Because user-level permissions don't trust even the network administrator with this information, encryption (answer b) would safeguard the files kept on the server as well as let the lawyers send Internet email securely. Gateway Service For NetWare would be required for access to the remaining NetWare servers, but it would not provide the required security.

Question 2

> The XYZ Graphical Design firm is building a new, state-of-the-art facility to house its growing business. It is going to use a combination of NetWare and Windows NT servers on its network and would like all servers to reside on a 100 Mbps backbone. The rest of the company will be using 10 Mbps Ethernet for now, but may require higher bandwidths in the future. What is the appropriate cabling type for this situation?
>
> ○ a. RG-58 A/U
> ○ b. UTP CAT3
> ○ c. UTP CAT4
> ○ d. UTP CAT5

Answer d is the correct choice. CAT5 cabling is suitable for 100 Mbps bandwidth and is less expensive to install than fiber optics. RG-58 A/U is a coaxial cable used for Thinnet Ethernet networks and is not suitable for higher bandwidths. Therefore, answer a is incorrect. CAT3 unshielded twisted-pair is capable of carrying 10BaseT, but it's not recommended for higher bandwidths. Therefore, answer b is incorrect. CAT4 is not a deployed wiring standard. Therefore, answer c is incorrect.

Question 3

Consider the following situation:

You work for a medical clinic that supports patients around the clock. You are installing twisted-pair Ethernet in a new wing of the building. There will be 25 machines in the addition, but that number is expected to double in the first year. There has been some concern about disaster recovery due to recent events in the news. Due to patient confidentiality, tape backups are kept on site. Cost is not a consideration.

Required Result:

- Increase the level of fault tolerance for your file servers to the highest degree possible.

Optional Desired Results:

- You want to plan for the expected growth.
- You need to maintain a high level of security.

Proposed Solution:

- Implement a RAID 5 disk array for all file servers in the clinic.

Which results does the proposed solution produce?

○ a. The proposed solution produces the required result and produces both of the optional desired results.

○ b. The proposed solution produces the required result and produces only one of the optional desired results.

○ c. The proposed solution produces the required result but does not produce any of the optional desired results.

○ d. The proposed solution does not produce the required result.

The correct answer is d. The proposed solution would not be completely fault tolerant in the case of the failure of more than one drive. The correct solution would be to install RAID 1 array, which is complete disk mirroring. Another option would be to maintain hot spares for all network equipment.

Question 4

> You want to connect a small Token Ring network with an Ethernet network, both of which use NetBEUI. You want to implement filtering to control network traffic. Which device should you use to accomplish this?
>
> ○ a. A repeater
>
> ○ b. A router
>
> ○ c. A gateway
>
> ○ d. A bridge

The correct answer is d because a bridge can connect two network segments and provide filtering to limit network traffic. The answer cannot be b because NetBEUI is not routable. A repeater cannot connect two dissimilar media access schemes and a gateway will not provide filtering. Therefore, answers a and c are also incorrect.

Question 5

> You are the administrator for a small insurance office with a 27-node LAN. You currently have a single 10Base2 Ethernet segment installed in your office, running Novell NetWare 3.12, to which all networked devices are attached. Your boss announced at the last staff meeting that business is booming and your office will be adding four more agents next month. You plan to add four machines to the existing segment. How will you accomplish this?
>
> ○ a. A T-connector
>
> ○ b. A router
>
> ○ c. A repeater
>
> ○ d. A bridge

The correct answer is c, because there can be no more than 30 stations per 10Base2 segment. If you added a thirty-first station using a T-connector, as mentioned in answer a, you would have experienced intermittent problems or a complete network failure. A router or bridge, although they can link Ethernet segments, is not the best solution here.

Network Planning And Design

Question 6

> Your company has merged with the Enormous Corporation. You have implemented Microsoft Mail for the company's email and have spent a considerable amount of training dollars on your end-users. The new parent corporation email standard is cc:Mail. What device will be required to connect the dissimilar email systems, so that your users can retain their current mail system and communicate with the new administration?
>
> ○ a. A gateway
> ○ b. A router
> ○ c. Microsoft Services For Lotus
> ○ d. A MIME repeater

The correct answer is a. A gateway is needed to provide conversion because those functions would typically be performed at the highest layer of the OSI model, the Application layer. A router would simply route data packets, without application translation. Microsoft Services For Lotus and MIME repeaters do not exist.

Question 7

> You have been hired as a consultant for the new Widget manufacturing company. This company will be moving into a pre-fabricated building in a month, and you must have the cabling in place for a twisted-pair Ethernet network. The four divisions of the company are Accounting, Administration, Sales, and Assembly Line. The company wants to give the employees a lot of latitude to use network resources freely, but accounting doesn't want anyone to see how much commission the sales staff makes. You have selected Microsoft Windows NT as your network operating system. Which security model should you implement?
>
> ○ a. Domain-level security
> ○ b. Inherited-rights security
> ○ c. Share-level security
> ○ d. User-level security

The correct answer is c, share-level security. This level of security involves assigning a password to selected shared resources, giving the owner of the share control over access permissions for other users. Domain-level security and inherited-rights security do not exist in a Windows NT network. User-level security (access permissions) is very extensive, providing a great deal of control over access rights, but it usually requires administrative overhead that may not be appropriate for a small network, especially one where the culture supports less security, rather than more.

Question 8

> The auditing firm of Dewie, Cheatam & Howe has hired you to install a temporary network for a two-month assignment. The company will be setting up seven computers in an unused boardroom that is not presently cabled for network use. What topology should you choose?
>
> ○ a. Bus
>
> ○ b. Mesh
>
> ○ c. Ring
>
> ○ d. Star-bus

The correct answer is a because a bus topology is the easiest and cheapest to install. There are no widely available commercial mesh topologies, which disqualifies b from further consideration. Both ring and star topologies usually require ancillary equipment, making them too expensive (and therefore less suitable) for a temporary network.

Question 9

> Because its new operations in Las Vegas have been successful, the Dewie, Cheatam & Howe accounting firm has decided to open another local office in Phoenix and relocate some of its employees from the corporate main offices in Hawaii. A high-speed data link will be needed to connect each of the mainland locations to the main offices on the islands. The company wants to take advantage of its low-cost T1 rates to link both voice and data on the same carrier signal. What type of device should the firm use?
>
> ○ a. A repeater
> ○ b. A bridge
> ○ c. A gateway
> ○ d. A multiplexer

Answer d is correct. A repeater will not aggregate various channels onto one data stream, which is the primary requirement. Neither a bridge nor a gateway will combine multiple signals over a single transmission link, but a multiplexer, answer d, will. This can be implemented in software, but is usually a combination of software and hardware.

Question 10

You have been managing a successful, efficient network for more than two years at your division of the Enormous Corporation. But because of the last mega-merger, your end-users have been complaining of slow network response times and strange, unrepeatable errors. Mr. Scrooge, your CFO, doesn't believe in spending money on frivolous software monitoring and administration tools. Fortunately, you have installed a Microsoft Windows NT network. What tools would you use to detect the potential problem(s)?

○ a. A network analyzer
○ b. Performance Monitor
○ c. A cable tester
○ d. User Manager For Domains

The correct answer is b. Performance Monitor is the only network monitoring tool that comes built-in to Windows NT. Although the User Manager For Domains is also built-in, it does not include problem diagnosis capabilities.

Need To Know More?

 Chellis, James, Charles Perkins, and Matthew Strebe: *MCSE: Networking Essentials Study Guide, 2nd Edition*. Sybex Network Press, San Francisco, CA, 1998. ISBN 0-7821-2220-5. Chapter 5, "Designing the Local Area Network," contains excellent coverage of the various topics contained within this chapter.

 Microsoft Press: *Networking Essentials, 2nd Edition*. Redmond, WA, 1997. ISBN 1-57231-527-X. Unit 1, Lesson 3, "Network Design," discusses all of the topics in this chapter in great detail.

 Search the TechNet CD (or its online version through **www.microsoft.com**) using the keywords "Planning," "Token Ring," "Thinnet," and related product names. The Windows NT *Concepts and Planning Manual* also includes useful information on networking concepts.

Network Operations

Terms you'll need to understand:

- ✓ Network operating system (NOS)
- ✓ Preemptive multitasking
- ✓ Cooperative multitasking
- ✓ Time slicing
- ✓ Client software
- ✓ Redirector
- ✓ Designator
- ✓ UNC naming
- ✓ Server software
- ✓ Windows NT Server
- ✓ Network services
- ✓ Network printing

Techniques you'll need to master:

- ✓ Understanding network operating systems
- ✓ Installing a network operating system
- ✓ Exploring and implementing network printing

Network operations have many components, including the types of services and applications provided, the process of installing and configuring these services, and devising and implementing a network management plan. Before you have an operational network, you must first perform a few necessary actions. First, you need to install a NOS. Then, you must enable a network resource or service, such as network printers, network shares, or networked applications. We discuss all of these issues in detail throughout this chapter.

Network Operating Systems

Prior to the invention of the network operating system, the functionality of network communication had to be added to an existing operating system. This addition usually came in the form of some sort of communication software packages or OS add-on used to extend the functionality of standalone operating systems to be shared with other users. For a system to communicate in a networked manner, the original OS and the NOS extensions had to be present on a single computer. Microsoft's LAN Manager is an excellent example of this type of technology. It was an add-on to MS-DOS, Windows 3.x, and OS/2 computers to enable networked communications.

It wasn't long before true NOSs—which were able to manage the activities on both standalone computers and network communications—replaced OS add-ons. Such network operating systems include Novell's NetWare and Microsoft's Windows NT.

It is important to understand that a computer's operating system is what controls the activities of that computer's hardware components. The OS controls things like memory, CPU, storage devices, and peripherals. The operating system governs interaction between a computer's hardware and software. This control is so precise that for applications to run correctly, they must be written within the control parameters of an OS, and are not portable to other OSs. For example, an application, such as Microsoft Excel written for Windows NT 4, will not function on an AS/400 computer.

A NOS's activities are broad, numerous, and complex. Therefore, NOSs require a lot of computing power. To get the most power out of a hardware configuration, many network operating systems, and some non-network operating systems, make use of a process called multitasking, which allows an operating system to run numerous processes—control more than one task—simultaneously. A true multitasking OS is able to support as many simultaneous processes as there are CPUs. However, when a computer only has one CPU, multitasking can be simulated through a technique called time slicing.

Time slicing involves dividing CPU computing cycles (hundreds to millions of cycles per second) between multiple tasks. You do this by giving each task a certain amount of process cycles, then halting that task to make the next task active. This process repeats until each task is finished. Users perceive this process as multiple applications operating simultaneously, but in fact, humans just can't perceive the small increments of each time slice.

It is important to note that there are two types of multitasking:

Preemptive The operating system controls which processes are allowed access to the CPU and for how long. Once the assigned time slice expires, the current process is halted and the next process is given its computing time.

Cooperative The operating system cannot stop a process; once CPU control is given to a process, it retains control until the process is complete. During this time, no other process is allowed to access the CPU.

A true high-performance NOS employs preemptive multitasking. Otherwise, the NOS couldn't complete many time-dependent tasks and would fail to complete tasks repeatedly.

Client Software

To allow clients to access the network, client network software must be installed on computers that regular users will utilize. This software is referred to as the client because it is the NOS component that accesses resources located on a network server. Three of the most important components of client software are redirectors, designators, and UNC pathnames.

Redirectors

There are actually two types of redirectors in use on any network: the client redirector and the server redirector. Both redirectors operate at the Presentation layer of the OSI model. When a client makes a request for a network application or service, the redirector intercepts that request and examines it to determine if the resource is local (on the requesting computer) or remote (on the network). If the redirector determines that it is a local request, the redirector forwards the request to the CPU for immediate processing. If the request is for the network, the redirector forwards the request across the network to the appropriate server. Basically, redirectors hide the complexity of accessing network resources from users. After a network resource is defined, users can access that resource without knowing its exact location.

Designators

A designator is a piece of software that manages the assignment of drive letters to both local and remote network resources or shared drives, which aids in network-resource interaction. When an association is made between a network resource and a local drive letter (also known as mapping a drive), the designator keeps track of the assignment of that drive letter to the network resource. Then, when users or applications access the drive, the designator substitutes the resource's network address for the drive letter before the request is sent to the redirector.

UNC Pathnames

Redirectors and mapping network drives are not the only methods used for network-resource access. Most modern NOSs, including Windows NT and Windows 98, also recognize Universal Naming Convention (UNC) names. UNC naming is a standard way to name network resources. These names take the form of \\servername\sharename.

UNC-aware applications and command-line activities use a UNC name in place of drive-letter mapping.

Server Software

For a computer to act as a network server, you must install a specific portion of the network operating system that enables the machine to both host resources and distribute those resources to network clients. Although a client computer only requires a redirector, a server is much more complex. Many software pieces work together to give a computer the ability to share its resources with others.

An important issue for network servers is the ability to restrict access to network resources. This is called network security. It provides the means to control which resources users can access, the extent of that access, and how many users can access that resource simultaneously at any given time. This control provides privacy and protection, and maintains an efficient networking environment.

In addition to providing control of network resources, a server does the following:

- Provides logon authentication for users
- Manages users and groups
- Stores management, control, and auditing tools for network administration
- Provides fault tolerance for protection of network integrity

Combined Client/Server Software

A number of NOSs, including Windows NT, have software components that enable the capabilities of both the client and the server on a computer. This enables computers to host and use network resources, and can be found predominantly on peer-to-peer networks. In general, this type of NOS is not as powerful and robust as a full-fledged NOS. The main benefit of a combined client/server NOS is that important resources located on a single computer can be shared with the rest of the network. A drawback is that, if a single computer hosts multiple resources that are accessed heavily, the computer takes a pretty serious performance hit. If this happens, you should consider transferring such resources to a dedicated server to improve overall performance.

Installing A NOS

Many important aspects of your network must be considered before you contemplate a NOS installation. Keeping the following issues in mind will both give you a better understanding of the final result of an operational network and make your installation run smoothly:

- Hardware compatibility
- Network media type
- Network size
- Network topology
- Server requirements
- Operating systems on clients and servers
- Network file system

- Network naming convention
- Network storage device organization

In the following section, we step through the installation of Windows NT Server to give you a better idea of how this process works.

Installing Windows NT Server

In comparison with other network operating systems, Windows NT Server 4 is relatively easy to install. With the proper preparation, the Windows NT Setup Wizard simplifies the installation process through the use of a graphical interface. Because this book is aimed at general networking topics, we don't provide information on each detailed step involved in the setup process. However, we do include the major installation steps to give you some insight into the architecture and simplicity of Windows NT Server 4.

The initial portion of the installation—bootstrapping—is the most difficult portion due to the many options from which you must choose. These options include the following:

- **Complete baseline or use of existing OS** Computers that don't already have an existing operating system installed require drive partitioning and a Windows NT-compatible CD-ROM; an existing OS may not require new partitioning and can use a non-Windows NT-supported CD-ROM.

- **Floppy-assisted or floppy-less** For computers without an existing OS, it's best to begin the setup with the three setup floppies; the floppy-less installation is simpler for systems with direct network access or direct access to a CD-ROM.

- **Network or local** If the computer has a network-compatible OS already installed, the Windows NT distribution files can be stored on a network-shared CD-ROM or directory; a local installation requires that the distribution files be accessed from a CD-ROM or copied to a local hard drive.

 Regardless of the installation type you choose, all of these options require that WINNT.EXE (or WINNT32.EXE for NT OSs) be launched to start the setup process (the floppy-based installation launches this utility as part of the boot process).

The initial portion of the Windows NT Server installation process is text-based. At this time, Windows NT asks you how to configure hard drives, format file systems, and name the system directory. After that, Windows NT copies the distribution files temporarily into a directory on the destination partition. After that, you reboot the computer and Windows NT enters the GUI portion of the setup.

The graphical portion of the Windows NT setup is controllable through the use of a mouse or keystrokes (Tab, arrows, and Enter). Here, you define computer and domain names, enter the CD key, select the server type (PDC, BDC, or member server), assign a password to the Administrator account, and select environment and desktop components. Setup then copies some files from the temporary folder it created to the destination folder you defined. After that, you move on to the network phase of the Windows NT setup.

During the networking portion of the Windows NT setup, Windows NT's communication components are installed and configured. It is here that you install NIC drivers, select which protocols to install, configure those protocols, and configure network bindings information. After completing this portion, setup then copies numerous files to the final destination folder and deletes the temporary folder.

After these files are moved, you define the time zone and display settings, then reboot. Once the computer is rebooted and the Administrator logs in, the Windows NT Server installation is complete.

Network Services

Network services are the basic resources that are required on all networks and are the foundation of network applications. Networks simply would not exist without them. As we've already mentioned, the main reason to implement a network is to share resources. The two most common network services are printers and directory shares. Although these are the most commonly implemented resources, the range of possible network services is extremely broad. There are many applications and resources that you can add to any NOS to extend its usefulness.

As discussed, all hardware devices require the use of a driver to communicate with an operating system. You can think of a network service as either a driver for software or the network itself. There's usually some kind of administrative tool for the installation and removal of network services included in a NOS. For example, Windows NT Server has the Network applet (located in the Control Panel). By using the Services tab of the Network applet, you can quickly and easily add and remove all of the Microsoft bundled network services and any services that a third-party vendor distributes.

Once a network service is in place, you can control its operation parameters in two ways. First is through a global services administrative tool—such as Windows NT's Services applet—where you can start and stop all the active network services, and modify basic operational parameters. Second, in some cases, the installation of a network service will add a new administrative tool for the exclusive management of the new service, such as RAS for Windows NT.

Network Printing

Network printing is the capability of network clients to access and utilize a printer hosted by a networked print server (assuming that clients have the correct access permissions). It's important to know that the redirector also takes part in network printing by intercepting print requests, interpreting them, and sending them to the proper print server or network-attached printer.

To begin, you must first install a printer on a server or as a direct network-attached device. After you have installed the printer and it is properly functioning, the logical representation of the printer within the NOS can be shared, which is as simple as adding the print resource to the list of available network resources.

In addition to requiring proper access permissions to a printer, most networked client workstations require the installation of local printer drivers, although, in some cases, workstations are able to access the printer drivers from the print server itself. Either way, you must install a new, shared logical printer that points to the printer share. After you have created this logical device, network clients can send print jobs to the printer by directing applications to print to the defined redirected port. The redirector then takes over by taking care of the complicated network communications involved with sending the print job to the remote printer.

Each NOS has a different method for setting up such shared resources, but it is generally straightforward. Just keep in mind that you need to know which clients require local access to print drivers, as opposed to those that can access them directly from the server. Also, you must manage users so that those who need it have proper access permissions to the shared printer.

Implementing Networked Applications

Network applications are specially designed applications that allow multiple, simultaneous users on numerous computers connected over a network to access and use them. In the early days of networking, the older, single-user applications were enhanced to allow for multiple-user access. But it wasn't long before new applications that could only exist as network applications were developed.

Most network applications operate differently. There are three types of architectures within network applications:

➤ **Centralized** The application operates on a server, and all clients interact with the central application through client-side user-interface terminals.

➤ **Client/server** Various portions of the application reside on both the server and the client, which allows the activities of multiple users to be processed on the server.

➤ **File-system sharing** The application resides on each client, and all clients share a database file or a storage directory for centralized storage of application information.

Network applications not only provide improved communication, but they are also easier to manage than standalone applications, especially on large networks. For example, rather than having to update software on each workstation, you can update some software on a server, and that information is automatically disseminated to workstation computers across the network. Network applications also save money: Standalone applications require that you purchase a complete version per user, whereas networked applications are able to host multiple users with the purchase of multiple-user licenses. However, there are drawbacks to networked applications as well. If performance over the network is poor or bandwidth is limited, the performance of that application is degraded accordingly. Also, networked applications are often unusable if the network is inoperable. These limitations, however, do not weigh as heavily when compared to the headaches associated with managing multiple, standalone applications.

Practice Questions

Question 1

> Multitasking is:
> - a. The installation of more than one protocol.
> - b. The method of computing in which multiple processes operate simultaneously by sharing the CPU.
> - c. The act of binding two or more services to a single protocol.
> - d. The activity of accessing a directory shared over a network link.

Answer b is the correct choice. Multitasking is the process of allowing multiple processes to operate simultaneously. Most NOSs allow for the installation of multiple protocols. Therefore, answer a is incorrect. Answer c is incorrect; binding services has nothing to do with multitasking. Finally, answer d is incorrect because accessing shared resources is a common task for any NOS.

Question 2

> When a NOS/OS maintains control of the CPU by assigning specific time slices to processes, it is called cooperative multitasking.
> - a. True
> - b. False

The answer is b, false. In cooperative multitasking, once CPU control is given to a process, it retains control until the process is complete. During this time, no other process is allowed to access the CPU.

Question 3

> What is the function of a redirector?
> - a. Maintains a group appointment list
> - b. Maps directory shares to local drive letters
> - c. Associates protocols, NICs, and services in order of priority
> - d. Forwards requests to local or remote resource hosts

Answer d is the correct choice. A redirector intercepts network requests, analyzes them, and forwards them to the correct hosts. Answer a is incorrect; a networked scheduling application would manage group appointments. Answer b is incorrect; you can map drives through most server-based tools. Answer c is incorrect because associating priorities is a services-management process.

Question 4

> Which of the following has the proper format for a UNC name?
> - a. (sharename)->servername
> - b. \\servername\sharename
> - c. sharename://servername/path
> - d. servername, sharename

Answer b is the only correct answer. The proper syntax of UNC naming is \\servername\sharename.

Question 5

> What are printer shares and directory shares considered to be?
> - a. Groupware
> - b. Network applications
> - c. Network services
> - d. Network protocols

Answer c is the correct choice. Printer shares and directory shares are network services. Printer and directory shares are not groupware. Therefore, answer a is incorrect. Likewise, they are not network applications. Therefore, answer b is incorrect. Answer d is incorrect because these are not network protocols.

Question 6

Which of the following issues must you address before setting up a NOS? [Check all correct answers]

❑ a. Responsibilities of the server
❑ b. Naming conventions
❑ c. Client applications
❑ d. Organization of storage devices

All of these answers are correct; you must consider all of these factors before installing a NOS. The "trick" to this question is that you must understand and select each correct answer. If not all correct answers are selected, you get the whole thing wrong!

Question 7

The Universal Naming Convention (UNC) provides a way for networked computers to identify each other's resources. Which of the following is included in a UNC name?

○ a. Domain name
○ b. Share name
○ c. User name
○ d. Workgroup name

Answer b is the only correct answer. UNC names are in the form of \\servername\sharename.

Need To Know More?

 Chellis, James, Charles Perkins, and Matthew Strebe: *MCSE: Networking Essentials Study Guide, 2nd Edition*. Sybex Network Press, San Francisco, CA, 1998. ISBN 0-7821-2220-5. Chapter 6, "Configuring the Network Server," discusses the concepts covered in this chapter.

 Microsoft Press: *Networking Essentials, 2nd Edition*. Redmond, WA, 1997. ISBN 1-57231-527-X. Unit 5, Lesson 15, "Network Operating System Setup," discusses the topics covered in this chapter in great detail.

 Search the TechNet CD (or its online version through www.microsoft.com) using the keywords "NOS," "installation," and "network services."

Network Administration And Support

Terms you'll need to understand:

- ✓ User accounts
- ✓ Passwords
- ✓ Event auditing
- ✓ Local groups
- ✓ Global groups
- ✓ Trust relationships
- ✓ Emergency Repair Disk (ERD)
- ✓ Registry
- ✓ Performance Monitor
- ✓ Network Monitor
- ✓ System management

Techniques you'll need to master:

- ✓ Setting up users and groups
- ✓ Making sure your network is secure
- ✓ Monitoring network performance

Not all of network administration is about hardware installation and troubleshooting. Once you've got the hardware in place and prepared to do its thing, you still need to ensure that the network is performing as expected, and that people can get to the resources they need, without getting to (or tampering with) resources they don't. In this chapter, we discuss the important points of network administration.

Managing Networked Accounts

The main task of network management is pretty basic: Make sure all users can access what they need, but can't get to what they don't or shouldn't. Okay, so this simple concept isn't always easy. We'll use Windows NT Server's User Manager For Domains as a framework for this subject, but the main idea is much the same no matter what tools you're using.

Managing User Accounts

There are three main points to managing user accounts. You must ensure that:

- Users have only the rights they need.
- Their accounts are secure.
- You know what those users are doing, within predetermined limits.

Creating User Accounts

The first step in managing user accounts is, of course, to create an account. Windows NT Server comes with two predefined accounts: an Administrator account for management duties and a Guest account for those who don't have an official account. However, it's unlikely that you'll want to use either of these for regular users. One account is too powerful for the average user, and the other is only useful if more than one person knows its password, which makes this option extremely insecure.

Before you begin creating accounts, however, you've got some decisions to make regarding the following:

- **Passwords** Should the user be able to change the password? How often should that password be changed? How many letters should it be? How often should users be able to reuse passwords? Should failed attempts to log on lead to lockouts?

- **Logon hours** Should users be restricted to logging on during certain hours of the day or only on certain days?

> **Auditing** Should user actions (logon, logoff, object access, and policy changes) be tracked? To what degree?

Passwords

For security reasons, it's best that users change passwords regularly. However, you will want to limit the frequency to some extent so users don't forget their passwords. If a user does lose track of his current password, it's fairly simple to fix with the User Manager For Domains—just open that user's account information, assign a new password, and then change the settings so that the user must change the password when signing on. More important, if you've adjusted passwords so that they may not be reused too frequently, it does you no good if an enterprising user just cycles through eight passwords to use "GoFish" again for the tenth time. Which brings up another point—Windows NT passwords are case sensitive, so you should take advantage of this fact to make them harder to guess. You should also include numbers in your passwords to make them less susceptible to dictionary attacks (password guessing programs that run through an entire dictionary to guess a password). But you shouldn't make passwords so difficult to guess that users start writing them down on sticky notes attached to their monitors.

What about account lockouts? It may seem unfriendly to lock out a user after a certain number of failed logon attempts. However, it foils automatic logon programs and good guessers if further attempts are refused after the specified number of attempts. Although it is an inconvenience, a valid user who has forgotten the password will have to find the network administrator to log on.

How long should passwords be? Theoretically, Windows NT can handle passwords up to 128 characters long, but dialog boxes won't accept more than 14 characters. Longer is generally better, especially because a minimum letter count avoids users using one space as their password (and pressing the spacebar once to gain access). We recommend a minimum of eight characters for password length.

Logon Hours

What about restricting logon hours? This isn't always necessary, and in some companies, it might even be undesirable. But in a tightly regulated office, it's another handy way of making sure that intruders can't break in and log on after working hours. However, the opportunities for a hacker to steal a password are limited if an account is locked when the account's owner is out of the office and unlocked only when he or she is in.

Using Windows NT, you can restrict logon hours by day of the week, hours of the day, or both. What happens if a user is logged on past his or her logon hours? This depends on the OS the user has. If it's Windows NT Workstation, and you have checked the option to break the connection when logon hours are over, then he or she will be forcibly disconnected. If it's another operating system, such as Windows 98, the user simply won't be able to log back on if disconnected.

With Windows NT, you can set logon hours individually, so you don't have to set everyone's account to the same schedule.

Auditing

One way to keep track of what's happening on the network (or, more accurately, on the server) is to configure the server so that certain actions such as object accesses, changes to the security information, logons and logoffs, and the like, are recorded for later review.

How much you audit depends on how much information you can usefully store. Although you could conceivably log every activity on the network, you'd probably end up storing so much information that you couldn't use it. Often, it's enough to record failures so that you know what people were unsuccessful at. Of course, if you have reason to suspect unauthorized access, then it's time to start recording successes as well.

Setting User Rights

A more specific matter that you need to consider is which user rights you should assign. Windows NT Server and Windows NT Workstation both come with predefined groups to which you can assign users and to give them a set of rights without having to handpick them. For example, Windows NT Server comes with the predefined local groups described in Table 8.1.

The Replicator group is not included in this list because it's not a user group; rather, it is used for the Replicator service to dynamically replicate specified folders across the network.

Table 8.1 Windows NT's built-in groups.

Group	Rights
Administrators	Complete control over the computer and domain.
Account Operators	May administer user and group accounts for the local domain.
Backup Operators	Can back up and restore files to which they normally do not have access.
Guests	Permitted guest access to domain resources.
Print Operators	May add, delete, and manage domain printers.
Server Operators	May administer domain servers.

In addition to the local groups are some global groups (groups meant to be used in more than one domain): Domain Administrators, Domain Users, and Domain Guests. These groups are essentially the same as the local groups with similar names, with some caveats about group membership that we'll explain in the following section on group accounts.

Using predefined groups like these makes it easy to assign rights to new user accounts, but you're not limited to these options. Rather, you have the choice of assigning extra rights on an individual basis (for example, if necessary, you could add the right to create printers to Carla's account—although Carla is a member of the Users group and ordinarily would not have such a right). Another choice is to assign a user to more than one group, like Users and Print Operators. Just remember that rights are cumulative: In cases where rights conflict (that is, one group has the right to do something but another group does not), the most restrictive right (i.e., No Access) takes precedence.

In addition to the groups to which you can assign users, there are some other groups to which users are automatically added, and which you cannot delete. These groups are described in Table 8.2.

Table 8.2 Groups in Windows NT that cannot be deleted and have users automatically assigned.

Group	Membership
Everyone	Everyone currently logged on to the domain.
Interactive	Everyone logged on to the domain locally.
Network	Everyone logged on to the domain via the network.

It's very important to remember the existence of these groups. For example, all members of the group Everyone have Full Control access to objects by default—they can add to, delete from, and change them. Sometimes, this is exactly what you want, but do recall that the Everyone group includes everyone from the network administrator to the intern who started last week. Be aware of who's got what rights on your network.

Managing Group Accounts

You can, of course, add and delete rights for groups just as you can for users. You can even create entirely new groups to provide exactly the rights that you need, or add groups to other groups (subject to the restrictions explained in the following section). Once your network expands beyond a single domain, however, you can use groups to make other domains accessible to your users.

Global Groups And Local Groups

It's impossible to talk about managing group accounts in a Windows NT context without getting into the concept of global and local groups. The concept is at first difficult to grasp, but quickly becomes second nature.

| Global groups are those intended for use in more than one domain. Their membership may include individual users.

| Local groups are those intended for use in the local domain. Their membership may include individual users and global groups.

Trust Relationships

One reason you would want to add a global group to a local one is for cross-domain communication. As you know, Windows NT Server networks are organized into administrative units, called domains, for security reasons and to manage from a central point the resources and accounts for that portion of the network. By default, the resources for one domain are not accessible to those whose accounts are in another domain. This is all very well and good, but sometimes it's desirable to let members of one domain access resources on another.

That's where trust relationships come into play. With them, you can establish "trust" (one-way or two-way) between domains so that their members may use the resources of a domain to which they don't belong. A domain must first "permit" another domain to trust it before the trust is actually established. For two domains to trust each other—that is, for the members of both domains to be able to use each other's resources—a two-way trust must be established, with each domain trusting the other as a separate action.

What do local and global groups have to do with all this? To establish the trust, you have to give the members of Domain A an account on Domain B. There are three ways of doing this:

- **Method 1** Add each user individually to Domain B's user-account database.

- **Method 2** Add each user's Domain A account to a global group on Domain A, and give that group rights on Domain B.

- **Method 3** Add the Domain A user accounts to a global group, and then add that group to a local group on Domain B.

Although the reasons why the third method is the easiest choice are probably pretty clear, let's walk quickly through the decision process. The first method works, but it's slow and it's a pain, and if you ever add new users to Domain A, you have to remember to add them to Domain B as well; the account databases are not shared, and Domain B's will not be updated to reflect the changes.

The second method makes a little more sense, because you don't have to make as many changes, but you're still taking an unnecessary step.

The third method, on the other hand, is the simplest way from an administrative standpoint. Add the users of Domain A to Domain Users (a global group) and then add that group to the Users group on Domain B. Any changes to the membership of Domain A will immediately be reflected in Domain B (as long as the accounts in question are part of the global group).

Dealing With Changes To Users And Groups

Every time you make a change to a user account or group account under Windows NT, that change is reflected in the Registry database and recorded in the two hive files that make up the security information of the Registry: Security and SAM. Therefore, it is extremely important to back up the contents of the Registry, preferably during your daily server backup. Although you could technically re-create all the account information for your domain if you had to, it's much easier to keep backups so that you don't.

As you know, one important aspect of disaster recovery for Windows NT is making sure that changes are reflected in the Emergency Repair Disk (ERD) that you can use to restore your installation if necessary. When you do so with the RDISK utility, it's important to be sure to include the /S switch to the command when you run it, and to include the security hives as well as the other ones. By default, this information is not saved when you update the Repair directory and ERD.

Managing Network Performance

At this point, then, your network users are all set to go. It's not yet time to relax, however, because you've still got to worry about the performance those users will see. In this section, we'll talk about network performance, including what you're looking for and how you can use Windows NT and other tools to get that information.

Network Performance Characteristics

Just what are you looking for when it comes to monitoring your network? Obviously, you want to be sure that the cables are in one piece and the network cards aren't conflicting with anything. But beyond the bare minimum of making sure the hardware works, what is there to monitor?

- Data read from and written to the server each second
- Connections currently maintained to other servers
- Errors in accessing data
- The number of files network users have opened
- Queued commands
- The number of collisions per second on an Ethernet network

Data Reads And Writes

The number of bytes read from and written to the server provides a useful measure of how busy the server is, particularly if this count increases over time. You can also count the amount of data that cannot be read or written. This is because (on a Windows NT network) the server will attempt to take large data streams as streams of raw data, not as sets of packets. If the server refuses to accept many such streams of raw data, it's a possible indication of memory problems on the server, because a certain buffer is needed to accept the stream.

Queued Commands

The number of commands that are awaiting execution is one measure of how busy a server is. This number should never be too high—not much more than the number of network cards in the server; otherwise, it will represent a bottleneck.

Collisions Per Second

Only one node on an Ethernet segment can broadcast at a time. When more than one attempts to do so, there is a collision of the two packets, and you must resend them both. Although the time to resend is fairly short for the first failed attempt, it increases exponentially for further failed attempts (and the chance of a repeated collision is fairly good for the first couple of retries); this slows down network transmission. High collision rates are not a good thing.

The rate of collisions per second can actually tell you something about your network's physical topology. One of the main causes of network collisions is a cable segment is too long for the nodes to hear that another node is already transmitting. Nodes normally "listen" to determine if other nodes are transmitting before they transmit their data. However, the nodes can only "hear" over a certain distance, so a high rate of collisions may indicate that you need to include a repeater in your network segment. Even if it's not a matter of a segment being too long, a high rate of network collisions indicates a problem somewhere in the segment, and you must track it down.

The propagation delay problem that causes excess collisions is not usually that severe. The main cause of collisions is when high utilization rates mean that random backoff and retry on retransmissions induces further collisions. Also, collisions and utilization have nothing to do with each other, except that as the "knee" of the utilization curve is crossed (between 56 and 60 percent for Ethernet) collisions go up enormously, and eventually swamp real traffic.

Security Errors

Although there may be innocent explanations, high rates of failed logons, failed access to objects, and failed changes to security settings may all indicate a security risk on the network. Perhaps a hacker is attempting to break into the system or a user is trying to access objects to which he or she has been denied access. Either way, it's something to watch, and it's a good idea to set up auditing so you can see who's causing the errors. This is also a good time to drag out the protocol analyzer to see where the errors are coming from, in case someone is being spoofed.

Server Sessions

You can tell a bit about server activity by observing the rate at which connections to the server are made and how those connections are broken, whether by a normal logoff, by an error, or by a server timeout. The last two cases may indicate that the server is overloaded and is either refusing connections or can't service them quickly enough. More RAM in the server may do the trick, or you may need to update other hardware.

Monitoring Network Performance

You need to monitor network performance, but how do you do it? If you're running Windows NT Server, you already have three tools that you can use to monitor your system: the Event Viewer, the Performance Monitor, and the Network Monitor.

The Event Viewer

From the User Manager For Domains, you can choose to audit certain events. When you do so, the event logs are stored within the Event Viewer, which is part of the basic set of Windows NT administrative tools. The Event Viewer maintains three logs: one for security information, one for system information, and one for events generated by applications.

Of the three logs, the first two are the most important to our current discussion. The Security log records security events based on the filters you set up in the User Manager For Domains, so it's the most useful for getting information about failed attempts to log on or access data. The System log records events logged by Windows NT system components, and therefore is the most useful for nuts-and-bolts information about how your network is running, and whether all the hardware is working properly. For example, if you've recently installed a new network card and it's not working, you can check the System log of the Event Viewer to see whether an interrupt conflict has been recorded. In addition, the System log notes when services are stopped and started, so you can be sure that all necessary services are running.

The Performance Monitor

Unlike the Event Viewer, which records individual events, the Performance Monitor is best for recording and viewing trends. For the purposes of monitoring your network, you'll be most interested in collecting data for the following objects:

➤ Logical or physical disk on the server

➤ Network interface

- Any of the protocol counters (there are several)
- Redirector
- Server
- Server work queues

However, because running the Performance Monitor takes up resources that you'll probably want to save for servicing client requests, it's a good idea to monitor the server remotely, from a Windows NT Server machine that's not as busy. This will increase network traffic, but the performance hit won't be as bad as the strain on memory would be from running the Performance Monitor from the server.

The Network Monitor

Unlike the Event Viewer and Performance Monitor, the Network Monitor is not automatically installed during Windows NT setup; you must install it separately as a network service. Once it is installed, it becomes a fairly capable software-based protocol analyzer. As such, it monitors the network data stream and records the source address, destination address, headers, and data for each packet. Network Monitor can only capture as many frames as there's room for in physical memory (and it always leaves 8 MB free for other programs). Therefore, it's best to prepare some kind of filter to ensure that you get all the data you need without crowding it out with data you don't. You can filter data packets based on the transport protocol used to transmit them, by source and destination address, or by data pattern, looking for specific ASCII or hexadecimal streams in the data at a certain point in the data.

For security reasons, Network Monitor detects other installed instances of Network Monitor agents on the network, showing the name of the computer on which they are running, the name of the person logged in, what the agents are doing at the moment, the adapter address, and the version number. Some instances of Network Monitor may not be detected if there's a router between your part of the network and the Network Monitor, if the router does not support multicasting, but if the monitor can see you, you can see it.

Total System Management

The network is a major bottleneck when it comes to network performance, but it's not the only one. In addition to thinking about network conditions, you should also consider what's happening on the server side, particularly when it comes to hard disk space and the amount of available memory.

Hard Disk

Of the three tools that come with Windows NT Server, the Performance Monitor is most useful when it comes to monitoring disk information on a Windows NT network. You'll be looking at the following:

- Remaining disk space

- Speed at which requests are serviced (both in terms of throughput and the amount of data being transferred)

- How often the disk is busy (both in terms of how often it's running and the average number of requests queued)

When monitoring disks, notice whether you're monitoring the physical disk object or the logical disk object; each may represent something different. Also, notice that not all counters will add up to 100 percent even if you do measure on a percentage basis. This is because the readings for multiple logical disks may very likely add up to more than 100 percent for the entire physical disk. Sometimes, you need to average the results among disks.

To use the disk-performance counters, you must first run DISKPERF from the command prompt. Otherwise, they'll all register as zero.

Memory Use

The other big issue with servers is the amount of memory they have to service the requests that come in. Windows NT is designed to page data out of memory when the data is not in use, or when it needs the memory for other, more recently used data. If it needs the data, it lets a page fault occur to get the data back in memory. However, if the server has to page too much data, installing more memory would be a good idea.

There are two kinds of page faults. Soft page faults occur when data is removed from a program's working set (the set of data that the process is actively using) and is moved to another area in physical memory. Thus, when that data is needed, it's a very fast operation to get it back into the working set. Hard page faults—when the data has gone unused for so long or there's such a shortage of physical memory that program data is actually stored on the hard disk—are another matter entirely. Reading data from disk takes quite a while longer than reading it from memory does, so if too many hard page faults occur, response time slows considerably. Thus, the best measure of memory shortages is the rate at which hard page faults occur.

Maintaining Network History

Both the Performance Monitor and the Event Viewer are able to prepare log data that you can use to keep long-term records of network performance and events. You can use this data to determine trends or notice when a new problem arises. Just as with any other troubleshooting techniques, you can't recognize a problem if you don't know what the solution looks like.

Be a little selective about the data you retain. One of the principal errors most beginning network administrators make is being too enthusiastic about archiving data, recording every burp and hiccup on the network and servers. The end result, of course, is that when the time comes to review this material there's an impossible amount of data to wade through and the history becomes useless.

Practice Questions

Question 1

> What user accounts are already built into Windows NT? [Check all correct answers]
>
> ❑ a. Administrator
> ❑ b. Replicator
> ❑ c. Backup Operator
> ❑ d. Guest

Answers a and d are correct. The Administrator and Guest user accounts are built into Windows NT. Answers b and c are incorrect: Replicator and Backup Operator are not user accounts built into Windows NT.

Question 2

> Which of the following are logs maintained by Event Viewer? [Check all correct answers]
>
> ❑ a. Security information
> ❑ b. Network information
> ❑ c. System information
> ❑ d. Application events

Answers a, c, and d are all correct. The Event Viewer maintains logs for security, system information, and events generated by applications. Answer b is incorrect; Event Viewer does not maintain a network information log.

Question 3

Where are user accounts created?

○ a. Server Manager

○ b. Network Monitor

○ c. User Manager For Domains

○ d. System Administrator

Answer c is correct. User accounts are created and maintained by the User Manager For Domains. Neither Server Manager nor Network Monitor are capable of creating user accounts. Therefore, answers a and b are incorrect. There is no tool called System Administrator. Therefore, answer d is also incorrect.

Question 4

Which of the following need to be considered before you begin creating user accounts? [Check all correct answers]

❏ a. Passwords

❏ b. Logon hours

❏ c. Groups

❏ d. Auditing

All of the answers are correct. You should consider password length and duration, what time of day users are allowed to log on, what groups they will belong to, and what type of auditing needs to take place on user accounts.

Question 5

> Which of the following can you track using Network Monitor?
> [Check all correct answers]
> ❑ a. Data packets based on the transport protocol
> ❑ b. Source and destination addresses
> ❑ c. Data patterns
> ❑ d. Disk reads and writes

Answers a, b, and c are all correct. You can filter data packets based on the transport protocol used to transmit them, by source and destination address, or by data pattern, looking for specific ASCII or hexadecimal streams in the data at a certain point in the data. You would use Performance Monitor to track disk reads and writes. Therefore, answer d is incorrect.

Need To Know More?

 Heywood, Drew: *Inside Windows NT Server, 2nd Edition*. New Riders, Indianapolis, IN, 1995. ISBN 1-56205-860-6. Chapter 16, "Windows NT Server and NetWare," explains the salient software, communications issues, and connectivity concerns that are likely to appear on the test.

 Minasi, Mark and Peter Dyson: *Mastering Windows NT Server 4, 5th Edition*. Sybex Network Press, Alameda, CA, 1997. ISBN 0-7821-2163-2. This book provides a good overview of Windows NT network-management tools and how to use them effectively.

 Zacker, Craig, Paul Doyle, et al.: *Upgrading and Repairing Networks*. Que Books, Indianapolis, IN, 1996. ISBN 0-7897-0181-2. Chapter 30 discusses network management.

 Search the TechNet CD (or its online version through **www.microsoft.com**) using the keywords "network performance," "user accounts," and "group accounts." The Windows NT *Concepts and Planning Manual* also includes useful information on network management and using the tools listed here.

Network Naming And Security

9

Terms you'll need to understand:

- √ Network names
- √ Accounts
- √ NetBIOS computer names
- √ Windows Internet Name Service (WINS)
- √ Domain Name Service (DNS)
- √ LMHOSTS file
- √ HOSTS file
- √ Security policy
- √ Virus protection
- √ Disaster recovery
- √ Backup
- √ Uninterruptible power supply (UPS)
- √ Redundant Array of Inexpensive Disks (RAID)

Techniques you'll need to master:

- √ Planning and implementing network security
- √ Enabling network auditing for security purposes
- √ Implementing a disaster recovery plan

As computers become increasingly capable of communicating with one another, and individuals become more knowledgeable about operating these computers, security becomes an issue of paramount importance. This chapter covers computer security relating to the following areas: network naming schemes, planning for network security, security models, additional security considerations, and disaster recovery.

Network Naming Schemes

Computers identify themselves to each other using various naming schemes. Each computer in a networked environment must be assigned a name so it can communicate with other computers on the network. Additionally, users on the network need names, as do the shared resources on the network. These network names can be divided into the following categories:

- Accounts
- Computers
- Resources

Accounts

An account is a compilation of all the information that pertains to a particular user or group on the network—normally consisting of a user name, password, rights and permissions, and group memberships. Accounts are created by the administrator, and are required to operate in most secure systems. It is in the best interest of network security for a user not to give other users his or her password, or any other account information that may be used to compromise sensitive data or operations.

Computer Names

One individual can have many titles simultaneously—a man may be called a father, boss, neighbor, or son, depending on who is addressing him. In much the same way, each computer in a network can have multiple names, depending on what process, protocol, or device is communicating with it at the moment. Because not all entities use or understand the same naming schemes, you need a system that allows for translation (resolution) of one naming/addressing type to another.

For instance, a data frame received at a computer's Physical layer contains information specifying that it is addressed to the computer's NIC address (or MAC address). The MAC address consists of hexadecimal code stored on a ROM chip on the computer's NIC; and at the physical level, this computer is known by this code. Numbering systems like this are easy for computers to understand, but they are very difficult for humans to use and remember. However, a user-friendly name like "PrintServer2" would be easy for people to use.

In a similar manner, remote systems using different equipment or protocols may have difficulty deciphering your naming and addressing scheme. To address this problem, various name resolution standards have been created to help transparently resolve the different names to one another, allowing internetwork communication to occur.

NetBIOS Computer Names

Every Microsoft computer uses a computer name, also known as the NetBIOS computer name, of up to 15 characters (see Figure 9.1). These names are part of the OSI Application layer interface to the network protocol stack on all networked Microsoft computers. Networks that use the TCP/IP protocol must resolve (or translate) the computer name into an IP address before networked communication can occur. The Windows Internet Name Service (WINS) and/or the Domain Name Service (DNS) can be used to resolve computer names to their corresponding IP addresses.

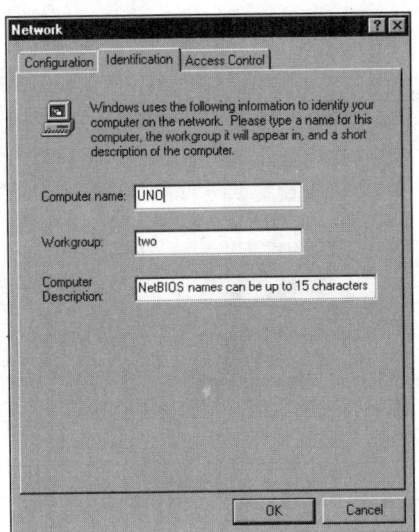

Figure 9.1 NetBIOS names can be set up to 15 characters in Microsoft computers. The name of this Windows 95 computer is "UNO."

Windows Internet Name Service

WINS is a service that resolves NetBIOS computer names to IP addresses. This service runs on a Windows NT Server on the network, and dynamically resolves NetBIOS computer names to IP addresses so that computers can communicate with each other. WINS is a client/server service whereby a client registers its computer name with the WINS server during its boot process. When a WINS client needs to locate a computer on the network, it can query the WINS server to obtain a computer name to IP address mapping (translation) for the computer with which it is going to communicate (see Figure 9.2).

Domain Name Service

DNS is similar to WINS in that it resolves computer names to IP addresses. However, in DNS, these names are called "host names" or fully qualified domain names (FQDNs). In general, NetBIOS computer names consist of a single part. In contrast, TCP/IP components rely on a naming convention know as the Domain Name System (DNS). An FQDN is a hierarchical naming convention using the format hostname.domainname, such as microsoft.com, spca.org, and utexas.edu, where the domain name is an indication of the type of organization. Windows NT combines the NetBIOS computer name with the DNS domain name to form the FQDN.

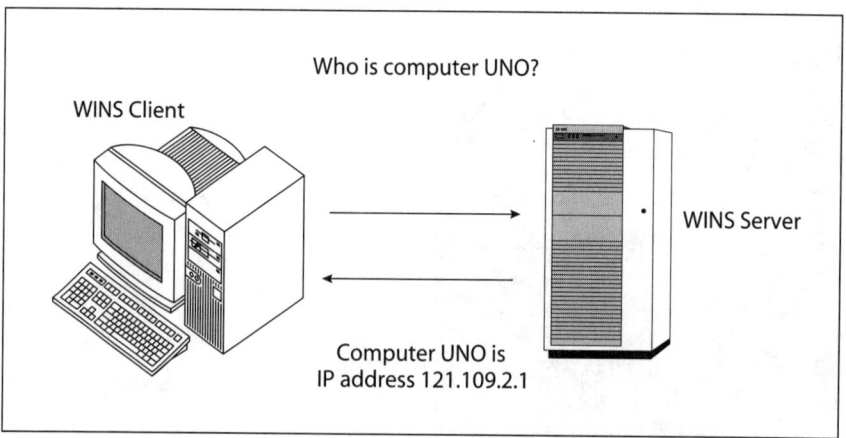

Figure 9.2 The WINS server can resolve NetBIOS names to IP addresses.

DNS also differs from WINS in that DNS is a static service, meaning that someone has to manually enter the names and IP addresses before the DNS server can resolve them. Figure 9.3 illustrates how the DNS server handles a request from the DNS client. The DNS server also can query other DNS servers to retrieve partial resolutions for the computer name. For instance, one DNS server may resolve the "microsoft.com" part of the name, while another resolves the "uno."

In addition to WINS and DNS, LMHOSTS and HOSTS files can be used to resolve names to IP addresses.

LMHOSTS And HOSTS Files

LMHOSTS and HOSTS files are normally maintained locally on the client computer. These files must be manually created and updated and placed in the appropriate directory (for instance, WINDOWS in a Windows 98 computer or WINNT\SYSTEM32\DRIVERS\ETC in a Windows NT computer). The LMHOSTS file is normally responsible for resolving NetBIOS names to IP addresses; the HOSTS file resolves host names and/or FQDNs to IP addresses.

Resources

Each resource is identified by a name. These names can be as vague or specific as the individual sharing the resource desires. "Printer connected to LPT 1" and "High-speed color thermal imaging printer on second floor,"

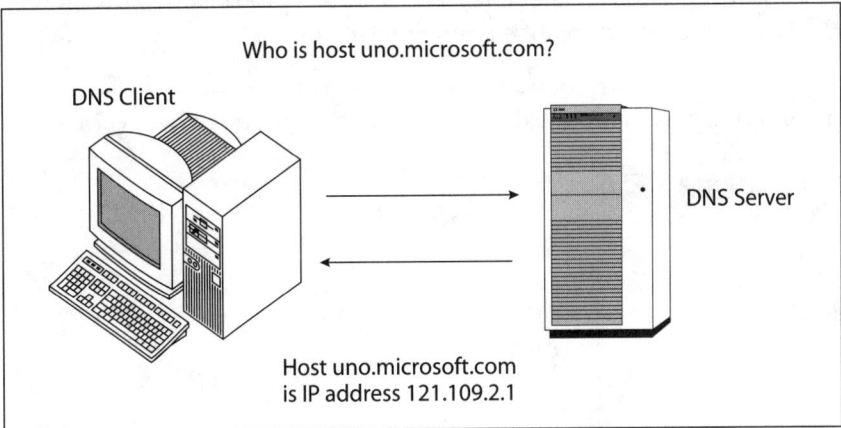

Figure 9.3 This graphic illustrates how DNS can resolve fully qualified domain names.

are both possible names for the same resource. Optimally, resource names should be chosen to make it easy for a user to tell what object (printer, shared file, or directory) is being accessed. Figure 9.4 illustrates the different types of resources you may see when browsing the network.

Planning For Network Security

If you don't take the time to plan your network, you can spend a huge amount of time, effort, and money correcting errors and redesigning later should you find that it isn't performing as you expected. This becomes an even larger issue in the area of security. You must create security policies and plans based on your organizational requirements. You should ensure that your network plan does the following:

➤ Addresses your company's needs

➤ Establishes policies that support those needs

➤ Provides the necessary amount of physical and logical security

Understanding Requirements

Your organization is different from every other organization in the world. It has a unique personality, style, and sense of direction. Your security plan must fit within your organization's style. Although you may think the CEO and everyone else should know your security ideas, remember that those ideas must support the direction of the organization. For instance, requiring diskless workstations in a public lending library probably won't fit in with the head librarian's vision of sharing information.

Look at your organization's vision. If it doesn't have one, look at other organizations in similar fields. Do you want an Internet presence? Do you

Figure 9.4 Shared resources are usually printers, drives, or directories made available by other computers on the network.

want one in the future? Is your data so sensitive that it must be kept absolutely private? Do you want to be able to remotely administer your site? You and your company's leadership must decide the depth of security for your network. Then, make the system as easy to use as possible, without violating your original security goals. Security threats to your network include:

- Unintentional damage
- Intentional damage
- Unauthorized access
- Electronic tampering
- Theft

Your security policy should address each of these threats in detail.

Setting A Security Policy

You are responsible for your organization's security policy. This policy must describe the who, what, when, where, and possibly the why of how your organization implements security. It is probably not a good idea, however, to describe exactly how your security is implemented.

You should maintain a network log, separate from your published security policy, which describes all actions you have taken in setting up and supporting your network. This is where your fellow administrators can look to see what has been implemented.

Many users feel that security policies are hindrances to getting work done, and will attempt to "get around" them. Don't immediately discard their ideas. Instead, review them, and after weighing the benefit of accomplishing work more easily against the benefit of additional security, you can decide whether to change the policy or leave it in place. Explain to the users why the system was or was not changed, and thank them for their suggestions.

Users can accidentally or unintentionally damage data, or the network itself. Policies must allow users to easily and efficiently accomplish their work without allowing them to cause any damage.

Physical And Logical Security

No matter how well you have your data protected electronically, it doesn't do any good if your computers can be carried out the front door of your building. You are responsible for all aspects of securing your network, including physically securing it.

In a peer-to-peer network that uses shared resources, each user is responsible for securing his or her computer. Your policy may be as simple as having users shut down their computers every night and locking their office doors. Some users may prefer to leave their computers on at night so they can obtain files from their home—you must decide if your security policy will allow for this type of situation. Again, you must balance the needs of the users with the need for secure network management policies.

In a client-server network, each user is allowed specific rights based on his or her needs and role within the organization. Like users in peer-to-peer networks, users in client-server networks need to take a degree of responsibility in keeping their personal workstations secure.

Servers

As the administrator, you must prevent internal and external sources from compromising your servers. A well-intentioned user can cause irreparable data loss by tinkering in the server closet. You should limit physical access to your servers, as well as limit the users and groups that can log on locally to the server.

Routers

Routers, much like servers, should be allowed limited access. A user might decide that, because the network was acting oddly, maybe turning the router off and back on could fix the problem. Depending on the make and model of the router, it may actually be okay to do this. Or it may delete the routing tables, and cause the router to "forget" what it is. Also, if your organization is large enough, a user may add his or her own network segments to your routers, possibly without your knowledge. This could be the first step in a major compromise of your network.

Cables

If your data is sensitive enough, you may have to limit the amount of electronic signals your cables emit, or ensure your topology doesn't radiate these signals. Also, it is possible for someone to tap directly into copper cable and thereby steal data. (During the mid-1970s, at the height of the Cold War, the United States government developed a wireless technology that can eavesdrop on the electromagnetic signals emanating from computers and network cabling.)

You should limit access to cable runs that carry sensitive data. If at all possible, use fiber optic cable, which is much more difficult to tap and does not emit electrical signals. Also, use the building structure to protect your cables. For instance, you may be able to run your cabling inside the walls of the building.

Security Models

Once you have physically secured your network, you must decide how you will secure it electronically. There are two basic types of account security that you can implement: share-level and user-level security, which we introduced in Chapter 6.

Share-Level Security

Share-level security is a security technique where each resource owner shares a resource under his or her control and creates a password to control access to this resource. An example of this would be a user with a color printer connected to his computer. He could share the printer over the network, and protect its use by placing a password on the use of the printer. Users who know the password can use the printer. Windows 3.11 and Windows 95 are examples of operating systems that use this technique. Both of these systems allow Read Only, Full, and Depends On Password access to the resource (see Figure 9.5), each of which is explained in the following:

- **Read Only** Users are only allowed to view files in the shared directory. They may not change, delete, or add files to the directory. They may copy files to their computers, and print (or execute) them.

- **Full** Users may create, read, write, delete, and change files in the shared directory.

- **Depends On Password** Shares using this feature allow users either Read Only rights, or Full rights, depending on the password the user provides.

User-Level Security

User-level security is a security technique where each user is assigned a unique user name and password. When users attempt to enter the network, they are prompted to provide their user name and password, which are compared to a security database on a remote server. This process is known as authentication. If the user name and password are correct, the server logs

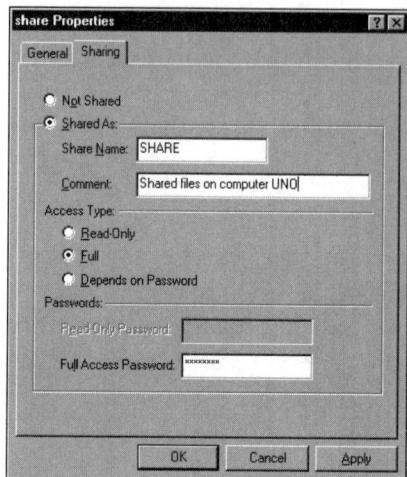

Figure 9.5 Share-level security provides password protection capabilities for shared resources.

the users on to the network. Rights and privileges are assigned based on the user ID and/or groups to which the user may belong.

In Windows NT, this technique is used to assign permissions. Although users may have access to parts of the network, they may or may not have permission to access certain resources, or their type of permission may limit their level of interaction with these resources. Those types of permissions are as follows:

- **Read** Similar to the Read Only permission in Windows 3.11 or Windows 95, the Read permission allows users to view and execute files in a shared directory. Users may not change, delete, or add files; however, they are able to print and copy files to their computers.

- **Execute** The Execute permission allows users to run files in the shared directory.

- **Write** The Write permission allows users to create, read, write, and change files in the shared directory. Users may not execute or delete files.

- **Delete** The Delete permission gives users the ability to delete files in the shared directory.

► **Full Control** Full Control access allows users to read, execute, create, write, change, and delete files in the shared directory.

► **No Access** Users are not allowed to access this directory if the No Access permission is set. When combined with other permissions, the No Access permission takes precedence. That is, if a user has Full Control and No Access to a particular directory, the user has No Access to the directory.

Account Management

To keep track of users and permissions, the administrator logically divides users and resources into manageable groups, and assigns permissions to each group.

For example, an organization consisting of Management, Engineering, Marketing, Accounting, and Human Resources could easily be grouped according to each specialty. In this instance, the administrator would create account groups (called global groups in Window NT) named: Management, Engineering, Marketing, Accounting, and Human Resources. Then, the administrator would place the users in each discipline into the appropriate group. As each group will need access to different resources, the administrator would create resource groups (called local groups in Windows NT) with the permission to access the following devices: High-speed printer, Color printer, Printer, CAD printer, After-hours printer, and Payroll printer. The administrator would then create account groups: High-speed printer with Management and Marketing; Color printer with Marketing; Printer with Accounting, Engineering, and Human Resources; CAD printer with Engineering; After-hours printer with Everyone; and Payroll printer with Accounting (see Figure 9.6).

Additional Security Considerations

The security measures that we've already mentioned are essential to your network's security. Other techniques you may consider implementing are auditing, diskless workstations, encryption, and virus protection.

Auditing

Auditing is a way to monitor network events and user actions. Primarily, auditing provides a log trail that shows who did what, and when, on the

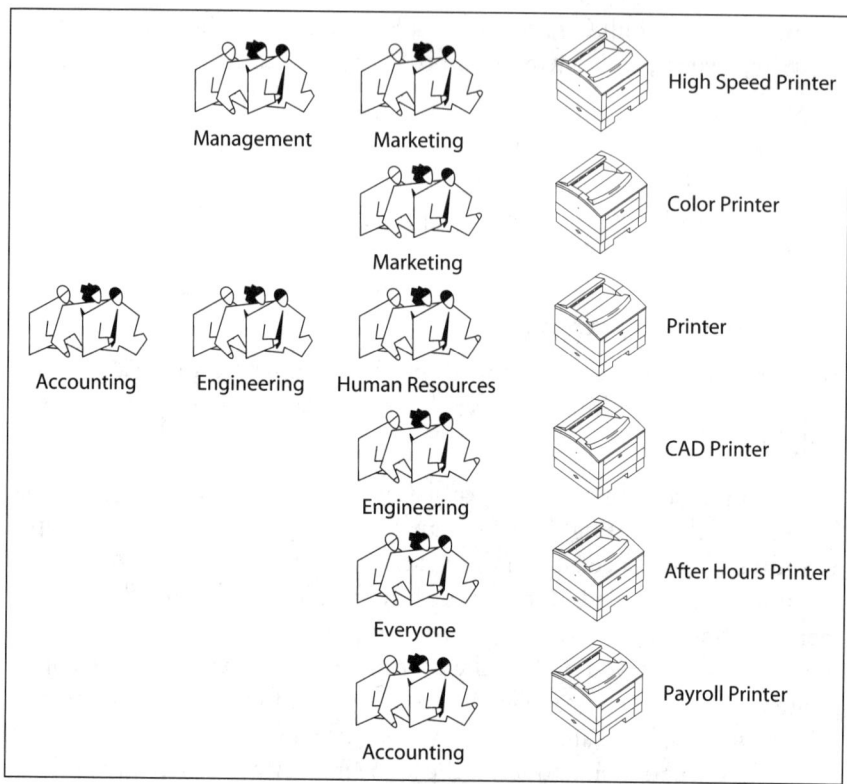

Figure 9.6 Users gain access to resources through their group memberships.

network. For instance, a large number of unsuccessful logon attempts over a very short period of time may indicate that an unauthorized user is attempting to gain access to your network. Other auditing functions provide the basis for informed decisions, such as where to place network resources or what additional resources may be necessary in the future. Windows NT comes with powerful auditing capabilities and allows the auditing of either the success or failure (or both) of the following:

- **Logon And Logoff** A user logged on or off, or made or broke a network connection to a server or to the local server.

- **File And Object Access** A user accessed a directory, file, or printer that is set for auditing. This event must be selected to audit file or print resources.

- **Use Of User Rights** A user exercised a right (does not include logon or logoff).

- **User And Group Management** A user account or group was created, changed, or deleted; or a user account was renamed, disabled, or enabled, or a password was set or changed.

- **Security Policy Changes** A change was made to the user rights, audit, or trust relationship policies.

- **Restart, Shutdown, And System** A user restarted or shut down the computer, or an event has occurred that affects system security or the security log.

- **Process Tracking** Tracks information for various events, such as program activation.

 Remember that you must enable auditing before you can track user actions. You must enable File And Object Access as shown in Figure 9.7 if you want to track the use of printers, files, or directories on the server.

Diskless Workstations

Diskless workstations have been in the news lately—more than they have ever been—with the hype surrounding the network computer. However, diskless workstations have been around for quite some time. They can be used in high-security environments, where data compromise is not allowed. With the advent of the Java operating system, diskless workstations (renamed "network computers") are being designed and marketed to appeal to a broader audience. Because these computers only run applications

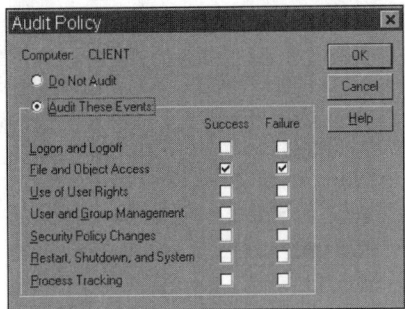

Figure 9.7 Windows NT allows you to enable auditing through the Windows NT User Manager application.

downloaded from the server, they could save maintenance costs associated with updating and installing applications on every computer in an organization. It is still undetermined if network computers will be accepted as viable replacements for the standard personal computer.

A diskless computer has a ROM boot chip that allows the client to initiate a session with the server. At startup, diskless computers broadcast their physical hardware address to the network. The Reverse Address Resolution Protocol (RARP) server does a reverse lookup of the client's assigned network address and sends boot information directly to the client. In addition, the server directs the client to challenge the user. Once the user provides proper authentication, the server allows the client to enter the network.

Diskless computers are sound investments for high-security environments. Because such computers do not have floppy or hard disks, users cannot download data and leave the premises. They are, however, useless if the network server is unavailable.

Encryption

Encryption is the act of changing a message into a format that only the sender and receiver can understand. Encrypting data prior to it entering the network interface card is the most secure means of sending data. Once the data reaches the intended recipient, it is unencrypted using a previously agreed-upon code, and returned to its original format.

The Data Encryption Standard (DES) is an encryption system created for the U.S. government. To use this system, both sender and recipient need access to complementary set of keys. To put it in simple terms, the sender uses a key to encrypt the data before it is sent, and the recipient uses a matching key to unencrypt the data. DES is the *de facto* standard for data encryption, but is vulnerable if an attacker can obtain a copy of the keys.

Pretty Good Privacy (PGP) is an encryption system much like DES (in both systems, the key is based on a numerical algorithm of specified length). However, PGP uses two linked keys. One key is used for encryption, and the other for decryption. The user safeguards the decryption key and publishes the encryption key. These keys are generated at the same time, using an algorithm that allows one to encrypt and one to decrypt. The keys cannot be used backwards. This allows the sender to obtain the recipient's public PGP key and encrypt a message to the recipient. Because the recipient has the only key that can decrypt the message (remember, the encryption key will not work as the decryption key) no one else can decrypt the message.

PGP encryption may be a more realistic alternative to encrypting every packet that leaves a computer. It allows the user to choose which data will be encrypted (sensitive email, for instance).

For a more secure environment, you may wish to obtain hardware that encrypts and decrypts data as it enters and leaves your computer.

Virus Protection

Although most viruses are only annoying programs that do not seriously harm a computer, some viruses can cause data loss. When we discuss viruses, we are really talking about four types of computer programs:

- **Viruses** Computer programs that make copies of themselves and "inhabit" an executable file. (Inhabiting a data file is pointless, because the processor does not execute data.)

- **Worm programs** These only make copies of themselves; they do not inhabit other files.

- **Trojan Horse viruses** Much like in the original story, viruses enter disguised as a totally different program. Only upon execution do we see what they really are. An example of this is the infamous AOL4FREE.EXE Trojan Horse. Many users believed it to be a downloadable America Online upgrade. Actually, on execution, it changed to the root directory of the host computer and, using the DOS DELTREE command, systematically deleted every file from the user's hard drive. Users could easily stop it by pressing CTRL+C, but many did not know this.

- **Macro viruses** These are a special subset of the virus family. Using the macro languages associated with many of today's powerful applications, it is possible to create a virus that infects data files. Although the data file itself is never processed, the macro code associated with the data file is. The Concept virus is an example of a macro virus that can spread through a data file attached to an email message.

Virus protection programs cannot prevent viruses. They can only prevent viruses from activating, correct damage done by a virus, and remove viruses from the system. The key to preventing viruses from activating is to have a multiphased plan that addresses the following issues:

- **What to do to prevent viruses from entering the network.** Limit user-loadable software, and create a strict policy in which all disks are scanned for viruses prior to being used.

- **How to check the network for any viruses.** Use a virus-checking program regularly to diagnose any inactive viruses that could be on your network. Ensure the program is updated regularly to reflect new viruses.

- **What to do when a virus is discovered.** Ensure that users know what to do if a virus is discovered. They should inform the Information Management staff, clean their hard drives, clean any other floppies, and inform their peers who may have received an infected disk or email.

Disaster Recovery

Although it is much more exciting to discuss data security and protection in terms of defending your network from intruders, in reality, it is much more likely that you will lose data due to some type of hardware failure. How many times have you thrown away a floppy that just wouldn't format properly or was acting strangely? Or, even worse, it was the file that had the big presentation on it, and it was the only available copy. No, a hacker probably didn't hack your disk. It was a physical object that had a mechanical failure.

Can you imagine what would happen if, despite all the warnings, someone in your office smoked a cigarette in the building, causing the sprinkler system to go off. It may seem amusing at first, until you remember that the sprinkler nozzle you'd been meaning to have the building superintendent remove from the server closet was fully functioning. After getting the key, you already know the network is down. And it will only come back up once you repair the damage caused by the sprinkler.

Data loss can have a disastrous effect on your organization. You are responsible for planning and implementing your disaster policy. It should cover problems caused by fire, data deletion and corruption, theft or vandalism, power fluctuations, server component failure, and natural disasters.

You can respond to most disasters with these three general techniques:

- Tape backup
- Uninterruptible power supply (UPS)
- Fault tolerance

Tape Backup

What are the first three rules of computing? Backup, backup, and backup. You may have heard this joke before, but its implications are absolutely clear. An administrator who does not back up mission-critical data is tempting fate. It is the easiest and least expensive means to protecting your data.

Planning a backup strategy is essential in every network. The plan must include what is deemed essential data, which must be backed up more often, and less essential data, which need not be backed up as often. Just as essential as planning and implementing backups is the act of testing the integrity of your system by performing regular test restores.

Components of network data backups are the hardware, software, the backup schedule, and the person(s) responsible for performing the backup.

Backup Hardware

Most backup hardware uses backup tapes; however, magneto-optical drives are becoming more widespread in backup operations. Your hardware will reflect your budget, but it should meet the following criteria:

- **Size** Can it back up the system effectively and have room to grow?
- **Speed** Can it back up the system in a timely manner?
- **Reliability** Can it be trusted to restore the data when the system has crashed?
- **Features** Does it include error detection and correction capabilities?

Backup Schedule

There are five types of data backup:

- **Differential** Backs up selected data that has changed since the last backup, without marking data as backed up.
- **Incremental** Backs up and marks selected data that has changed since the last backup.
- **Copy** Backs up all selected data without marking data as backed up.
- **Daily** Backs up only those files that were changed that day, without marking them as backed up.
- **Full** Backs up and marks all selected data, regardless of whether the data has changed since the last backup.

Depending on the network and the data sensitivity, backups could be performed daily, weekly, or even monthly. A good strategy is to make an incremental backup daily, with a full backup over the weekend. This maximizes backup throughput during hours of low network usage. It is also recommended to rotate the backup tapes. Using the same five tapes, labeled Monday through Friday, over the course of a year is probably not a good idea. You should also keep an additional full backup off site, in a secure location. If a fire destroys the building, the data would still be safe.

Backup Operators

Backup operations should be recorded with the date, time, and type of backup. This information should also be written in a network log. Backup operators should be well trained and dedicated to the important task of performing the system backup. For essential security, anyone who has access to your backup tapes should be well known and trusted.

Uninterruptible Power Supply

An uninterruptible power supply (UPS) is a large switched battery that connects between the wall outlet and the computer. If the AC power should fail, the UPS would detect the power loss and immediately begin supplying the computer with power. This occurs so quickly that the computer doesn't crash due to the power outage. Many UPSs have the ability to inform the computer that it is on battery power, and how long the anticipated battery life is. This allows the computer to calculate when to conduct a complete shutdown prior to total power failure. Most systems also will send administrative alerts when the computer changes from AC to UPS power.

In addition, most UPSs act as line conditioners. The voltage at a wall outlet, although rated at 110 to 120 volts, can fluctuate well above and below these levels. These varying levels can damage delicate electrical components. A UPS that also conditions the line ensures that the computer receives voltage within the proper range.

Many operating systems (including Windows NT) do not immediately write data to disk. The system caches the disk writes, and waits for processor idle time. Upon reaching a certain threshold, the data is written to disk. Although this system is the most efficient way for the system to operate, if the power should fail, all data still in the cache will be lost. The UPS provides the necessary time for the administrator to shut down the system safely (or for the system itself to shut down).

 Windows NT can have problems identifying UPSs during startup. When NTDETECT.COM sends a signal to the serial ports to detect attached hardware, it can cause some UPSs to switch off. To correct this, use the NO SERIAL MICE switch in the BOOT.INI file to stop NTDETECT.COM from sending the signal.

Fault-Tolerant Systems

Fault tolerance is a term used to describe the ability of a system to recover from failure. Fault-tolerant hard disks are defined by a series of specifications known as RAID (Redundant Array of Inexpensive Disks). The six RAID levels discussed in this section are:

- **RAID level 0** Disk striping without parity
- **RAID level 1** Disk mirroring or duplexing
- **RAID level 2** Disk striping with ECC
- **RAID level 3** Disk ECC stored as parity
- **RAID level 4** Disk striping with large blocks
- **RAID level 5** Disk striping with parity

Each of these levels describe how multiple physical hard disks can be used to increase system performance and/or fault tolerance; in addition, we include information on a concept called sector sparing.

RAID Level 0—Disk Striping Without Parity

Strangely enough, stripe sets (without parity) provide no fault tolerance. If any disk fails, all data is lost. However, disk throughput is high on a system that uses disk striping without parity. This occurs because the slowest element in the sequence of writing to disk is the hard drive. With two drives in a stripe set, one drive will receive data from the controller and begin writing to disk. The controller can immediately switch to the next disk and send it data, and that disk can begin saving the data. The first disk may not have completed the first write operation, and the controller may have to wait. As you increase the number of hard drives in the stripe set, more time is available for each drive to write to disk.

 RAID level 0 provides NO data redundancy. Its attraction lies in its ability to conduct read and write operations more efficiently than the other RAID levels.

RAID Level 1—Disk Mirroring Or Duplexing

RAID level 1 allows an operating system to save data to two separate hard drives. This level is normally associated with disk mirroring and disk duplexing. Disk mirroring uses two hard drives and one hard-drive controller. If one drive fails, the other hard drive is available with a complete set of all the data. Disk duplexing employs two hard drives, each of which has its own hard-drive controller (see Figure 9.8). This technique also provides redundancy for the hard-drive controllers. As in disk mirroring, if one drive fails, the other would still be available. However, in disk duplexing, if a hard-drive controller fails, or if a disk fails, all data is still available. A drawback to RAID level 1 is low-disk utilization. With two disks in a set, disk utilization is only 50 percent. If there are two 1-GB drives in a system with RAID level 1 active, there will only be 1 GB available for use.

Windows NT Server supports both disk mirroring and disk duplexing.

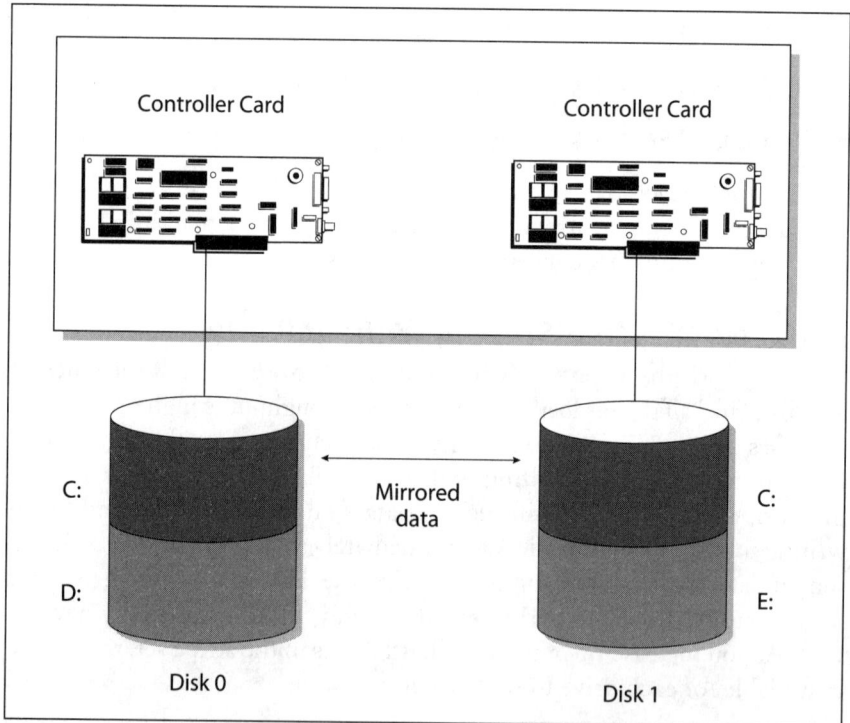

Figure 9.8 Disk duplexing is similar to disk mirroring, except each mirrored disk has its own controller.

 Disk mirroring uses only one controller for two hard drives, whereas disk duplexing uses a controller for each hard drive. Also, disk utilization for RAID level 1 is 50 percent.

RAID Level 2—Disk Striping With Error Correction Code

RAID level 2 implementations write data across a minimum of three disks linked to one controller, and Error Correction Code (ECC) is used to keep track of the data. The group of disks is called a "stripe set," and the process is referred to as data striping. As the data is being written to the stripe set, the ECC code is written to a separate disk. Because ECC uses more space than parity code and only provides marginal improvement in disk utilization, this level is seldom used.

RAID Level 3—Disk Striping With ECC Stored As Parity

RAID level 3 is similar to RAID level 2, except that the ECC is replaced with a parity-checking scheme. Instead of calculating ECC, the system checks the data by adding a mathematical formula to the data, where the number of ones in the data must always be the same. This data-checking system is known as parity checking. It allows the system to check to ensure the data is correct and uses less disk space than ECC. Only one disk is used to store parity data; if this disk fails, the data may not be recoverable, depending on the last backup.

RAID Level 4—Disk Striping With Large Blocks

RAID level 4 defines the method of writing entire blocks of data on each disk, rather than striping blocks of data across the disks in the set. RAID level 4 striping uses parity information to ensure the data is written correctly. The parity information is stored on one disk. As a result, each time data is written to the stripe set, the parity must be calculated and written to the parity disk. This system works well with the large data blocks, but is not efficient because the parity information must be written as the data is written. Windows NT does not support RAID levels 2, 3, and 4, but they can be supported as a hardware-based RAID implementation.

RAID Level 5—Disk Striping With Parity

This RAID level writes data and parity information across all disks in the stripe set, ensuring that the parity information associated with that data is not on the same disk as the data (see Figure 9.9). If a single disk fails, the parity information (in conjunction with the data still on the other disks)

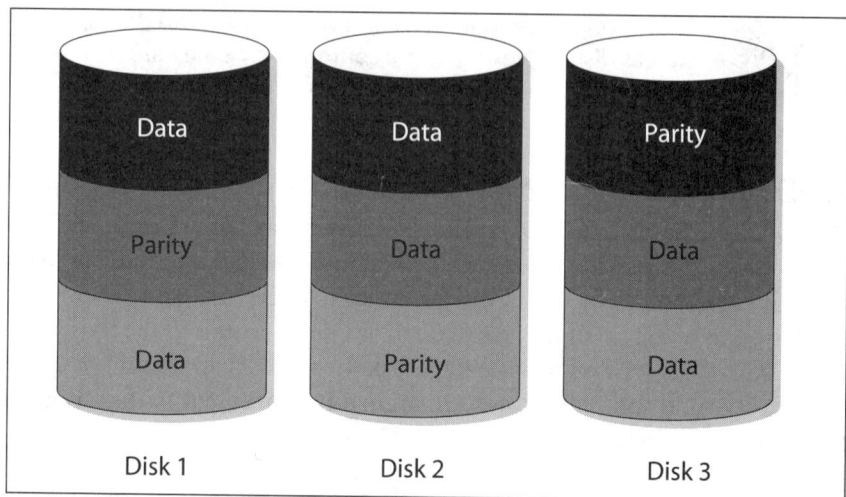

Figure 9.9 Disk striping with parity provides fault tolerance by writing parity information during each write operation—the disk controller writes the parity information in alternating locations in the set, which keeps parity information spread evenly across all disks in the stripe set.

can replace the missing data dynamically. However, if two disks fail at the same time, the stripe with parity cannot recover the information. The only solution in this instance is to restore from tape. RAID level 5 is supported by Windows NT and is a more efficient technique than levels 2, 3, and 4.

Because parity information must be written with each write operation, some of the drive space is occupied by parity information. This means that the usable drive space is equal to the size of all the drives in the system minus 1 divided by the number of physical disks in the system times the total space of all the drives in the system. For example: If a system is using four 3 GB drives, the total space on the set would be: 3 GB + 3 GB + 3 GB + 3 GB = 12 GB. The parity information would use 25 percent of the stripe set (1 divided by the total number of physical disks [4]), which is 3 GB. The total space available for data in this scenario would be 9 GB (or 12 GB minus 3 GB).

Another example: If a system is using six disks with 2 GB each, the total space on the set would be: 2 GB + 2 GB + 2 GB + 2 GB + 2 GB + 2 GB = 12 GB (same as the earlier example). The parity information would use one sixth of the stripe set (1 divided by 6), which is 2 GB. The total space available for data would be 10 GB (or 12 GB minus 2 GB).

Because the disks in a stripe set with parity must be the same size, the easy way to calculate the total space available for data is to add up the total available space on all of the drives and subtract the total available space on a single drive. As the number of disks in a stripe set increases, more space is available for data storage, because less space is necessary for the parity information.

Sector Sparing

Sector sparing is a fault tolerance technique where the hardware or the operating system checks the integrity of the disks prior to write operations. If it discovers a bad sector during a write operation, the bad sector is mapped out (marked unusable) and the data is written to a good sector. This technique only works on SCSI drives, unless the file system supports sector sparing (as does the Windows NT File System).

Table 9.1 Fault tolerance supported by Windows NT—hardware requirements.

RAID Level	Minimum Number Of Disk Drives	Maximum Number Of Disk Drives	Number Of Controllers
RAID 1:	2	2	1
RAID 1:	2	2	2
RAID 5	3	32	1 or more
RAID 0	2	32	1 or more

Practice Questions

Question 1

> The easiest and least expensive means to protect data is:
> - ○ a. Fault tolerance
> - ○ b. RAID level 5
> - ○ c. Disk mirroring
> - ○ d. Scheduled backups

The answer for this question is d. Backups are the easiest and least expensive way to protect data. Although various RAID strategies are very effective at providing fault tolerance, no other means is as easy, or as comprehensive.

Question 2

> Which of the following are normally associated with user-level security? [Check all correct answers]
> - ❑ a. Each user is assigned a unique user name and password
> - ❑ b. Windows 95
> - ❑ c. Windows NT
> - ❑ d. Users are allowed access to resources based on their user names and passwords

The answers for this question are a, c, and d. Systems with user-level security assign each user a unique user name and password, and assign resources based on privileges associated with the user. Contrast this with share-level security, where resource owners place passwords on resources. Windows NT is designed to support user-level security. Windows 95 is designed to support share-level security.

Question 3

You are consulting for a company that is installing NetBIOS as the only protocol. The network topology consists of a small 10BaseT LAN with 1 Windows NT PDC, 1 BDC, and 15 Windows NT Workstations. The company has functional areas named Management, Accounting, Engineering, and Information Systems. The administrator wants the computer name of each workstation to include the user's functional area, the word "workstation" or "server," and the number of the system.

Required Result:

- Ensure the computers can communicate.

Optional Desired Results:

- The system should be able to resolve FQDNs to IP addresses.
- The system should be able to resolve computer names to IP addresses.

Proposed Solution:

- Use the following system to name the computers:

Accountingworkstation1   Accountingworkstation2
Accountingworkstation3   Accountingworkstation4
Accountingworkstation5   Managementworkstation1
Managementworkstation2   Managementworkstation3
Managementworkstation4   Managementworkstation5
Managementworkstation6   Engineeringworkstation1
Engineeringworkstation2   Engineeringworkstation3
Engineeringworkstation4   Informationserver1
Informationserver2

Which results does the proposed solution produce?

- a. The proposed solution produces the required result and produces both of the optional desired results.
- b. The proposed solution produces the required result and produces only one of the optional desired results.
- c. The proposed solution produces the required result, but does not produce any of the optional desired results.
- d. The proposed solution does not produce the required result.

The correct answer is d. NetBIOS only allows 15 characters as computer names, with a 16th character used by the system. The system could easily be implemented by removing the word "workstation" or "server" from the proposed computer names. DNS resolves FQDNs to IP addresses. WINS resolves computer names to IP addresses.

Question 4

> Disk striping without parity requires how many disks to implement?
> - a. One
> - b. Two
> - c. Three
> - d. Four

The correct answer is b. Disk striping without parity only requires two disks to implement. Disk striping with parity requires a minimum of three disks. Both techniques can use up to 32 disks in Windows NT.

Question 5

> Fault tolerant systems include which of the following? [Check all correct answers]
> - a. Disk duplexing
> - b. Sector sparing
> - c. Data encryption
> - d. RAID level 0

The correct answers are a and b. Disk duplexing is a fault-tolerant method that uses two disk controllers and two disk drives. Although sector sparing is not a RAID level, it does supply fault tolerance to systems by detecting bad sectors, attempting to save the data in the bad sectors to a good sector, and identifying the bad sector as unusable. Data encryption secures data from being read; it does not secure it from being lost or damaged. RAID level 0 provides no fault tolerance.

Question 6

> Your UPS shuts off every time your Windows NT computer boots. What should fix the problem and still maintain protection from power failure? [Choose the best answer]
>
> ○ a. Bypass the UPS and plug your computer directly into the wall outlet.
>
> ○ b. Push the spacebar to invoke The Last Known Good Configuration.
>
> ○ c. Use the NO SERIAL MICE switch in the BOOT.INI file.
>
> ○ d. Reboot using the Emergency Repair Disk.

The correct answer is c. During boot, NTDETECT.COM attempts to identify all system peripherals. This includes sending a signal to the serial ports. This signal may shut off some manufacturers' UPSs. Answer a does nothing to protect your machine from a power failure; therefore, answer a is incorrect. If the problem is recurrent, then the LKGC won't fix the problem; therefore, answer b is incorrect. Like answer b, the ERD won't fix the problem; therefore, answer d is also incorrect.

Question 7

> A company is installing an Internet Web server and is very concerned with how quickly data images can be read from the server and sent to potential clients. What disk management system would you want to enable? The company is not as concerned with losing the data as it is about the speed at which the data can be read.
>
> ○ a. RAID level 1—disk duplexing
>
> ○ b. RAID level 2—disk striping with ECC
>
> ○ c. RAID level 1—disk mirroring
>
> ○ d. Raid level 0—disk striping without parity

The correct answer is d. Disk striping without parity is much quicker than the other choices at Read and Write operations, because no parity information is calculated or written to disk.

Question 8

> A user wants to share a directory on his computer with coworkers, and does so using a password to protect the contents of the directory. This is an example of:
>
> ○ a. User-level security
>
> ○ b. Share-level security

The correct answer is b. Users assigning passwords to resources is an example of share-level security. Access to resources depending on rights that the administrator assigns is an example of user-level security.

Question 9

> You are consulting for a company that is using TCP/IP as the only protocol. The network topology consists of a small 10BaseT LAN with 1 Windows NT PDC, 1 BDC, and 15 Windows NT Workstations. Due to the nature of some of the data, the company wants to install some type of software-based fault-tolerant system.
>
> Required Result:
>
> - Ensure the data is immediately available in case of single disk failure.
>
> Optional Desired Result:
>
> - Ensure the system is inexpensive.
>
> Proposed Solutions:
>
> - Install disk striping without parity.
> - Schedule and conduct frequent data backups.
>
> Which results do the proposed solutions produce?
>
> ○ a. The proposed solutions produce the required result and produces the optional desired result.
>
> ○ b. The proposed solutions produce the required result but do not produce the optional desired result.
>
> ○ c. The proposed solutions do not produce the required result.

The correct answer is c. Although the backups are present, the data would not be immediately available in the case of a single disk failure. The administrator would have to restore the backup data before it could be used. This would be an excellent solution if the company installed disk striping with parity. RAID level 5, disk striping with parity, is software that Windows NT supports. A hardware-based RAID solution would not need to be purchased.

Need To Know More?

Chellis, James, Charles Perkins, and Matthew Strebe: *MCSE: Networking Essentials Study Guide, 2nd Edition*. Sybex Network Press, San Francisco, CA, 1998. ISBN 0-7821-2220-5. Chapter 8, "Administering Your Network," contains excellent coverage of the various topics contained within this chapter.

Microsoft Press: *Networking Essentials, 2nd Edition*. Redmond, WA, 1997. ISBN 1-57231-527-X. Unit 6, Lesson 23, "Avoiding Data Loss," discusses all of the fault-tolerance topics in this chapter in greater detail.

Rutstein, Charles B.: *National Computer Security Association Guide to Windows NT Security: A Practical Guide to Securing Windows NT Servers & Workstations*. McGraw-Hill, 1997. ISBN 0-07-057833-8. This is the best guide to NT security on the market.

Search the TechNet CD (or its online version through www.microsoft.com) using the keywords "RAID," "fault tolerance," "WINS," and "DNS."

You've made a smart decision to purchase an Exam Cram or Exam Prep certification study guide, The Smartest Way to Get Certified.™

And now, your decision is even smarter!
Please accept our thanks and...

Receive up to a $100 discount off the price of the Exam Cram! certification course of your choice!

REMEMBER,
when you take an Exam Cram Live! certification course, we guarantee you'll pass the certification exams the first time or your training is on us.*

1-800-809-3243
or www.certizone.com

This card is worth $25 off the price of any course. You may redeem up to four cards with original sales receipts from four different books, for a maximum discount of $100 per course. Your discount will be provided immediately at the time of your registration. Not valid with any other promotion. Offer expires 12/31/99.

*For information about the CertiZone Guarantee and for details on all of our courses, please visit us at www.certizone.com.

Exam Cram Study Guides Come Alive!
Introducing Exam Cram Live! MCSE Certification Courses from CertiZone

Why enroll?
Because our authors are your instructors!

- One instructor has authored or co-authored over 85 books for the industry.
- One instructor helped develop the new, soon-to-be-released Network+ certification test.
- Many of our instructors have authored "Exam Cram" study guides.
- All of our instructors have many years of training experience.

Plus, we guarantee you'll pass your certification tests!
Class locations nationwide.

Just $999 Guaranteed*

*For information about the CertiZone Guarantee and for details on all of our courses, please visit us at www.certizone.com.

Wide Area Networks

Terms you'll need to understand:

- √ Analog and digital connections
- √ Packet and circuit switching
- √ Public Switched Telephone Network (PSTN)
- √ Dial-up lines and dedicated (leased) lines
- √ X.25 Network
- √ Integrated Services Digital Network (ISDN)
- √ Frame relay
- √ T1 and T3 lines
- √ Switched 56 lines
- √ Switched Multimegabit Data Services (SMDS)
- √ Asynchronous Transfer Mode (ATM)
- √ Fiber Distributed Data Interface (FDDI)
- √ Synchronous Optical Network (SONET)

Techniques you'll need to master:

- √ Understanding the differences among WAN technologies
- √ Implementing various WAN technologies

Sometimes, a local area network (LAN) is not sufficient to completely blanket an organization with communications capabilities. This condition generally occurs when multiple LANs in different geographical areas must be interconnected, or on large campuses or in industrial parks where distance limitations for conventional LAN technologies prevent their use. This chapter discusses wide area network (WAN) technologies used to interconnect such geographically dispersed systems. In this chapter, we concentrate on those WAN issues that are most commonly used in modern networks.

WAN Terminology

As your local area network matures, you will probably notice a decrease in its responsiveness. Excessive use causes printers to slow down, email to take longer, and applications that move large amounts of data across the network to bog down. When this happens to your LAN (not *if*), you should plan for expansion, especially if your company covers a wide geographical area. You can usually interconnect multiple smaller LANs within a single building by using routers, which we'll cover later in this chapter, and bridges, which we introduced in Chapter 5. Likewise, if you have several buildings located close together, you can convert a collection of smaller LANs into one large internetwork using the same kind of equipment. But, when offices are located in multiple cities or across international borders, you must make other arrangements. You are now ready to consider introducing a WAN into the mix.

A wide area network can span a city, a state, a continent, or even the globe. The technologies used to accomplish such a feat are usually quite similar to those used to build LANs, despite their differences in distance and scope. Typically, WANs consist of several LANs interconnected through high-speed communications links, usually called "WAN links." Such WAN links may rely on telephone carriers, cable TV companies, long-haul fiber optic cables, line-of-sight or satellite microwave systems, or long-haul packet-switched networks. Routers and bridges can also work together with other connectivity devices to ensure that data is transmitted quickly, safely, and securely across WAN links. Amazingly, if a WAN is constructed correctly, most users may not even notice that a WAN is involved in the network.

Owning and operating the physical links that comprise a WAN is usually beyond the financial means of most companies, so they typically lease services (and, sometimes, equipment) from communications service providers, also known as communications carriers. Such carriers include local and long-distance telephone companies such as BellSouth or AT&T, cable operators such as Time Warner, and companies that operate long-haul fiber optic networks such as MCI WorldCom. The longer the distance a WAN link spans, in fact, the higher the probability that more than one communications carrier is involved in transporting the signals between the linked sites. Companies pay for such connections—often called leased lines or leased WAN links—month to month.

Leased WAN links generally use one of the following technologies to make the necessary connections:

- **Analog connections** These use conventional telephone lines, with voice-signaling (modem) technologies
- **Digital connections** These use digital-grade telephone lines, with digital technologies all the way
- **Switched connections** These use multiple sets of links between sender and receiver to move data

Switching (as in switched connections) refers to finding a path for data transmission across a number of potential links between sender and receiver. On the other hand, analog and digital connections require a fixed connection to exist, at least for the duration of each communication session. Switching methods include both circuit switching and packet switching. Essentially, when data is received on an incoming line, the switching device must find an appropriate outgoing line on which to forward it. These switching devices are usually called routers, based on the functions they perform.

Circuit Switching

The most common example of circuit switching is a typical telephone conversation. When you call someone, the phone company maps out and reserves a single communications line between you and the person you are calling. This may involve allocating lines in several central offices (and through multiple long-distance carriers, in the case of a long-distance call). These lines remain allocated for the duration of a call. When your conversation is done, the lines that the various central offices reserved for your call (as well as the long-distance carriers, if your call used them), are freed, and other callers can use those resources.

However, if you call the same party numerous times in a day, you probably won't be connected through the same set of lines. In fact, it's highly unlikely. This points out one of the weaknesses of circuit switching: The

United States and other first-world countries enjoy reliable telephone-line service. But the same is not true of emerging and third-world countries. If you try to connect regularly with one of these countries, the chances of a reliable, clear connection decrease dramatically.

Data transmission through circuit switching is an all-or-nothing process. It either succeeds or fails. A popular analogy of circuit-switched transmissions is the transportation of goods by train. All of the merchandise is loaded on one train, which takes it from Point A to Point B. During this journey, many detours or mishaps may occur. Any deviation in the delivery affects the entire shipment. On a train, everything moves, or it all stands still.

 Circuit-switched networks can be inexpensive but they are generally slow and not exceptionally efficient for transmitting data, especially in large amounts, or when delivery time is a serious concern (for voice or video traffic, for instance).

Analog Connectivity

The Public Switched Telephone Network (PSTN) can provide data communications as well as voice communications. PSTNs exist worldwide and are usually run by government agencies or private organizations. The PSTN is not new; it has been around for about 100 years. At PSTN's inception, it handled only voice communications over analog lines. As such, the PSTN was not well equipped to provide data transmission. But, with new technologies like high-bandwidth fiber optic cables, microwave transmissions, and satellite relays, the PSTN has become much more reliable for data transmission.

Analog transmission consists of sending streams of continuously modulated data, rather than two signals (one for zeros and another for ones), as with digital transmissions. Such continuity is important to permit phones to reproduce the human voice intelligibly; however, this signaling method must essentially be worked around for data transmission. Here's a tidbit of information: "Modem" stands for "modulator/demodulator," which explains the technology used to convert a digital signal to its analog equivalent for transmission, and then to convert that analog signal back to its digital form upon reception.

There are two predominant types of analog lines used for data communications: Dial-up lines work like ordinary phone lines in that a connection is made on demand, by dialing; dedicated lines act more like regular network cables in that once the connection is brought up, it's left up and running pretty much all the time.

Dial-Up Lines

Dial-up lines are voice-grade lines for which you use a modem to connect to another modem that is attached to another computer. These lines are usually limited to a 56 Kbps rate, and frequently you will have to contend with noise on the line. There is no consistent quality because the line is being allocated from the PSTN's pool of voice lines. Thus, a dial-up session is only as good as the circuits it contains.

Dedicated/Leased Lines

As an organization grows, dial-up service may no longer suffice for its communication needs. Ordinary phone lines must handle voice, modem, and fax traffic, with varying results. When demand begins to outstrip the supply of available outside lines, when you try to connect, the line may be busy more often than not. Assuming that the computer is under your control, and you can cover the extra costs involved, you can change this situation by signing up for a dedicated (or leased) analog line that you can use just for data communications. A leased line is faster and more reliable than a dial-up line, but is also more expensive because it's always available whether it's in use or not. Line conditioning (a service that reduces delay and noise on the line, allowing for better transmissions) can make the leased lines even more reliable, and is often part of a leased-line package, or you can obtain it from the service provider at an additional cost.

How, then, can you decide whether to use dial-up or dedicated lines for data communications? Cost is certainly a factor, as is frequency of use and reliability. If your users need to connect only occasionally, dial-up lines make the most sense because they're inexpensive; slow connections or busy signals that occasionally inconvenience usually persist for only a short time. But, if your users need greater reliability, guaranteed access, or higher bandwidth, the benefits that a leased line can deliver will usually be worth the added expense (figure about two to three times the monthly cost of a normal business line, plus some additional fees for line conditioning and setup).

Digital Connectivity

There will come a time when even the enhanced capabilities of a leased analog line won't be able to satisfy your data-transmission needs. Fortunately, there are numerous digital alternatives available. When you need a faster, more secure method of data transmission, take a look at Digital Data Service (DDS) lines. DDS lines use a point-to-point synchronous method that can transmit at 2.4, 4.8, 9.6, and 56 Kbps. DDS is available from most large communications carriers.

For even higher bandwidth—and higher monthly expenses—high-speed digital lines offer nearly error-free transmission. Such lines are available in numerous forms, including full and fractional T1, T3, and Switched 56. They don't require modems but they do require different devices for each end. These are called channel service units/data service units (CSU/DSU), and they make the necessary changes from the digital signals used on network media to that which is in use on digital telephony media for transmission, and reverse the process upon reception.

Packet Switching

Data sent via packet switching is broken down into small pieces of information called packets. Each packet consists of a piece of the data to be transmitted and certain header information that contains the destination address. Packets are sent one at a time, and rely on special network protocols to find a path between sender and receiver, and to deliver them to their proper destinations. It's highly likely that not all packets will travel the same route from source to destination, nor will they arrive in the same order as they were sent. If a packet gets lost or damaged during transmission, it is a relatively easy task to ship out a replacement. But, it is pretty certain that all packets will ultimately arrive at their proper destinations, and be reassembled into whatever original form the sent data may have taken.

Although the analogy for circuit switching is one of loading goods onto a train, packet switching is more like using a fleet of trucks. Goods are broken down into truckload lots, printed on a shipping manifest, and sent to the destination. Each driver is free to choose his or her route, but is expected to attempt to deliver each shipment in a safe and timely manner. As each truck arrives at the destination, the particular lot is checked off a master list. If a truck breaks down or loses its way, a phone call to the source ensures reshipment of an identical lot of goods. As soon as all lots have arrived, they are reassembled into their original configuration and handed over to the receiver. Packet-switching networks, which work as in the truck example, are fast and efficient, yet fairly economical, because they use high-speed transmission lines on a per-transaction basis.

So far, we have been dealing with basic networking technologies. Let's move on to more advanced technologies that are required to meet the demand for faster, more efficient data transmissions. At first, such technologies were built atop existing media such as telephone lines, but later on, new methods and media—such as fiber optic cable, microwave, and satellite—emerged.

The following sections cover a number of such advanced technologies, including X.25 networks, Integrated Services Digital Networks (ISDNs), frame relay, T-connector services (T1 and T3), Switched 56, Asynchronous Transfer Mode (ATM), Fiber Distributed Data Interfaces (FDDIs), Synchronous Optical Networks (SONETs), and Switched Multimegabit Data Services (SMDS).

X.25 Networks

The X.25 specification was written in the mid-1970s to provide an interface between public packet-switched networks and their customers. It specifies how devices connect over an internetwork. Early X.25 networks transmitted data over analog telephone lines, an unreliable medium that introduced numerous transmission errors. This led the designers of X.25 to incorporate extensive error-checking and packet-retransmission mechanisms to compensate for damaged or missing data. This improved reliability to acceptable levels, but it also resulted in relatively slow transmission speeds that peaked at 64 Kbps. Although a 1992 revision to the X.25 specification increases its maximum throughput to 2 Mbps, this faster version is not yet widely deployed.

Although the X.25 specification was written for use with public or private networks, it has become strongly associated with public data networks (PDNs), marketing as a service by large commercial providers such as AT&T, General Electric, and Tymnet (and most of the PSTNs outside the United States). PDNs were originally used to provide connections between remote terminals and mainframe computers, but now provide relatively low-cost LAN connections. Such links have proved to be particularly useful for credit card processing and other applications where the amount of data is small, and a variable response rate does not pose severe difficulties.

X.25 is not responsible for describing how data moves through the network. It is only responsible for delivering data up to the WAN and receiving it from somewhere else on the WAN. You can imagine the WAN as an amorphous cloud—an ever-changing environment with no standard set of circuits, nor fixed paths between any two points. The best path is determined as needed.

Connection of a LAN to an X.25 network usually requires customers to lease lines that reach between the LAN and a commercial PDN. The actual PDN connection may pass through a computer with an X.25 interface, or through a standalone device called a packet assembler/disassembler (PAD). Whatever type of attachment is used, X.25 networks provide proven, reliable, and nearly error-free connections, but their popularity is waning because of their slow speeds and the evolution of newer and faster technologies such as frame relay and ATM.

Because of its error checking and retransmission of erroneous or lost data packets, X.25 is one of the slowest of the advanced WAN technologies, but it is also one of the most broadly available and affordable options. It remains pervasive outside Europe and the United States.

ISDN Networks

In 1984, a new kind of network called the Integrated Services Digital Network (ISDN) was specified. Although it was heavily hyped and received lots of attention in the 1980s, it hasn't been until the 1990s that ISDN has staked out a measurable piece of the communication-services marketplace.

By design, ISDN's primary goal is to integrate voice and data services by replacing analog telephone lines with digital equivalents that are suited for both voice and all kinds of digital traffic, including data, video, and other digital data streams. Although ISDN is available in many locations, it is used considerably less than PSTN lines. This is due in part to the higher costs of ISDN connections, but also because ISDN does not always offer a sufficient boost to bandwidth compared to PSTN lines (which can support data throughput as high as 115 Kbps including compression). ISDN offers nominal bandwidth of 64 Kbps per channel, and most ISDN lines offer nominal bandwidth of 128 Kbps, because channels are often used in pairs (with compression, some vendors claim throughput as high as 400-plus Kbps across two ISDN bearer channels).

The ISDN specification process took several years; because networking technology moved so rapidly simultaneously, by the time the ISDN standard was finalized, it was already out of date. Today's LANs offer speeds of at least 10 Mbps and are being replaced with 100-Mbps technologies. Offering 64-Kbps service to businesses in the 1980s was a serious proposition. In the 1990s, ISDN might have been completely bypassed, had it not been for individuals and small businesses that need to connect to the Internet.

Although some users are lucky enough to have Internet access at their workplaces, many users are relegated to home or office Internet access via modem, at speeds of 56 Kbps or slower. Because of the cost of ISDN devices, a twofold speed increase is helpful for individuals, but may not be fast enough for LAN-to-Internet connections.

Fortunately, you may purchase ISDN in two different forms:

- The Basic Rate Interface (BRI) targets home users or small businesses. A BRI consists of two bearer channels, also called B-Channels (64 Kbps), and a data channel, also called a D-Channel (16 Kbps), for a total of 144 Kbps of bandwidth. Each of the B-Channels may be used to transmit and receive either voice or data. The D-Channel is used for call setup and control (and sometimes for X.25 or fax communications). With the proper equipment and software, both B-Channels may be combined into a single virtual channel with a data transmission speed of 128 Kbps.

- The Primary Rate Interface (PRI) targets service providers and large organizations. A PRI uses a full T-1 line with 23 B-Channels and a single 64-Kbps D-Channel. Users with access to a PRI can use B-Channels individually, in pairs (typically for incoming BRI connections), or aggregated in any combinations up to all 23 channels together.

ISDN makes it possible to access the Internet at nearly three times the current speed of a modem. Home and small-business users have shown themselves to be willing to use ISDN to enjoy the rapid downloading of Web graphics, files, and email. Essentially, ISDN can be a cost-effective way to connect remote sites where occasional connections are required, and bandwidth needs remain relatively modest.

Remember, though, that ISDN is a type of dial-up service. In most cases, if an ISDN connection is to be used as a dedicated line, Internet Service Providers charge significantly more for such service. On-demand ISDN access is as cheap as $20 a month at some ISPs, but it's rare to find monthly fees for a dedicated line with two B-Channels at less than $300. Because communications carriers often charge per-minute usage fees, in addition to basic service charges, the carrier costs for a dedicated ISDN line can range from a low of $70 per month, to a high of $876 per month (at 2 cents per minute of connect time).

ISDN is a dial-up technology that furnishes voice and data at speeds up to 128 Kbps. Although it took a long time to get to the marketplace, it now enjoys widespread use as a source for Internet connectivity.

Frame Relay

Frame relay evolved from X.25 and ISDN technology. Like X.25, frame relay is a packet-switching network service, but unlike X.25, it doesn't perform error checking or accounting functions. Frame relay expects that the media it traverses will deliver high-quality transmission characteristics, and that error checking will be handled at either end of a connection, most likely in hardware.

Frame relay uses variable-length packets in a packet-switching environment. It establishes a logical path that's called a Permanent Virtual Circuit (PVC) between end-points. PVCs take fixed paths, so a PVC is the equivalent of a dedicated line in a packet-switched network. The path is fixed, so network nodes don't have to waste time calculating routes. Frame relay connections operate at speeds between 56 Kbps and 1.544 Mbps because they use PVCs, and there is no built-in error checking. Frame relay services are gaining popularity: They are much faster than other networking systems at performing basic packet-switching operations, and customers can specify exactly what amount of bandwidth they want to pay for.

You can establish frame relay services to meet any bandwidth requirement. When an organization arranges for a frame relay connection with a provider, it contracts for a Committed Information Rate (CIR), a guaranteed minimum data-transmission rate for the connection. CIRs are available in 64-Kbps increments. Frame relay connections are also popular because they are one of the least expensive types of medium-speed WAN connections. A frame relay connection costs significantly less than a dedicated leased line or an ATM connection.

Frame relay connections to a network require you to use a frame relay-compatible CSU/DSU to create the physical connection to the WAN, and a router or bridge to move traffic from the LAN to the WAN, and the WAN to the LAN, as needed.

Frame relay costs less than a dedicated line or an ATM connection and provides data transmission rates of up to 1.544 Mbps over conventional or fiber optic media.

T1 And T3 Lines

In the early days of the PSTN, a single telephone line could only carry a single telephone conversation. As the use of telephones increased, and demand for more lines grew, the telephone companies desperately sought a solution. In the 1960s, Bell Labs developed a process called multiplexing (or muxing) that could take several transmissions, aggregate them across one high-speed cable, transmit them, and then separate them at their destinations. This process gave birth to the T-carrier system.

The basic unit of the T-carrier system is the T1 line, perhaps the most widely used type of all high-speed digital lines. T1 is a point-to-point transmission technology that consists of 24 64-Kbps channels for a total transmission capability of 1.544 Mbps. Each of the channels may be used as a separate voice or data communications channel, or channels may be combined to provide higher transmission rates. For example, combining 3 channels yields 192 Kbps, and combining 22 channels yields 1.31 Mbps.

A faster commercial T-carrier line is called a T3. It is the equivalent of 28 T1 lines and handles a data rate of 44.736 Mbps. A T3 is the highest-capacity leased-line service available from most communications carriers, and is designed to transport large amounts of data at high speeds between two points. T3 lines can also be horrendously expensive; prices of $30,000 per month or higher are the norm. T1 lines use standard copper wire, whereas T3 lines require fiber optic cables or microwave-transmission equipment.

Installation and monthly service charges for leased T-carrier lines are high; for those reasons, service providers allow customers to lease portions of a T-carrier line's bandwidth through services called Fractional T1 (FT1) and Fractional T3 (FT3). For example, a customer could lease from 1 to 24 of the 24 64-Kbps channels of a T1 line; or anywhere from 2 to 27 T1-width channels of a T3 line.

Connecting a T1 line to your network is similar to connecting a DDS or frame relay line. You will need a T1-compatible CSU/DSU, and a bridge or router. To distribute the T1's bandwidth between voice and data traffic, you will need a multiplexer/demultiplexer to combine voice and data signals for transmission, and separate them upon reception. You can lease T1 or T3 lines, either full or fractional, from telephone companies, long-distance carriers, or other service providers, and you are billed at a flat monthly rate, once you pay for installation and equipment.

T1 lines are the most common high-speed connectivity in use today. They can transmit up to 1.544 Mbps. One nice feature is that a user can lease a fraction of the T1 line as needed. T3 lines are 28 times the size of a T1 (roughly 45 Mbps), and can be consumed in fractions as well.

Switched 56

When customers demanded 56-Kbps dial-up service that was less expensive than dedicated lines, telephone companies and service providers began offering the Switched 56 service. In reality, a Switched 56 line is nothing more than a circuit-switched version of a standard 56-Kbps DDS leased line. As customers pay only for connection time, resulting costs are usually significantly lower than those of a dedicated line.

Both ends of a connection must be equipped with Switched 56-compatible CSU/DSUs that can dial and connect to each other on demand. In many areas where ISDN is not yet available, Switched 56 offers an attractive alternative. In areas where both services are available, it's often wise to make a cost comparison between ISDN and Switched 56, and choose the one that's cheaper (especially in areas where per-minute ISDN-usage charges can contribute significantly to line-operation costs).

Switched 56 is merely a circuit-switched version of a standard 56-Kbps line. This is good for customers because they only have to pay for what they use.

Asynchronous Transfer Mode (ATM)

ATM is an advanced packet-switching technology that transmits data over LANs or WANs in fixed-length 53-byte chunks, called cells, at speeds of up to 622 Mbps. ATM can accommodate voice, data, fax, realtime video, CD-quality audio, imaging, and multimegabit data transmission.

Unlike frame relay, which uses variable-sized packets, ATM cells have a fixed length of 53 bytes. Of these 53 bytes, 48 bytes contain data and 5 contain header information. Because data packets of uniform length are much easier to transport than random-sized packets, ATM can use network equipment to switch, route, and move cells much more quickly than the same equipment could handle randomly sized frames.

ATM is like frame relay because it assumes noise-free lines and leaves error checking to devices at either end of a connection. Also, ATM creates a PVC between two points across an ATM network as part of setting up a communication session. The primary speeds for ATM networks are 155 Mbps and 622 Mbps. The 155-Mbps speed was chosen because high-definition television signals are transmitted at this speed. The 622-Mbps speed was chosen to permit four 155-Mbps channels to be sent simultaneously through the same connection.

You can use ATM with existing media designed for other communications systems such as coaxial, twisted-pair, and fiber optic cable. Because these traditional network media do not support all of ATM's capabilities, you can also use ATM with T-3 (45 Mbps), FDDI (100 Mbps), Fiber Channel (155 Mbps), and OC-3 SONET (155 Mbps)—we'll discuss these last three and OC shortly. ATM can even interface with frame relay and X.25.

ATM offers theoretical throughput speeds of up to 2.4 Gbps (OC-48) but is usually constrained to 622 Mbps because of the type of fiber optic cable used for current long-haul cable installations. Experimental fiber optic technologies have already surpassed transmission rates of 10 Gbps in laboratory environments, so ATM has obviously not reached its "speed limit"—it's just waiting for faster transport equipment and improved media!

ATM is a packet-switched technology that transmits data in fixed-length, 53-byte cells. Theoretically capable of speeds of 1.2 (OC-24) and even 2.4 Gbps (OC-48), it usually transmits in the 155 Mbps (OC-3) to 622 (OC-12) Mbps range.

About Optical Carrier Levels, T-Carrier Rates, And More

The Optical Carrier rating level for standard ATM technologies is customarily abbreviated as OC-n, where n is a multiplier applied to the basic OC level 1 rate (OC-1) of 51.84 Mbps. OC-1 describes the basic transmission rate for SONET communications. Table 10.1 (seen later in this chapter) summarizes most of the WAN service types that we cover in this chapter, along with their common abbreviations, basic characteristics, maximum throughput rates, and associated transmission technologies.

FDDI

Fiber Distributed Data Interface (FDDI) is not really a WAN technology but is used to connect LANs via a high-speed, token-passing, one- or two-way counter-rotating ring. FDDI supports both LED- and laser-generated LAN communications across fiber optic cable. FDDI networks are quite reliable because fiber optic cable doesn't break as easily as other cable types, is difficult to wiretap because the cable doesn't emit any signals, and is immune to electrical interference.

FDDI is not like a regular Token Ring network because more than one computer at a time can transmit a token so that multiple tokens can circulate on the ring at any one time. The token-passing system is used in a dual-ring setting. Traffic in the FDDI network consists of two similar data streams moving in opposite directions around two counter-rotating rings. The primary ring usually carries the traffic. If the primary ring fails, FDDI automatically reconfigures the network so that data flows onto the secondary ring, and moves the data in the opposite direction. Redundancy is one of the key advantages of this particular dual-ring topology.

FDDI can achieve data transmission speeds of up to 100 Mbps. FDDI is not suitable for WANs because the maximum ring length is 100 kilometers or about 62 miles; however, it can interconnect LANs that will be connected to form a WAN, and is also clearly suitable for deployment in metropolitan area networks (MANs).

FDDI networks are very reliable because the cable cannot be wiretapped, and is not susceptible to electromagnetic interference. In addition, FDDI's dual-ring architecture increases its reliability.

SONET

After the breakup of AT&T in 1984, local telephone companies were faced with trying to connect to many long-distance carriers, all with different interfacing schemes. Bell Communications Research developed SONET, the Synchronous Optical Network. SONET is a fiber optic WAN technology used to deliver voice, data, and video at speeds in multiples of 51.84 Mbps (known as OC-1, as documented in Table 10.1). SONET's main goals were to create a method by which all carriers could interconnect, and to unify differing standards used in Europe, the United States, and Asia—especially Japan.

SONET has unified these groups with a new system that defines data rates in terms of Optical Carrier (OC) levels. The basic OC-1 level specifies a data rate of 51.84 Mbps, and is based on the DS1 basic rate defined for SONET. The most common level is OC-3 or 3 multiplied by 51.84 Mbps or 155.52 Mbps. OC-3 is the most common SONET implementation in use today, even though the specification defines OC-48 at 2.48 Gbps.

SONET is a fiber optic WAN technology used to deliver voice, data, and video at speeds up to 622 Mbps, and beyond.

SMDS

Switched Multimegabit Data Services (SMDS) is a switching WAN technology introduced in 1991 that provides data transmission in the range between 1.544 Mbps (T1 or DS1) to 45 Mbps (T3 or DS3). SMDS offers high bandwidth at reduced network costs. Like ATM, SMDS uses a fixed-length cell of 53 bytes for data transmission. Like ATM and frame relay, it provides no error checking, leaving that up to devices at the connection points.

An SMDS line with appropriate bandwidth can connect to a local carrier and provide connections between all sites without requiring call setup or tear-down procedures to be invoked. ATM and convention digital technologies require that such procedures be enacted for every PVC used, which saves time and money.

Note: SMDS *is a competitor to X.25 but is not in widespread use because of high equipment costs.*

Table 10.1 Common WAN service types, with salient details.

Abbreviation	Expanded Form	Transmission Rate	Applies To	Remarks
BRI	Basic Rate Interface	2 64-Kbps channels	ISDN	Total bandwidth 144 Kbps (2B +16 Kbps data channel)
DS0	Digital Service, level 0	64 Kbps	Digital telephony	Defines basic digital channel used to classify capacities of digital lines and trunks
DS1	Digital Service, level 1	1.544 Mbps, U.S. 2.048 Mbps, Outside the United States	Digital telephony	In the United States, based on a Bell standard, same as T1; 2.048 speed based on ITU standard
DS3	Digital Service, level 3	44.736 Mbps	Digital telephony	Same as T3, equivalent to 28 T1s

(continued)

Table 10.1 Common WAN service types, with salient details (continued).

Abbreviation	Expanded Form	Transmission Rate	Applies To	Remarks
E1	European Trunk Line, level 1	2.048 Mbps	Digital telephony	Equivalent to T1 in most of the world, but the E stands for Europe in the abbreviation
T1	Level 1 Trunk Line	1.544 Mbps	Digital telephony	Uses two pairs of TP phone cable. Used in the United States, Canada, Hong Kong, Japan
T3	Level 3 Trunk Line	44.736 Mbps	Digital telephony	Often rounded to 45 Mbps
OC-1	Optical Carrier level 1	51.840 Mbps	ATM, SONET	Permits direct electrical-to-optical mapping
OC-3	Optical Carrier level 3	155 Mbps	ATM, SONET	
OC-12	Optical Carrier level 12	622 Mbps	ATM, SONET	
OC-24	Optical Carrier level 24	1.2 Gbps	ATM, SONET	
OC-48	Optical Carrier level 48	2.4 Gbps	ATM, SONET	
PRI	Primary Rate Interface	1.544 Mbps	ISDN	23-B + 64 Kbps channel, same overall bandwidth as a T1, DS1
Switched 56	Switched 56	56 Kbps	Digital telephony	On-demand, moderate-speed digital telephone service

Practice Questions

Question 1

> What is the most widely used type of high-speed digital link in the United States?
>
> ○ a. T1
> ○ b. T3
> ○ c. E1
> ○ d. Switched 56

The correct answer is a; T1 lines are the most common high-speed digital links used in the United States today. Answer b names the 44.736-Mbps T3 (DS3) service, whose costs start at around $30,000 per month from most carriers—still a bit too expensive for widespread deployment. Answer c, E1, names the most common European digital trunk line, unheard of and unused in the United States. Switched 56 is quite common, but doesn't really qualify as a high-speed digital link, so answer d is also incorrect.

Question 2

> What role does the D-Channel play in basic-rate ISDN?
>
> ○ a. Signaling and link management data
> ○ b. 128 Kbps data only
> ○ c. Voice, data, or videos
> ○ d. 16 Kbps only

Answer a is correct. The primary function of the data channel in ISDN, whether basic or primary rate, is call management, which literally translates into signaling and link management data. If you recall the ISDN discussion earlier in the chapter, the BRI D-Channel is also sometimes used for fax or X.25 traffic as well. The bandwidth of the D-Channel is 16 Kbps on a BRI, so answer b is clearly incorrect. The D-Channel is only used for call control and some limited types of narrow-bandwidth data transmission. On telephone circuits, digitized voice requires 64 Kbps (or at least one B-channel), data and video usually do best when they can use both B-channels; thus, answer c is also incorrect. Although answer d accurately describes the bandwidth of a D-Channel, it fails to name what it's used for, which explains why that answer is also incorrect.

Question 3

> Which of the following WAN technologies was originally intended to replace analog phone lines?
>
> ○ a. ATM
>
> ○ b. T1
>
> ○ c. ISDN
>
> ○ d. Frame relay
>
> ○ e. FDDI

The correct answer to this question is c, the Integrated Services Digital Network, or ISDN. ATM offers bandwidth that typically starts at 155 Mbps; because a digital voice channel needs only 64 Kbps, this is a major case of overkill, and would be way too expensive to replace analog phone lines. Therefore, answer a is incorrect. Even T1, which includes only 24 voice line channels of 64 Kbps is too expensive and offers too much bandwidth for replacing less than a sizable bank of telephone lines. Therefore, answer b is incorrect. Frame relay, answer d, comes in increments of 56 Kbps, and is sometimes used to aggregate voice and data traffic, but was not ever intended to replace analog phone lines either. Finally, FDDI is not a form of digital telephony at all (and is not considered a WAN technology in some circles anyway); also, at 100 Mbps; it's another case of overkill for replacing analog voice channels. Therefore, answer e is incorrect.

Question 4

> Which of the following WAN technologies can transmit data at more than 100 Mbps? [Check all correct answers]
>
> ❏ a. Switched 56
>
> ❏ b. ATM
>
> ❏ c. ISDN
>
> ❏ d. T1
>
> ❏ e. SONET OC-12

Answers b and e are the only correct answers to this question. Although answer b, ATM, comes in many flavors, standard implementations begin at 155 Mbps and increase from there; thus, ATM is a correct answer. Like ATM, SONET comes in many flavors, some of which are slower than 100 Mbps; however, answer e's specification of OC-12 (622 Mbps) specifically states that it transmits faster than 100 Mbps. The key to answering this question lies in knowing the speeds associated with these technologies. Answer a, Switched 56, offers 56-Kbps speeds for each channel; clearly, this is less than 100 Mbps, which makes this answer incorrect. Even ISDN PRI offers only 1.544 Mbps (BRI tops out at 144 Kbps); therefore, answer c is incorrect. T1 lines offer a maximum of 1.544 Mbps (same number of 64 Kbps channels as a PRI, in fact), making answer d incorrect.

Question 5

Which of the following statements best describes frame relay technology?

○ a. It transmits fixed-length packets at the Physical layer through the most cost-effective path.

○ b. It transmits variable-length packets at the Physical layer through the most cost-effective path.

○ c. It transmits fixed-length packets at the Data Link layer through the most cost-effective path.

○ d. It transmits variable-length packets at the Data Link layer through the most cost-effective path.

Because frame relay uses variable-length, not fixed-length, packets, only answer d is correct. Only the physical interfaces and media operate at the Physical layer of the OSI model. Thus, answers a and b are both incorrect because they situate packet handling where only frames may go.

Question 6

> Which of the following WAN technologies is actually a protocol suite that uses packet assemblers and disassemblers (PADs)?
>
> ○ a. X.25
> ○ b. ISDN
> ○ c. ATM
> ○ d. Frame relay

Answer a is the only correct answer. The real clue to this question comes from its mention of Packet Assemblers/Disassemblers (PADs)—of all the technologies mentioned in this question, only X.25 uses PADs. Only X.25, the oldest WAN technology discussed in this chapter, actually incorporates its own specific protocol suite to manage addressing, transport, and delivery of the information that it carries.

Question 7

> What two ring configurations can be used on an FDDI network? [Check all correct answers]
>
> ❑ a. Single rotating ring
> ❑ b. Single virtual ring, implemented as a star
> ❑ c. Dual counter-rotating rings
> ❑ d. Dual parallel-rotating rings

Answers a and c are the correct choices. Answer a is the only correct single-ring answer. FDDI can use either a single-ring or a double-ring configuration, where the topology is a true ring. For dual rings, FDDI uses counter-rotating rings to speed delivery times, not parallel-rotating rings (the option for answer d), so only answer c of the two dual-ring possibilities is correct. Answer b is incorrect; even though for most other topologies, the ring is virtual (and the star actual) as with IBM Token Ring networks.

Question 8

> Of the following networking technologies, which define data rates in terms of Optical Carrier (OC) levels? [Check all correct answers]
>
> ❑ a. SMDS
>
> ❑ b. FDDI
>
> ❑ c. ATM
>
> ❑ d. SONET
>
> ❑ e. ISDN

Answers c and d are correct. Both of the highest-speed technologies listed here—namely ATM and SONET—describe their data rates using Optical Carrier levels. SMDS supports variable data rates up to DS3 levels, and is not described in terms of Optical Carrier levels. Therefore, answer a is incorrect. FDDI is strictly 100 Mbps, and makes no reference to OC levels. Therefore, answer b is incorrect. ISDN describes its data rates in terms of DS0 64-Kbps bearer channels (and for BRI, a 16-Kbps data channel as well; for PRI, the D-Channel is also 64 Kbps). Therefore, answer e is incorrect as well.

Need To Know More?

This chapter covers a huge range of topics. We offer some of our favorite resources, but these only scratch the surface of what's available. Be sure to visit www.amazon.com and check out its "Search by Author, Title, Keyword" capabilities for all these topics—new publications keep showing up all the time, and most of the topics covered in this chapter are hotbeds of publication activity!

Bezar, David D.: *LAN Times Guide to Telephony*, Osborne/McGraw-Hill, Berkeley, 1995. ISBN: 0-07-882126-6. One of the best all-around references on computer telephony, with especially informative coverage of digital telephony, trunk lines, and digital data services.

De Prycker, Martin: *Asynchronous Transfer Mode, 3rd Edition*, Prentice-Hall, London, 1995. ISBN: 0-13-342171-6. Although the material is a bit dated, this book contains one of the best overviews of ATM signaling and cell handling we've ever seen. Recommended for those who need to learn the details of this technology.

Michael, Wendy H., William J. Cronin, Jr., and Karl F. Pieper: *FDDI: An Introduction*, Digital Press, Burlington, MA, 1993. A short, clear, and understandable introduction to FDDI terminology, technology, and hardware.

Parnell, Tere: *LAN Times Guide to Building High-Speed Networks*, Osborne/McGraw-Hill, Berkeley, 1996. Good chapters on ATM, SONET, and SMDS, among numerous other topics of interest to those who seek to construct the fastest networks possible.

Sheldon, Tom: *LAN Times Encyclopedia of Networking, 2nd Edition*, Osborne/McGraw-Hill, Berkeley, 1997. An outstanding all-around reference on networking topics of all kinds, Sheldon's articles on all of the technologies covered in this chapter will make valuable supplements to the information covered in any of the Networking Essentials study guides or training materials available.

Tittel, Ed, and Dawn Rader: *Computer Telephony: Automating Home Offices and Small Businesses*, AP Professional, Boston, 1996. ISBN: 0-12-691411-7. A good review of computer telephony terminology and technology, with good coverage of digital telephony of all kinds.

 Tittel, Ed, Steve James, David Piscitello, and Lisa Phifer: *ISDN Clearly Explained*, 2nd *Edition*, AP Professional, Boston, 1997. ISBN: 0-12-691412-5. A thorough overview of ISDN terminology and technology, coupled with in-depth reviews of SOHO ISDN adapters, modems, and routers.

 For more information on any of the technologies covered in this chapter, visit your favorite search engine, or **www.search.com**, and use its name as a search term to find countless sources of additional information.

 The ATM Forum, which operates a Web site at **www.atm.forum.com**, is the ultimate source of information about ATM online.

 Ray LaRocca, of the FDDI Consortium, has written an excellent tutorial on the subject that you can find at **www.iol.unh.edu/training/fddi/htmls/index.html**.

 The folks at Teletutor have put together a terrific online X.25 tutorial that you can download at **www.teletutor.com/x25.html**.

 Lucent has put together a nice tutorial on Internet access that includes significant discussion of SONET, which you will find at **www.webproforum.com/lucent/index.html**.

 Online resources on ISDN abound, but nowhere is there a better place to start than Dan Kegel's truly amazing repository of ISDN pointers and information, which you will find at **www.alumni.caltech.edu/~dank/isdn/**.

Problem Diagnosis And Resolution

11

Terms you'll need to understand:

- ✓ Troubleshooting
- ✓ User and account management
- ✓ Performance tuning
- ✓ Network operations
- ✓ Physical plant
- ✓ Security policies
- ✓ Auditing
- ✓ Disaster planning and recovery
- ✓ Capacity planning
- ✓ Network modeling

Techniques you'll need to master:

- ✓ Evaluating and troubleshooting network problems
- ✓ Preparing for successful software and hardware upgrades and maintenance
- ✓ Auditing events on the network

Even in the most smoothly planned, designed, and executed system, problems will occur simply because of the complexity of a network. Just like children, a network system is conceived, born, and continues to grow and change throughout its existence. Unlike children, some even outlive their usefulness. But there are tools that allow you to observe components of the network, help you to determine what is normal, and alert you when there might be problems. There are certain preventive measures you can take to avoid common problems before they happen and there are established troubleshooting procedures to follow when difficulties do occur.

In this chapter, we discuss some approaches to proactive network management, such as the use of management utilities, network monitoring and baselining, performance management, and preemptive troubleshooting. Following will be a discussion of prevention through careful planning, which includes backup systems and methodologies, elimination of security risks, standardized components and procedures, documentation, and training. Finally, we work through some common troubleshooting tips and techniques.

Approaches To Network Management

Network management can be defined as the act or process of regularly managing or supervising a network's execution, usage, and conduct. Administration is a daily, ongoing process. An effective administrator must continually deal with and be an expert at:

- User and account management
- Performance tuning
- Network operations
- Software/hardware upgrades and maintenance
- Physical plant, including cabling, data, and telecommunications
- Security policies and auditing
- Disaster planning and recovery
- Capacity planning
- Network modeling

Network administrators need both breadth and depth of knowledge. Although you can't be an expert at *everything*, you are generally expected to be one at all times. So Microsoft included several tools with Windows NT to assist you in managing daily operations. Knowing how to use these tools and including them in your management regimen will make your life easier and your job saner.

Introduction To Network Management Utilities

A network administrator must be able to use all the tools at his or her disposal in order to properly detect, analyze, and correct problems. It is important to know what you started with, how it's changing, how to expand it painlessly, and what to do when it fails. Gathering and analyzing data, known as baselining, will give you the foundation to measure the network's reaction to changes and stresses. Practicing preemptive troubleshooting regularly will help to prevent problems. Microsoft Windows NT includes such tools as the Performance Monitor, the Network Monitor, and the Event Viewer to assist in a smooth-running operation.

Baselining Your Network

Now that we've discussed what network management is, let's further examine baselining, an often overlooked but effective tool for general network administration and for troubleshooting problems. As we already mentioned, baselining is the practice of taking snapshots of your network and its various components at predetermined time intervals in order to establish a basis for trend comparison. Certain events are monitored and information about those events is recorded. You may then use the raw data to construct a graphical representation of the information so that it will be easier to compare and analyze trends, which simplifies your monitoring and planning tasks.

What should you baseline? Such classes as security, applications, and the system itself. The following tools are included with Windows NT operating system and can be used to assist in network monitoring.

Event Viewer

In the early days of networking, events on the server could be accurately judged by the sounds and various lights on the server. Things will never be that simple again, so Microsoft included the Event Viewer to log critical and informational events that affect the daily operation of your servers and your network environment. The Event Viewer can be an alert service for critical events, such as loss of power, or an information service, which logs and records non-critical events, like low disk space on the volume or a failed logon attempt. The Event Viewer utility allows an administrator to view, sort, filter, and search for specific events in the log.

> The Event Viewer can be used to monitor such activities as unsuccessful logon attempts, but you must enable logon auditing first. You can see a report of unsuccessful logon attempts with the Event Viewer's Security log.

Network Monitoring

Administrators monitor network performance and activities in order to detect bottlenecks (or to prevent them from happening), to improve performance based on the existing configuration, to forecast capacity requirements, and to avoid problems. One of the tools readily available and most widely used for monitoring events on the TCP/IP network is the Simple Network Management Protocol (SNMP).

In SNMP, clients load a special program, known as an agent, in memory. These agents monitor the network for "gets," "sets," and "traps." A special management program polls the agents and downloads the information from their management information base (MIB), where the information has been stored. Because various network-management services are used for different types of devices or for different network-management protocols, each service may have its own set of objects. The MIB refers to the entire set of objects that any service or protocol uses. The management program not only collects the data, but it also presents the information in the form of maps, graphs, and/or charts; it also packages the information to send to designated databases for analysis.

A community is a cluster of hosts to which the computer or device running the SNMP agent belongs. SNMP security allows the administrator to specify the communities and hosts a computer will accept requests from, and to specify whether to send an authentication trap when an unauthorized community or host requests information. Should the agent receive a request for information from an unidentified source, it will send a trap to the designated trap destination that indicates the failed authentication.

> In an SNMP environment, the agent is the program loaded on a client machine or a networked device to monitor network traffic and to report events to the management program console.

Performance Management

Microsoft defines performance as time per transaction, where a transaction is a request or an action a user or a system wants to perform. We may envision performance as pure, raw power and speed; if you notice the response, it's too slow! System bottlenecks, such as inadequate bandwidth, slow NICs, slow server buses, or poor hard disk subsystems, may affect performance. Too much happening at once—too many processes for the CPU, too much data for the buffers, or too many transactions for both—may also influence performance. Excessive paging, disk thrashing, high utilization percentages, and sluggish server response will result. Performance tuning is the fine art of identifying these bottlenecks, correcting them in a non-intrusive manner, and moving on to identify the next bottleneck.

Performance Monitor charts historical as well as realtime performance data to identify both trends over time and bottlenecks in the system. It also monitors the effects of system or configuration changes, and determines system capacity limits. Four views are available in the Windows NT Performance Monitor:

- **Chart** Realtime as well as historical; might be useful to analyze why an application is performing poorly, to discover intermittent problems, or to inform you where to increase capacity.

- **Alert** Tracks up to 1,000 alerts; notifies you when a counter is outside the range of permitted values; selected by the administrator.

- **Log** Historical only; instrumental in capacity planning.

- **Report** Realtime view of performance of selected counters in a columnar format.

You can monitor numerous items. Each object that you can monitor contains subcategories, called counters. Performance Monitor actually reports on the counters, instead of the objects directly, in all views except Log view. Here are the objects that can be measured with Performance Monitor:

- Cache
- Logical disk
- Memory
- Objects
- Physical disk

- Process
- Processor
- System
- Thread
- Network-related objects
- Printers

 **TIP** Through performance monitoring, the network administrator can identify bottlenecks and gauge the results of network changes.

Preemptive Troubleshooting Through Preventative Maintenance

Normally, we would include in our annual budget money for auto, house, and life insurance. We think nothing of having our vehicles and household items regularly serviced and maintained. We may visit our family physician annually for general checkups. Likewise, we should budget time and money to regularly maintain and check up on our network systems. There are many simple but effective ways to proactively manage your assets.

A network file server is not a PC on steroids, but many of the same preventative maintenance principles may apply. Although Windows NT is generally self-tuning, that only goes so far. Regular, documented activities such as virus checking/detection and cleaning, disk defragmentation, disk checking (CHKDSK), and deletion of temporary files help preserve disk space that is necessary for performance and general health. The AT command can be very helpful in automating a lot of these routine checkups. You can use the tools supplied with the NOS, or there are many third-party products available. Some may be useful in keeping tabs on disk quotas—limiting runaway processes or disk hogs and providing accountability. You should, however, make sure that any add-on products are certified to be compatible with your NOS and hardware.

Be aware that corrupted or virus-infected files are usually backed up in their corrupted state, so check those restore processes as part of your routine maintenance procedures. Add to your baseline measurements by checking for such things as free disk space, number of user and group accounts, and backup times. We were able to pinpoint a WAN problem many times just by noticing the backup time had increased dramatically. Recording disk-space usage and user accounts will help you plan for growth. It is wise to keep a log book to record these activities and their outcomes by date. By keeping things neat, orderly, and accounted for, you may prevent many common problems.

Prevention Through Planning

You have established the need for a network, perhaps through an organized process as a consultant for a client firm, through joint development efforts with a team of your fellow employees, or just because of circumstances outside your control. As part of the planning process, you then proceed to identify the benefits and set priorities for those outcomes that are viable. As you do this, you must take into account the human factors involved in a network installation, because these can affect the system just as much as hardware or software.

When you are in the pre-planning stage, you should consider the health of the entire network: Don't forget to include provisions for training, documentation, and transitioning. Consider such issues as your company's history (how the organization responds to change), projected growth, operating policies (how difficult it will be to acquire what you need), working environment, office systems and procedures (who will provide frontline and backup support), and the people who will be using the final product (what kinds of training will you require).

Contingency planning involves identifying the costs of a failure and the likelihood that any one component will fail. It may be easy to identify the cost of replacing or repairing a lost server, gateway, hub, router, or their individual components. It is much more difficult, however, to measure the cost of downtime in terms of lost sales, competitiveness, customer goodwill, employee productivity and confidence, perishables, and contractual obligations.

When planning, keep in mind that you need to minimize a single point of failure in any system. That is, try to limit the components whose failure will result in the loss of the computer or the network. The components most likely to cause network downtime are failed servers, faulty or inadequate power systems, lack of climate control, faulty wiring, insufficient cabling, failed intermediate devices, lost telecommunications, and buggy software. For each of these components, consider fault tolerance, redundancy, additional vendor support, and quick repair or replacement.

Standardization

Standardization is another technique of smart network administration. By limiting the number of components in a system, you will also limit the complexity. NICs, gateways, routers, hubs, servers, access devices, and so on, all carry a certain amount of excess baggage, in the form of documentation, staff technical training, software drivers and firmware, and spares and replacement parts.

Another technique is to centralize as many of the events associated with network connectivity as you can, including centrally accessible logon scripts, profiles, and policies. Using WINS and DNS servers for browsing services or centrally located HOSTS and LMHOSTS files reduces the amount of administrative overhead substantially. Another helpful tool that is not widely deployed in heterogeneous shops is Dynamic Host Configuration Protocol (DHCP) services. Not only can DHCP control the assignment of IP addresses, but it also lends some administrative control through the use of DHCP options, configured using the DHCP Manager, and makes the movement of TCP/IP clients much easier.

Finally, even though it may cost a little more up front, there is something to be said about purchasing industry-standard components and devices. Not only will doing so reduce administrative and technical burdens, but you will have a greater chance of choosing items from the Microsoft Hardware Compatibility List. This is extremely important in the real world. You may have purchased the highest level of support agreement that exists, but if you call for technical support on products that aren't on that list, you will be refused in some way or another.

Backing Up

The first line of defense against a network disaster is a reliable, current backup. Backups are also useful for archiving seldom-used data that must be saved for legal or historical purposes, allowing the administrator to recover that disk space for other uses. Clearly and completely document your backup system, policies, and procedures. Depending on the nature of your organization, backups may be included in an audit or needed in case of an extreme emergency. It's also wise to keep a secondary backup system offsite in "hot standby" mode, ensuring the restoration of data in a catastrophe.

Even in the most fault-tolerant environment, you still need backups to protect your data from the following:

Problem Diagnosis And Resolution

- User errors
- Sabotage and virus infections
- Software malfunctions
- Catastrophes
- Disk corruption

Data recovery will be easier and less time-consuming if your backup operations are based on good planning, reliable, high-quality hardware, and consistent, easy-to-use software. You must make sure the system you choose will both back up the type of data you have in the available amount of time and restore it reliably.

 Your primary defense against data loss is the implementation of an effective, efficient backup system with an appropriate schedule and methodology. Use fault-tolerant systems, such as RAID 1 or RAID 5, in addition to—not at the exclusion of—data backups.

In Chapter 9, you learned about the different backup strategies. Now let's consider various backup approaches. The two extremes you need to consider when planning an appropriate backup strategy are the small, simple network with less than 10 computers and one with high-powered servers that store huge amounts of data that need to be available on a twenty-four-hour-a-day, seven-day-a-week basis. Here are some guidelines for the small networks:

- Test your backup capability frequently and record the results. Adjust your procedures as needed.
- Store tapes in a safe environment—offsite—and have trusted individuals maintain them.
- Ensure the backup media will hold the amount of data to be backed up.
- Ensure the backup system will cooperate with the computer in which it's installed.
- Standardize all of your backup systems with the same media, hardware, and software.
- Verify that the media works in all the backup devices.
- Test your restoration capability frequently and record the results. Make adjustments as necessary.

- Implement a standard labeling scheme for the tapes and logs, which includes, at minimum, date, type of backup, amount of data backed up, and server backed up.
- Make sure all details of the backup are documented in a log, and send a copy of the log offsite at regular intervals.
- Rotate your media in a scheme that supports your organizational goals and objectives.
- Back up critical data and important servers, such as domain controllers and mission-critical application servers, on a daily basis.
- Test your backup and restoration capability frequently and record the results. (We cannot stress this enough!)

Circumstances are more difficult for larger networks, where the health and availability of the server are critical to the functions of the organizations. For large amounts of data, it is often difficult to back up in the allotted amount of time. If the server must be running and available 24 hours a day, you must choose backup software that can back up open or locked files. These types of software make a backup of the file's image, because you cannot really back up an open or locked file. Other creative solutions we've seen include:

- Disconnecting all users prior to backup and keeping them out until the backup has completed. In Windows NT Server, you can automate this task using the AT command.
- Pausing the Server service, which logically removes the server from the network.
- Ensuring all files are unlocked or closed, which usually requires cooperation of the application and/or programming team.
- Replicating the data to a duplicate server or extra volume that has no connected users, and backing up that machine. When choosing this method, make sure permissions and file attributes are replicated along with the data.

Security

It's important to plan to minimize the effects of human error or deliberate acts of sabotage, with the former being the most common. This usually involves a lot of common sense and a little diligence. Servers, as well as critical devices and peripherals, should be kept in an adequately cooled, sufficiently powered environment that limits access. If anyone can walk up to your server, he or she can walk off with it or find a way to fool with it. Ensure that only trained, trusted individuals have access to those critical resources, either locally or remotely. This includes password protecting any server or device that can be remotely administered.

Other common-sense considerations include password-protected screen savers on servers, locked enclosures, diligent virus checking, and virus-detecting software that stays resident on users' desktops but doesn't interfere with the computer's operations.

One item that is often overlooked is a regular audit of security enforcement. Special software programs accomplish this, or a resourceful network administrator can make use of the tools at hand. As we have already mentioned, Windows NT includes such tools as the Event Viewer to assist in security auditing.

Finally, include security measures in your network plan. Determine what levels of restrictions allow your users to do their jobs without interference and undue burden but still maintain the security and integrity of your data. A complete network operating system allows the network administrator to determine and manage what the users can and cannot do. In Windows NT, this is accomplished through the use of user- and share-level security as well as through user profiles. Auditing makes sure that these levels of security are not compromised as changes occur in the network.

Upgrades

Information technology changes daily, promises the networking environment we all want, and renders a lot of what's installed obsolete. We upgrade to:

- Keep up with changing technology.
- Keep up with changing user needs.
- Incorporate new technologies to meet changing user needs.
- Prepare for growth and change.

Here are a few guidelines for when you are preparing to upgrade software or hardware, particularly on a critical server or device:

- Make sure your documentation is current and complete.
- Make sure you have two reliable, full backups of data, as well as system configurations.

- Be sure to keep a separate backup of critical files like Registries, boot partitions, and system files.
- Have Emergency Repair Disks current, tested, and handy.
- Test the upgrade as many times as possible before deploying it in a production environment.

Documentation

No one will ever know your network as well as you, especially the intricate ins, outs, and exceptions that lace every installation. Cover your assets! Document *everything*. Create a log book for every server and backup system, your users, network, cabling systems, vendor services, pertinent telephone numbers, scheduled maintenance, MIS policies and procedures, troubleshooting tips, escalation procedures, and WAN diagrams—and maintain detailed information about your software. This is your second line of defense in the disaster planning and recovery process and your first reference source when troubleshooting problems.

There is a wide variety of vendor-supplied and third-party documentation products available for every NOS and every system's individual needs, but you can usually achieve the most effective documentation through a combination of effective tools and due diligence on the part of the MIS staff. The documentation process should begin with the conception phase and become a routine part of system administration. As part of the documentation process, include such information as where the documentation is stored, who has access, how often it should be updated, and what is included in the documentation process itself.

Training

If your users can't utilize your network effectively, it is useless to them. If you and your staff lack the proper skill sets and knowledge to effectively monitor, maintain, and manage the network, the project is doomed to failure. Your organization must realize that the investment in training is an investment in success. It's as important as the network design and must become an integral part of planning and implementation.

Train the administrators and backup operators first, because their functions are critical to the inception of the networking system. You can accomplish this in many ways, but perhaps the most effective is a round of formal classes, where personnel are trained at each phase of development, then allowed to cement their new knowledge with experience before taking on the next phase. This training should begin in the planning stage and continue throughout the lifetime of the network.

There are usually many available training options. Formal, instructor-led classes are offered in most metropolitan areas and network vendors are usually happy to assist their clients with training opportunities whenever possible. Vendors and user groups are good sources of practical, hands-on training as well as general knowledge, in-depth tips and techniques, and sharing of experiences. Time and time again, whenever we hear an especially knowledgeable speaker give a productive training session, the first question from the attendees will be about the source of the instructor's practical knowledge. Most will usually cite direct experience first, then credit a user community second.

On-site training may seem prohibitively expensive, but it may prove to be the most productive in the near term. This can be an option when time and resources are the constraining factors and usually offers a good return on the investment. Independent training companies and even large organizations like Microsoft are increasingly offering on-site as well as self-paced training.

Finally, look to the Web. Even prestigious universities are offering MIS degrees via the Internet, and training opportunities are boundless and cost effective, both in terms of time and money.

Although lack of time may be an obstacle to effective training, the most common barrier may be the corporation itself. It may be afraid to send MIS staff to training for fear of losing its investment as soon as the individual is certified, or the company may cite lost time and lack of adequate backup resources as reasons for not training end-users. It should be stressed that rewarding, long-term gain will definitely compensate for minor, short-term losses.

Troubleshooting Networks

The following sections detail some specifics on how to troubleshoot your network. Common areas to consider when troubleshooting include: how to go about troubleshooting (methodology), as well as special tools and resources that can be used for troubleshooting purposes.

Methodology

Network troubleshooting shares a lot of the same principles as the scientific method: A five-step, structured approach will usually lead to problem resolution. First, set the problem's priority by determining its impact. In most situations, you will be fighting many fires at once. Second, collect as much information as possible about the obvious as well as the not so obvious. Question users, employ all the available tools, and turn to special resources for help. Next, develop a list of all possible causes and conduct tests to isolate them. Finally, identify the solution by the process of elimination.

In general, to troubleshoot a problem, it is best to begin with a series of standard questions. Your first question should always be: "Did it ever work correctly?" Next ask: "When did it last perform satisfactorily?" And finally, "What has changed since then?" (This is where diligent documentation efforts will pay off in platinum.) Other useful questions include: "what works?"; "what doesn't work?"; "how are these items related?"; and "whom and what has this problem affected?"

If you don't have time to stop, gather information, and study a problem, then you have no choice but to rely on well-documented, well-practiced procedures for problem elimination. Just like a well-trained paramedic, your MIS staff should rehearse a series of escalation procedures often enough that their reactions to crisis situations become automatic. In these cases, emergency responses may not allow for scholarly contemplation until the system is functional and the crisis is resolved. It is best to plan early from the start for these types of situations.

Special Tools

It may be necessary to bring in special hardware or software when troubleshooting problems or determining performance bottlenecks. The following tools are very effective:

- **Protocol analyzer** Captures data packets on a network segment and provides detailed data about them, analyzes and simulates trends, and distinguishes protocols. Also known as a network analyzer.
- **Cable tester** Detects cable breaks, shorts, faults, and distance limitations.
- **Time-domain reflectometer (TDR) or an optical TDR** A super cable tester, can also provide the location of the break, short, or fault, as well as lack of proper termination.

► **Power monitor** Can log fluctuations in electrical power.

► **Oscilloscope** Electronic measurement device that determines the amount of signal voltage (amperage) per unit of time for display on a monitor. Can detect shorts, cable bends or crimps, opens, or loss of signal power.

► **A Volt/Ohm meter and/or Digital Volt Meter (DVM)** Can be used to detect resistance in cables, terminators, and barrel connectors. Cables and barrel connectors should provide zero (or very little) resistance. Terminators for 10Base2 and 10Base5 networks should provide 50 Ohms of resistance. Components that display incorrect resistance should be replaced.

You must know the capabilities of each of these devices. In particular, the protocol (network) analyzer has the capability to capture and decode packets, perform trend analysis and simulation, and distinguish protocols. Most network monitors and cable-testing devices work at the Physical layer of the OSI model.

Support Resources

Access to online services, such as CompuServe and MSN, and to the Internet is essential for research and troubleshooting as well as for sources of the most current software and firmware updates. These services also offer the best in-road to technical support departments through email and public list servers. Vendors and technical consultants are usually very happy to participate in these types of communications because it allows them time to reply without pressure, and provides maximum exposure to their skills.

Subscriptions to most major industry periodicals are free for the qualified individuals who renew annually. Other types of subscriptions, such as to knowledge bases like TechNet, Cisco Support Solutions CD, or Novell Support Connections, should be maintained for all operating systems and hardware installed at your site. Subscriptions to third-party technical-reference services have saved many weekends for the short-handed network administrator. The absolute best, daily reference source and tool kit for Microsoft networks and operating systems will be the *Resource Kits*, which provide lots of detailed information, tools, and valuable insight; they are a lot of value for a small investment.

Outsourcing may be a viable option for your company. This affords many organizations access to resources on an "as-needed" basis, without the burden of training and maintaining full-time, highly skilled staff. Outsourcing options can range from remote monitoring services and server administration to electronic software distribution and asset management. These organizations price their services to be competitive and they survive on volume, which translates into a wealth of experience and effective tools for the end-user, as well as a personnel resource that knows and is in tune with your particular environment and corporate culture. A trusted value-added reseller (VAR) or maintenance provider can usually be called upon for consulting services on a time-and-materials basis for special projects, freeing you for project management, research, or the skills that only you can provide the organization.

Troubleshooting Hardware Problems

You've learned some general troubleshooting techniques that should apply in most situations. Now let's turn our attention to some more specific categories of troubleshooting. The largest percentage of network makeup is hardware, so we can start with this category. Hard disks, NICs, hardware configurations, and startup problems fall into this category.

For network-related problems, it is usually best to start with preemptive planning. Ask the following questions in the design and implementation phase as well as when confronted with problems:

- Is the current or proposed hardware on the network operating system vendor's compatibility list?
- Are all pertinent drivers current? What access to drivers is available?
- Does the machine have enough of the appropriate memory?
- Is there enough free hard disk space to support storage needs?
- Is the CPU powerful enough?
- Are the buses compatible?
- What IRQs are available?

For current situations, check cabling: You can trace 95 percent of all network-related problems to cabling faults. Check for loose, lost, broken, or compromised cables and connections; proper cable lengths, resistance, and termination; and most importantly in elusive situations, electrical or magnetic interference.

Isolate the hardware and simplify its configuration as much as possible. For a quick determination of whether the problem is hardware or cabling, attach the PC directly to a port on the hub with an adapter cable known to be good. To determine hardware conflicts, remove all unnecessary cards from the PC and reinstall them one at a time until the problem occurs again. You can try to segment the network in order to troubleshoot one section at a time.

Troubleshooting Software Connection Problems

You should have cleared up or prevented 99 percent of your problems with proper planning, preventative maintenance, user training, painstaking documentation, and wizardry monitoring. Software-related problems are the final obstacle to a properly operating network system:

- Protocol mismatches
- Application conflicts or misconfiguration problems
- Accounting, security, and rights issues
- Client server/problems

Sometimes, the server you are trying to connect to isn't up. More often, however, the client simply isn't connecting to the network or isn't communicating with it properly. The client must be running at least one of the server's protocols: NetBEUI, TCP/IP, or NWLink. When Novell's NetWare is included in the network soup, the most common troubleshooting tip involves using the proper frame types. In a NetWare environment, the two devices attempting to communicate must be using the same frame type. The default frame type is 802.2. You can set this using the Advanced tab on the NWLink protocol's Properties sheet.

In TCP/IP networks, misspelling the computer's NetBIOS name is another common problem. In some cases, the FQDN may have been misspelled or the IP address mistyped in the DNS entry or HOSTS file. It may be that the WINS server is down and there is no LMHOSTS file accessible to you.

Finally, most problems are user-oriented: Did the user enter the correct password? Is the account locked? Does that user have an account on that server? Does that user have rights to access those files or that application?

 The most effective way to configure the binding order of multiple transport protocols on a computer is to place the most frequently used protocol at the top of the binding order.

Handling Network Performance Problems

We've determined that bottlenecks somewhere in the system cause most performance problems, so performance tuning will involve continually finding the source of traffic congestion, relieving it, and moving on to the next problem. A lot like untangling the knots in a very long rope, relieving bottlenecks in one part of the system may cause others to occur elsewhere.

Again, start with the basic troubleshooting process of elimination. Ask yourself:

➤ Have I (or others) changed anything?

➤ Did this occur all at once or gradually?

➤ What new application or device has been added?

➤ At what rate have new users and machines been added to the network?

➤ Do my servers have enough disk space and RAM to do their jobs?

➤ Is the CPU operating at full capacity?

Performance tuning in a TCP/IP network may involve adjusting the send or receive window size or the network packet size. Reducing the receive or send window size may cause performance to degrade due to increased acknowledgments on the network. Reducing the receive window size is usually the safest route. Increasing the network packet size can reduce the number of reads and writes in a given time period and improve overall performance.

Practice Questions

Question 1

> Your server has slowed down considerably over the last month and you suspect additional RAM may be needed due to a SQL installation that occurred at about the same time. What instrument would you use to confirm your suspicions?
>
> ○ a. Network Monitor
>
> ○ b. Performance Monitor
>
> ○ c. TDR
>
> ○ d. Cable tester

Answer b is correct. You would need Performance Monitor to determine whether or not the server had adequate RAM. The number of the page faults per second counter would be high in this case, which indicates the application can't find the requested data or code page in memory. Although you would use the Network Monitor to analyze traffic to and from the server, it would not indicate the need for more RAM. Therefore, answer a is incorrect. Answers c and d are incorrect because you use these devices to test the cabling.

Question 2

> The XYZ Graphical Design firm just built a new, state-of-the-art facility to house its growing business. It has been using a combination of NetWare and Windows NT Servers on its network and all servers are on a 100 Mbps backbone. The rest of the company is using a 10 Mbps Ethernet. Things were just fine until the company changed janitorial services, and now the network is experiencing intermittent problems. What is the appropriate troubleshooting tool for this situation? [Check all correct answers]
>
> ❑ a. Advanced cable tester
>
> ❑ b. Protocol analyzer
>
> ❑ c. Sniffer
>
> ❑ d. TDR
>
> ❑ e. All of the above

The correct answer is e, all of the above, because these types of problems are generally related to a crimped cable somewhere in the system. In reality, the TDR would be the best tool, as it can actually pinpoint the location of the fault. A protocol analyzer would be able to determine the source of excessive collisions or beaconing. The sniffer is a third-party vendor protocol analyzer.

Question 3

> Consider the following situation:
>
> You work for a medical clinic that supports patients around the clock. You are installing a twisted-pair Ethernet in a new wing of the building. Some concern has been expressed about security due to recent events in the news, and the CFO suspects someone may be trying to intrude into the network. You check the Event Viewer's Security log daily but find no reports of unsuccessful logon attempts. What could be wrong?
>
> ○ a. There are no unsuccessful logon attempts.
>
> ○ b. Auditing was not enabled for that server.
>
> ○ c. You have insufficient rights to view the Security log.
>
> ○ d. The Security log doesn't record incidents of unsuccessful logon attempts.

The correct answer is b. In order for security auditing to be recorded in the Security log, auditing must be enabled on the server. Answer a is incorrect, because it's extremely rare to have a perfect set of users who never forget passwords. An unsuccessful logon attempt would be recorded in this case. If you are able to view the Security log on a daily basis, then you obviously have sufficient rights; therefore, answer c is incorrect. Answer d is incorrect because the Security log does record those events for which auditing has been enabled. Time stamps and computer names from which the unsuccessful attempt was made would help you track possible security breaches.

Question 4

> A sliding window specifies how many packets should be received before an acknowledgment (ACK) is returned on a TCP/IP network. To improve network performance, how would you change the relationship of the send to receive packets?
>
> ○ a. The send packet should be larger than the receive packet.
>
> ○ b. The receive packet should be larger than the send packet.
>
> ○ c. The send packet should be the same size as the receive packet.
>
> ○ d. Packet size has no relationship to performance.

The correct answer is a. The send window's size indicates how many packets the sending computer can send before requesting an ACK; the receive window's size indicates how many packets can be received before sending an ACK. To be certain the sender is not idle while waiting for an acknowledgment, the send packet should be larger than the receive packet.

Question 5

> You are the administrator for a small insurance office with a 27-node LAN. You currently have installed in your office a single 10BaseT Ethernet segment that runs a Windows NT application server and a Novell NetWare 3.12 file-and-print server, to which all networked devices are attached. You purchase four machines to add to the existing segment. After they are all installed and configured, one of the four machines cannot locate the file server. What is the most likely cause?
>
> ○ a. You have exceeded the number of machines allowed on the segment.
>
> ○ b. A router will be needed because of protocol mismatches between NetWare and Windows NT.
>
> ○ c. The frame binding is incorrect.
>
> ○ d. The frame type on the client PC is incorrect.

The correct answer is d. For two computers to communicate via NWLink, they must be using the same frame type. The frame type is the format used for header content and data information. Only one computer is affected, so it makes more sense to reconfigure that machine rather than the server and all the rest. The number of devices allowed on 10BaseT is 1,024, so answer a is wrong. There is no such thing as a protocol mismatch between NetWare and Windows NT, or a frame binding. Therefore, answers b and c are also incorrect.

Question 6

> You are trying to connect to a Windows NT Server on your subnet and are receiving the error message that the file cannot be found. It worked yesterday. You check to make sure the WINS server is up and find out that the other users on your subnet can contact that server. You can PING the server's IP address. What is the most likely cause of the problem?
>
> ○ a. An SMTP gateway is down.
> ○ b. There is no LMHOSTS file.
> ○ c. You've typed the name incorrectly.
> ○ d. Your router is not configured as a BOOTP agent.

The most likely cause is answer c, human error. Answer a is incorrect because the SMTP gateway is used to link dissimilar email systems. Answer b is incorrect because the WINS server is operating correctly, so the LMHOSTS file is not needed. As the server is on your subnet, there is no need for a router, making answer d incorrect as well.

Question 7

You are installing a NIC in a new laptop and have connected it to the network. It cannot see the file server, and your floppy drive has stopped working. What is the mostly like cause of the problem?

○ a. Protocol mismatch

○ b. Faulty cabling

○ c. IRQ mismatch

○ d. NICs will not work in a laptop

The correct answer is c. Although your first response might be b, because cabling causes the greatest majority of network connectivity problems, the more likely cause is answer c. It is most likely that the NIC was preset to the same IRQ as the floppy drive. There are very sophisticated NICs for laptops; they usually fit in a PCMCIA slot.

Question 8

The auditing firm of Dewie, Cheatam & Howe has hired you to determine the cause of a problem on its network. Upon arriving, you question the client about the problem and discover it is related to performance degradation. What device would you use to determine if the problem is excessive broadcast traffic?

○ a. Bridge

○ b. Router

○ c. Gateway

○ d. Protocol analyzer

The correct answer is d. The protocol analyzer will be able to pinpoint the source of the broadcast storms. A router would be used to filter out broadcast traffic, so answer b would not be correct. A bridge would be used to segment network traffic but couldn't be used to filter broadcasts. A gateway would be used to connect dissimilar systems.

Question 9

> Because its new operations in Las Vegas have been so successful, Dewie, Cheatam & Howe has decided to upgrade its network with a new accounting package. What should its first course of action be? [Check all correct answers]
>
> ❏ a. Document the current network.
>
> ❏ b. Come up with a deployment plan.
>
> ❏ c. Back up the servers.
>
> ❏ d. Create Emergency Repair Disks.

All answers are correct. The first action should be to produce a concise, detailed plan for deployment that takes into account user training, fault tolerance, and disaster recovery. Therefore, answer b is correct. But as part of the disaster recovery plan, items a, c, and d would also need to be carried out.

Question 10

> Which of the following statements is true about Simple Network Management Protocol (SNMP) agents?
>
> ○ a. They isolate and resolve problems with broadcast storms.
>
> ○ b. They monitor traffic and report the source of broadcast storms.
>
> ○ c. They monitor, log, and audit ICMP messages.
>
> ○ d. They monitor network traffic and behavior in key network components.

The correct answer is d. The SNMP agents loaded on the client devices would monitor network traffic and behavior for the key object and record them in the MIB. A management console would then poll the MIB for its information. A protocol analyzer would be used to isolate broadcast storms, and a router or similar device could be used to resolve problems due to broadcast storms, making answers a and b incorrect. ICMP is a maintenance protocol used to build route tables, assist in problem determination (PING and TRACERT), and adjust flow control to prevent router or link saturation, so answer c is incorrect.

Need To Know More?

Chellis, James, Charles Perkins, and Matthew Strebe: *MCSE: Networking Essentials Study Guide, 2nd Edition*. Sybex Network Press, San Francisco, CA, 1998. ISBN 0-7821-2220-5. Chapter 12, "The Basics of Network Troubleshooting," contains many useful pointers as to how to successfully troubleshoot a network.

Microsoft Press: *Networking Essentials, 2nd Edition*. Redmond, WA, 1997. ISBN 1-57231-527-X. Unit 8, "Solving Network Problems," and Appendix C, "Network Troubleshooter," contain excellent coverage of the various topics contained within this chapter. There are also "Troubleshooter" exercises throughout the book's chapters that reinforce the chapter's topic.

Microsoft Press: *Windows NT Server Networking Guide*. Redmond, WA, 1996. ISBN 1-57231-344-7. Chapter 2, "Network Security and Planning," contains helpful information about security policies.

Microsoft Press: *Windows NT Server Resource Guide*. Redmond, WA, 1996. ISBN 1-57231-344-7. Part III, Chapter 8, is devoted to general troubleshooting and each individual chapter has a troubleshooting section particular to the chapter's topic. The Microsoft *Resource Kits* are designed with the network administrator in mind and are an excellent reference for test taking as well as daily use.

Search the TechNet CD (or its online version through **www.microsoft.com**) using the keywords "Performance Monitor," "Network Monitor," "advanced administration," "troubleshooting," and related terms. The Windows NT *Concepts and Planning Manual* also includes useful information on networking concepts.

Sample Test #1

In this chapter, we provide pointers to help you develop a successful test-taking strategy, including how to choose proper answers, how to decode ambiguity, how to work within the Microsoft testing framework, how to decide what you need to memorize, and how to prepare for the test. At the end of the chapter, we include 55 questions on subject matter pertinent to Microsoft Exam 70-058: "Networking Essentials." After this chapter, you'll find the answer key to this test; after that, you'll find yet another sample test, followed by another answer key. This gives you two opportunities to prepare!

Also, remember that you can take three adaptive practice exams on Networking Essentials online at **www.coriolis.com/cip/core4rev/** (the password is NEPTOL61982) to help you prepare even more. Good luck!

Questions, Questions, Questions

There should be no doubt in your mind that you are facing a test full of specific and pointed questions. Networking Essentials is an adaptive exam, which means that you must study hard to be able to answer as many questions as possible correctly, so you won't have to guess (which can cause problems even when you guess correctly, because you'll wind up facing a harder question next). The test will consist of somewhere between 15 and 35 questions (on average) and take somewhere between 20 and 60 minutes.

For this exam, questions belong to one of five basic types:

➤ Multiple-choice with a single answer

➤ Multiple-choice with multiple answers

➤ Multipart with a single answer

➤ Multipart with multiple answers

➤ Pick one or more spots on a graphic

Always take the time to read each question at least twice before selecting an answer, and always look for an Exhibit button as you examine each question. Exhibits include graphics information related to a question. An exhibit is usually a screen capture of program output or GUI information that you must examine to analyze the question's contents and formulate an answer. Thus, the Exhibit button brings up graphics and charts used to help explain a question, provide additional data, or illustrate page layout or program behavior.

Not every question has only one answer; many questions require multiple answers. Therefore, it's important to read each question carefully, to determine how many answers are necessary or possible, and to look for additional hints or instructions when selecting answers. Such instructions often occur in brackets, immediately following the question itself (as they do for all multiple-choice, multiple-answer questions).

Picking Proper Answers

Obviously, the only way to pass any exam is to select enough of the right answers to obtain a passing score. However, Microsoft's exams are not standardized like the SAT and GRE exams; they are far more diabolical and convoluted. In some cases, questions are strangely worded, and deciphering them can be a real challenge. In those cases, you may need to rely on answer-elimination skills. Almost always, at least one answer out of the possible choices for a question can be eliminated immediately because it matches one of these conditions:

- ▶ The answer does not apply to the situation.
- ▶ The answer describes a nonexistent issue, an invalid option, or an imaginary state.
- ▶ The answer may be eliminated because of the question itself.

After you eliminate all answers that are obviously wrong, you can apply your retained knowledge to eliminate further answers. Look for items that sound correct but refer to actions, commands, or features that are not present or not available in the situation that the question describes.

If you're still faced with a blind guess among two or more potentially correct answers, reread the question. Try to picture how each of the possible remaining answers would alter the situation. Be especially sensitive to terminology; sometimes the choice of words ("remove" instead of "disable") can make the difference between a right answer and a wrong one.

Only when you've exhausted your ability to eliminate answers, but remain unclear about which of the remaining possibilities is correct, should you guess at an answer.

 Because Networking Essentials is an adaptive test, if you can't figure out the answer, you'll have to guess to be able to move on to the next question. That's why guessing is your technique of last resort!

Decoding Ambiguity

Microsoft exams have a reputation for including questions that can be difficult to interpret, confusing, or ambiguous. In our experience with numerous exams, we consider this reputation to be completely justified. The Microsoft exams are tough, and deliberately made that way.

The only way to beat Microsoft at its own game is to be prepared. You'll discover that many exam questions test your knowledge of things that are not directly related to the issue raised by a question. This means that the answers you must choose from, even incorrect ones, are just as much a part of the skill assessment as the question itself. If you don't know something about most aspects of networking, you may not be able to eliminate obviously wrong answers because they relate to a different area of networking than the one that's addressed by the question at hand. In other words, the more you know about the topic, the easier it will be for you to tell right from wrong.

Questions often give away their answers, but you have to be Sherlock Holmes to see the clues. Often, subtle hints appear in the question text in such a way that they seem almost irrelevant to the situation. You must realize that each question is a test unto itself and that you need to inspect and successfully navigate each question to pass the exam. Look for small clues, such as the mention of times, group permissions and names, and configuration settings. Little things like these can point at the right answer if properly understood; if missed, they can leave you facing a blind guess.

Another common difficulty with certification exams is vocabulary. Microsoft has an uncanny knack for naming some utilities and features entirely obviously in some cases, and completely inanely in other instances. Be sure to brush up on the key terms presented at the beginning of each chapter. You may also want to read through the Glossary at the end of this book the day before you take the test.

Working Within The Framework

The test questions appear in random order, and many elements or issues that receive mention in one question may also crop up in other questions. It's not uncommon to find that an incorrect answer to one question is the correct answer to another question, or vice-versa. Take the time to read every answer to each question, even if you recognize the correct answer to a question immediately. That extra reading may spark a memory, or remind you about a networking feature or function, that helps you on another question elsewhere in the exam.

Because you're taking an adaptive test, if you see something in a question or one of the answers that jogs your memory on a topic, or that you feel you should record if the topic appears in another question, write it down on your piece of paper. Just because you can't go back to a question in an adaptive test doesn't mean you can't take notes on what you see early in the test, in hopes that it might help you later.

Don't be afraid to take notes on what you see in various questions. Sometimes, what you record from one question, especially if it's not as familiar as it should be or reminds you of the name or use of some utility or interface details, can help you on other questions later on.

Deciding What To Memorize

The amount of memorization you must undertake for an exam depends on how well you remember what you've read, and how well you know the software by heart. If you are a visual thinker, and you can see drop-down menus and dialog boxes in your head, you won't need to memorize as much as someone who's less visually oriented. The tests will stretch your recollection of networking concepts, tools, and technologies.

At a minimum, you'll want to memorize the following kinds of information:

➤ The seven layers in the OSI Reference Model, and what each one does

➤ The OSI model layers where repeaters, bridges, brouters, routers, switches, and gateways operate, and what each device can (and can't) do

➤ The characteristics and components of the NetBEUI, TCP/IP, and IPX/SPX protocol suites

➤ The IEEE 802 networking specifications, and their associated networking technologies and how they access network media

If you work your way through this book and try to exercise the various capabilities of Windows NT and Windows 98 that are covered throughout, you should have little or no difficulty mastering this material. Also, don't forget that The Cram Sheet at the front of the book is designed to capture the material that is most important to memorize; use this to guide your studies as well.

Preparing For The Test

The best way to prepare for the test—after you've studied—is to take at least one practice exam. We've included one here in this chapter for that reason (and another in Chapter 14); the test questions are located in the pages that follow (and unlike the preceding chapters in this book, the answers don't follow the questions immediately; you'll have to flip to Chapter 13 to review the answers separately [see Chapter 15 for the answers to Chapter 14's sample test]).

Give yourself no more than 90 minutes to take the exam, keep yourself on the honor system, and don't look at earlier text in the book or jump ahead to the answer key. When your time is up, or you've finished the questions, you can check your work by consulting Chapter 13 or 15. Pay special attention to the explanations for the incorrect answers; these can also help to reinforce your knowledge of the material. Knowing how to recognize correct answers is good, but understanding why incorrect answers are wrong can be equally valuable.

Taking The Test

Relax. Once you're sitting in front of the testing computer, there's nothing more you can do to increase your knowledge or preparation. Take a deep breath, stretch, and start reading that first question.

There's no need to rush, either. You have plenty of time to complete each question. If you read a question three times and remain clueless, you'll have to guess and move on because you're taking an adaptive exam. Both easy and difficult questions are intermixed throughout the test in random order. Because you're taking an adaptive test, don't spend more than five minutes on any single question—if it takes you that long to get nowhere, it's time to guess and move on.

Set a maximum time limit for questions, and watch your time on long or complex questions. If you hit your limit, it's time to guess and go on to the next question. Don't deprive yourself of the opportunity to see more questions by taking too long to puzzle over answers, unless you think you can figure out the correct answer. Otherwise, you're limiting your opportunities to pass.

That's it for pointers. Here are some questions for you to practice on!

Sample Test #1

Question 1

Suppose the following situation exists:

A company hired you to build a network to support 20 PCs and an IBM mainframe computer. The office is already wired with shielded twisted-pair cabling.

Required Result:

- The network must accommodate all computers and provide fault tolerance.

Optional Desired Results:

- The network should support transmission speeds of 100 Mbps.
- The network must be easy to configure.

Proposed Solution:

- Implement an Ethernet network with 10BaseT cable.

Which results does the proposed solution produce?

- a. The proposed solution produces the required result and produces both of the optional desired results.
- b. The proposed solution produces the required result and produces only one of the optional desired results.
- c. The proposed solution produces the required result but does not produce any of the optional desired results.
- d. The proposed solution does not produce the required result.

Question 2

You need to connect two network segments that are 1,000 meters apart. Which of the following cable types can transmit data over 1,000 meters without using a repeater?

- a. RG-58 A/U
- b. Fiber optic
- c. CAT3 UTP
- d. CAT5 UTP

Question 3

Which of the following network protocols enables communication with an IBM mainframe computer?

○ a. FTP

○ b. RIP

○ c. DLC

○ d. MRP

Question 4

It is possible to install multiple transport protocols on a Windows NT Workstation computer. In what order should binding be set when multiple protocols are used?

○ a. When IPX/SPX is installed, it should always be at the top of the binding order.

○ b. When TCP/IP is installed, it should always be at the top of the binding order.

○ c. The most efficient protocol should be set at the top of the binding order.

○ d. The most frequently used protocol should appear at the top of the binding order.

Question 5

The new network administration intern installed a network interface card in her PC. After the installation, she notices that her floppy drive no longer works. What is the most likely cause of this problem?

○ a. There is an IRQ or I/O setting conflict.

○ b. There is a memory error.

○ c. The NIC uses bus mastering.

○ d. The wrong kind of bus slot was used.

Question 6

Which connector type is used to connect Thinnet to a NIC?

○ a. BNC barrel
○ b. BNC T
○ c. AUI
○ d. RJ-45

Question 7

Which one of the WAN technologies listed below can provide users with bandwidth on demand?

○ a. T1
○ b. X.25
○ c. ISDN
○ d. Frame relay

Question 8

Which RAID level creates a stripe set, but with no data redundancy?

○ a. RAID 0
○ b. RAID 1
○ c. RAID 2
○ d. RAID 3

Question 9

What occurs when the number of network broadcast messages is greater than the amount of available network bandwidth?

○ a. Crosstalk

○ b. Attenuation

○ c. Broadcast storm

○ d. Beaconing

Question 10

Which of the following is a transport protocol?

○ a. IP

○ b. IPX

○ c. SNMP

○ d. NetBEUI

Question 11

Suppose the following situation exists:

A company has hired you to connect networks in two separate office buildings that are located 2,000 feet apart.

Required Result:

- Provide a working network link that interconnects the two buildings.

Optional Desired Results:

- The network must support 100 Mbps transmission speeds.
- The network should be immune to interference.

Proposed Solution:

- Implement fiber optic Ethernet.

Which results does the proposed solution produce?

- ○ a. The proposed solution produces the required result and produces both of the optional desired results.
- ○ b. The proposed solution produces the required result and produces only one of the optional desired results.
- ○ c. The proposed solution produces the required result but does not produce any of the optional desired results.
- ○ d. The proposed solution does not produce the required result.

Question 12

You are the administrator for a network that has several NetWare clients that require access to a Windows NT Server. What must be installed on the Windows NT Server for this to be possible? [Check all correct answers]

- ❑ a. NWLink
- ❑ b. Client Service For NetWare
- ❑ c. File And Print Services For NetWare
- ❑ d. File And Print Services For Microsoft Networks

Question 13

Which of the following devices segment network traffic? [Check all correct answers]

❑ a. Gateway

❑ b. Bridge

❑ c. Multiplexer

❑ d. Router

Question 14

A newly installed computer on an IPX/SPX Thinnet Ethernet network appears to work fine, but it is unable to access the network, even though all other machines are able to use the network's services. What is the most likely cause of this problem?

○ a. Protocol mismatch

○ b. Incorrect frame type

○ c. Upper memory area conflicts

○ d. Faulty connectivity devices

Question 15

Which of the following statements describes a star topology?

○ a. It is less reliable than a ring topology.

○ b. All network computers get equal network access through the use of CSMA/CD.

○ c. It requires more cabling than a bus topology.

○ d. It is more difficult to troubleshoot than a ring topology.

Question 16

Which of the following devices can be used to reduce traffic bottlenecks on a network that uses the NetBEUI protocol?

- ○ a. Router
- ○ b. Multiplexer
- ○ c. Bridge
- ○ d. Gateway

Question 17

What type of network-access method should be implemented to provide centralized control of network transmissions?

- ○ a. CSMA/CA
- ○ b. CSMA/CD
- ○ c. Demand priority
- ○ d. Token passing

Question 18

Which of these hardware devices can be used to boost broadband signal strength across a long cable?

- ○ a. Repeaters
- ○ b. Amplifiers
- ○ c. Passive hubs
- ○ d. Time-domain reflectometers

Question 19

Which operating systems allow you to assign separate passwords to each shared resource? [Check all correct answers]

❑ a. Windows 95

❑ b. Windows NT Server

❑ c. Windows NT Workstation

❑ d. Windows For Workgroups

Question 20

When should you use DNS instead of WINS to resolve a computer name into an IP address?

○ a. When there is no LMHOSTS file

○ b. When there is no HOSTS file

○ c. When the name being requested has a period (.) in it

○ d. When the name being requested has a backslash (\) in it

Question 21

A Windows NT Server on the network is extremely slow and you suspect that it doesn't have enough RAM. Which counter would you measure in Performance Monitor to determine if this is the case?

○ a. Page Faults/sec

○ b. Disk Reads/sec

○ c. % Processor Time

○ d. Network Reads/sec

Question 22

What must be installed to enable Windows 95 client computers to access a NetWare server? [Check all correct answers]

- ❑ a. Gateway Service For NetWare
- ❑ b. An IPX/SPX-compatible protocol
- ❑ c. File And Print Services For NetWare
- ❑ d. Microsoft Client For NetWare Networks

Question 23

What topology should you use if you want to use routers to search among multiple active paths and decide upon the best path at any given moment?

- ○ a. Star
- ○ b. Bus
- ○ c. Ring
- ○ d. Mesh

Question 24

Which layer of the OSI Reference Model translates data formats?

- ○ a. Application
- ○ b. Data Link
- ○ c. Network
- ○ d. Presentation

Question 25

How does a router reduce broadcast storms on a network?

○ a. By only transmitting TCP/IP broadcast messages

○ b. By only transmitting SNMP broadcast messages

○ c. By blocking forwarding of broadcast messages

○ d. By using multiple routes to transmit broadcast messages

Question 26

Which of the following tools permits you to determine what particular devices may be causing network problems without requiring that these devices be turned off?

○ a. Protocol analyzer

○ b. Time-domain reflectometer

○ c. Transceiver

○ d. Volt-ohm meter

Question 27

Which of the following items should you check if your network is unable to resolve a Unix host name into a corresponding IP address?

○ a. DHCP

○ b. LMHOSTS

○ c. DNS

○ d. WINS

Question 28

Which of the following devices can be used to examine frame counts, collisions, and beaconing information?

- ○ a. Oscilloscopes
- ○ b. Volt-ohm meters
- ○ c. Time-domain reflectometers
- ○ d. Advanced cable testers

Question 29

Suppose the following situation exists:

You run a network that is divided into two segments that are connected by a bridge. The only protocol in use is NetBEUI. You recently added five workstations and network performance has decreased to an unsatisfactory level.

Required Result:

- Replace the bridge with a more efficient device.

Optional Desired Results:

- Continue using only NetBEUI
- Keep the costs to a minimum

Proposed Solution:

- Replace the bridge with an Ethernet switching hub to create a third network segment.

Which of the results does the proposed solution produce?

- ○ a. The proposed solution produces the required result and produces both of the optional desired results.
- ○ b. The proposed solution produces the required result and produces only one of the optional desired results.
- ○ c. The proposed solution produces the required result but does not produce any of the optional desired results.
- ○ d. The proposed solution does not produce the required result.

Question 30

Which of the following is a drawback of peer-to-peer networking?

○ a. A server failure can render a network unusable; at best, it results in loss of network resources.

○ b. Costs increase due to the requirements of dedicated hardware and specialized software.

○ c. When shared resources are accessed, the machine where the resource resides suffers a performance hit.

○ d. An expert staff is needed to manage the complex, special-purpose server software, which adds to the overall cost.

Question 31

Which layer of the OSI Reference Model establishes a route between sending and receiving computers?

○ a. Transport

○ b. Session

○ c. Network

○ d. Physical

Question 32

Of the following cable types, which is the most susceptible to crosstalk?

○ a. STP

○ b. CAT5 UTP

○ c. Coaxial

○ d. Fiber optic

Question 33

Which of the following is the most likely culprit when a computer's operating system is unable to detect a network card? [Choose the best answer]

○ a. Wrong frame type is set on the network card

○ b. Wrong IRQ is set on the network card

○ c. Wrong IRQ is set on the IDE controller card

○ d. Wrong protocol is bound to the network adapter

Question 34

Your network is experiencing heavy traffic and signal attenuation due to overly long cable distances between computers.

Required Result:

- Correct the signal attenuation problem.

Optional Desired Results:

- Reduce broadcast traffic that is present on your network.
- Filter network traffic to reduce the number of frames transferred across the network.

Proposed Solution:

- Install repeaters between distant segments.

Which results does the proposed solution produce?

○ a. The proposed solution produces the required result and produces both of the optional desired results.

○ b. The proposed solution produces the required result and produces only one of the optional desired results.

○ c. The proposed solution produces the required result but does not produce any of the optional desired results.

○ d. The proposed solution does not produce the required result.

Question 35

Which of the following are normally associated with user-level security? [Check all correct answers]

- ❑ a. Each user is assigned a unique user name and password
- ❑ b. Windows 95
- ❑ c. Windows NT
- ❑ d. Users are allowed access to resources based on their user name and password

Question 36

What is the function of a redirector?

- ○ a. To maintain a group appointment list.
- ○ b. To map directory shares to local drive letters.
- ○ c. To associate protocols, NICs, and services in order of priority.
- ○ d. To forward requests to local or remote resource hosts.

Question 37

Your company has two LANs, each of which uses a different protocol. You need to interconnect both LANs but do not want to configure additional protocols for either network. What kind of device could perform this task?

- ○ a. Bridge
- ○ b. Router
- ○ c. Brouter
- ○ d. Gateway

Question 38

Your UPS shuts off every time your Windows NT computer boots. What might fix this problem?

○ a. Bypass the UPS and plug your computer directly into the wall outlet.

○ b. Push the spacebar to invoke The Last Known Good Configuration during the boot process.

○ c. Use the **/NOSERIALMICE** switch in the BOOT.INI file.

○ d. Reboot using the Emergency Repair Disk.

Question 39

Which of the following can gather performance information from a router's MIB?

○ a. SNMP

○ b. Protocol analyzer

○ c. Network Monitor

○ d. Time-domain reflectometer

Question 40

A company is installing an Internet Web server and is concerned with how quickly data images can be read from the server and sent to potential clients. What disk-management system would you want to deploy for maximum performance? The company is not as concerned with losing the data as it is with the speed at which the data can be read.

○ a. RAID level 2

○ b. RAID level 5

○ c. Disk mirroring

○ d. Disk striping without parity

Question 41

You are installing a network card in a computer that has several devices configured. There is a printer on LPT 1, a mouse on COM 1, a modem on COM 2, and a SCSI host adapter occupying IRQ 5. The computer also has a sound card using IRQ 7. If your network card supports IRQs 3 through 5 and 9 through 11, which of the following IRQs could you use in this computer? [Check all correct answers]

- ❏ a. IRQ 3
- ❏ b. IRQ 4
- ❏ c. IRQ 10
- ❏ d. IRQ 11

Question 42

Which of the following WAN technologies uses packet assemblers and disassemblers?

- ○ a. ATM
- ○ b. ISDN
- ○ c. X.25
- ○ d. Frame relay

Question 43

You run a 10Base5 network that has three segments, each separated by a repeater. The trunk ends are terminated by 50-ohm terminators, and there are six in all. How many terminators should be grounded?

- ○ a. Two
- ○ b. Three
- ○ c. Six
- ○ d. None

Question 44

What limitation applies to a WINS server that doesn't make use of any other name-resolution methods? [Choose the best answer]

○ a. All computers must have an LMHOSTS file.

○ b. All computers must know the IP address of the WINS server.

○ c. It cannot perform name resolution for Internet computer names.

○ d. It generates more network traffic than NetBIOS broadcasts.

Question 45

Which of the following statements is true for HOSTS and LMHOSTS files?

○ a. A local HOSTS file is used as a local DNS equivalent.

○ b. A remote HOSTS file is used as a local WINS equivalent.

○ c. A local LMHOSTS file is used as a local DNS equivalent.

○ d. A remote LMHOSTS file is used as a local WINS equivalent.

Question 46

What is the maximum throughput on a V.35 combined circuit link with four 28.8 modems?

○ a. 1.44 Mbps

○ b. 28.8 Kbps

○ c. 115.2 Kbps

○ d. 144 Kbps

Question 47

Which of the following actions would most effectively reduce the number of network reads and writes?

- ○ a. Using TCP/IP instead of NetBEUI
- ○ b. Using Token Ring instead of Ethernet
- ○ c. Increasing the network packet size
- ○ d. Reducing the TCP window size

Question 48

Which Windows NT application may be used to identify any network users who have made unsuccessful login attempts?

- ○ a. Explorer
- ○ b. File Manager
- ○ c. User Manager
- ○ d. Event Viewer

Question 49

Which of the following is required to implement user-level security on a network that includes Windows 95 machines?

- ○ a. DNS server
- ○ b. WINS server
- ○ c. Windows NT Server
- ○ d. Master Browser

Question 50

Which of the following cable types can span distances greater than 100 meters, but no more than 185 meters?

- ○ a. 10Base2
- ○ b. 10Base5
- ○ c. 10BaseT
- ○ d. Fiber optic

Question 51

Which of the following devices is able to perform protocol conversions?

- ○ a. Gateway
- ○ b. Router
- ○ c. Bridge
- ○ d. Brouter

Question 52

Which of the following terms describes the process of communicating to the computers on a Token Ring network that a network error of some kind has interrupted token passing?

- ○ a. Jitter
- ○ b. Crosstalk
- ○ c. Attenuation
- ○ d. Beaconing

Question 53

Which of the following devices can reduce traffic bottlenecks on a NetBEUI network?

○ a. Gateway

○ b. Bridge

○ c. Router

○ d. Multiplexer

Question 54

Which OSI Reference Model layer is responsible for repackaging data bits into data frames?

○ a. Data Link

○ b. Network

○ c. Physical

○ d. Presentation

Question 55

Which of the following backup methods only backs up files that were created or changed since the last full backup and marks those files as archived?

○ a. Daily backup

○ b. Differential backup

○ c. Incremental backup

○ d. Normal backup

Answer Key #1

1. d
2. b
3. c
4. d
5. a
6. b
7. d
8. a
9. c
10. d
11. a
12. a, c
13. b, d
14. b
15. c
16. c
17. c
18. b
19. a, d
20. c
21. a
22. b, d
23. d
24. d
25. c
26. a
27. c
28. d
29. b
30. c
31. c
32. b
33. b
34. c
35. a, c, d
36. d
37. d
38. c
39. a
40. d
41. c, d
42. c
43. b
44. b
45. a
46. c
47. c
48. d
49. c
50. a
51. a
52. d
53. b
54. a
55. c

Question 1

Answer d is the correct response. The proposed solution does not produce the required result because an Ethernet network incorporates no built-in fault tolerance.

Question 2

Answer b is the right answer. Fiber optic cable is able to transmit data for up to 2,000 meters without a repeater. Although it is faster and more secure than coaxial or twisted-pair cable, fiber optic cable is more expensive and requires specialized installation expertise. RG-58 A/U (answer a) can only go 185 meters, CAT3 UTP (answer c) and CAT5 UTP (answer d) can only go 100 meters (but CAT5 can carry much more bandwidth than CAT3).

Question 3

Answer c is the correct choice. The Data Link Control (DLC) protocol enables client communication with IBM mainframes. It is also used to communicate with network-attached printing devices. FTP (answer a) is a TCP/IP file transfer protocol. RIP (answer b) may be one of several routing protocols, usually IP-based, but possibly IPX-based. MRP (answer d) is a common abbreviation for Manufacturing Resource Planning, and is not even a networking protocol.

Question 4

Answer d is the correct response. It is most efficient to bind the most frequently used protocol first. This reduces network response time and makes for faster network connections. There is no protocol sensitivity involved, but rather a matter of search order—the binding order defines the sequence of attempts when broadcasts for name resolution occur. If the most frequently used protocol does not occur at the top of the binding order, users will have to wait for timeouts on broadcasts on less frequently used protocols before they get to the one that's really needed. This explains why answers a, b, and c are incorrect—it's a matter of which protocol is most frequently used, not a matter of protocol type or efficiency.

Question 5

The correct answer is a. In general, when you encounter problems when installing new NICs, IRQ and I/O setting conflicts are usually to blame.

Most floppy disk drives are configured to use IRQ 6; if the NIC is also set for that IRQ, neither device will work, so the floppy disk controller will fail. Memory errors most commonly result in boot failures, which is why b is incorrect. Bus mastering involves letting an adapter control memory transfers instead of the computer's CPU; this has nothing to do with a floppy failure, which explains why c is incorrect. Likewise, it would be difficult (if not impossible) to seat a NIC in the wrong kind of bus slot; even so, this would not affect the floppy, so d is also incorrect.

Question 6

Answer b is correct. Thinnet Ethernet uses a BNC T-connector to connect the NIC to the cable. A BNC barrel connector (answer a) is used only to join two pieces of cable; it includes no place to attach a NIC. Answer c, AUI (attachment unit interface), is most commonly used to accommodate a transceiver cable, like those used for Thicknet Ethernet. Likewise, an RJ-45 connector (answer d) is typical of 10BaseT, and is not used for Thinnet Ethernet.

Question 7

The correct response is answer d. Frame relay uses private virtual circuits (PVCs) to transmit variable-length frames to provide bandwidth to users as needed. T1 (answer a) comes in a variety of flavors, but all flavors offer fixed bandwidth capabilities. X.25 (answer b) is a packet-switched technology that offers only modest bandwidth, with a fixed ceiling. ISDN (answer c) is a digital data transmission technology that offers two or more 64 K or 56 K Bearer channels to users, but each channel supports only a fixed maximum carrying capacity.

Question 8

Answer a is correct. RAID level 0 (disk striping) writes data to disks in fixed-size blocks, but does not record parity information. Although it offers the best performance, if you lose one disk in a stripe set without parity, all information is lost. RAID 1 (answer b) usually describes disk mirroring or duplexing, both of which included data redundancy. RAID 2 interleaves data, and writes checksum information to checksum drives. Because this latter function creates redundant data; answer c is also incorrect. RAID 3 is very much like RAID 2, except it stores parity rather than checksum data; but parity data also provides redundancy, so answer d is incorrect as well.

Question 9

The correct answer is c. A broadcast storm occurs when the number of broadcast messages overwhelms a network's carrying capacity. (Its effective bandwidth is swamped by such messages, in other words.) Because routers may be configured to block—rather than transmit—broadcast messages, routers can be used to prevent this type of network overload. Answer a, crosstalk, refers to the kind of interference that signals traveling on one set of wires can impose on another set running parallel (often within the same cable bundle). Answer b, attenuation, describes the effects of impedance on signal strength in cables—that is, the further they must travel, the weaker they become. Beaconing, answer d, is the technique used to elect a ring monitor on a Token Ring network whenever a new node enters the ring (or when the current ring monitor exits the ring).

Question 10

Answer d is the correct choice. Transport protocols include NetBEUI, as well as NWLink, TCP, and SPX. Answers a and b are incorrect because IP and IPX are network protocols, not transport protocols. SNMP is an application protocol. Therefore, answer c is also incorrect.

Question 11

The correct choice is a. The fiber optic Ethernet technology called 10BaseFL should be implemented. It works, which meets the required result. And because it can transmit data at 100 Mbps for over 2,000 feet, without susceptibility to interference, the proposed solution also delivers both of the optional desired results.

Question 12

Answers a and c are correct. A Windows NT Server must use the NWLink protocol and support File And Print Services For NetWare to service native NetWare client requests. Client Service For NetWare (answer b) permits Windows NT machines to access NetWare servers, which fails to meet the question's requirements. There is no product or service named File And Print Services For Microsoft Networks, making answer d incorrect as well.

Question 13

Answers b and d are correct. Both bridges and routers segment network traffic. The difference between the two is that a bridge can only see MAC addresses provided by the Data Link layer. A router can see network addresses transmitted by the Network layer. Routers are not usable with protocols such as NetBEUI; bridges are. But either type of device can segment networks on the basis of the kinds of addresses it can see. A gateway (answer a) provides translation between two sets of incompatible protocols and services, but provides no traffic segmentation. A multiplexer (answer c) permits multiple data streams such as voice, video, and data to be aggregated for transmission across a single line, but also provides no traffic segmentation.

Question 14

The correct answer is b. IPX/SPX protocols support four different frame types for Ethernet. Because Windows NT's auto-detect capabilities can only handle one of those types at a time, whenever multiple IPX frame types are used, NWLink must be manually configured to define all frame types in use, and the IPX network numbers where they appear. A protocol mismatch (answer a) is certainly a possible explanation for the problem, but is unlikely on a network that uses only one protocol suite. Upper memory area conflicts (answer c) will usually cause a machine to crash, but the question indicates that the machine is apparently working okay. Answer d points to faulty connectivity devices; this too is a possibility, but it is far less likely, because such failures on Thinnet Ethernet will usually cause the entire network to fail (and other machines still have network access).

Question 15

Answer c is the correct choice. Because star topologies are connected through a central hub, each computer requires a direct link to the hub, which uses more cabling than a bus topology, where computers are connected in a series, or to a common cable. Answers a and d are incorrect because in a ring topology, a single cable break could halt the entire network, which makes ring networks less reliable and difficult to troubleshoot. Answer b is incorrect because the CSMA/CD access method does not guarantee equal access to all network users; rather, it depends on detecting collisions and random backoff before trying to regulate traffic again (only token-based technologies can guarantee equal access).

Question 16

The correct choice is c. A bridge can be used on a NetBEUI-based network to reduce network traffic. Because NetBEUI is not a routable protocol, answer a is incorrect. Likewise, answers b and d are incorrect because multiplexers and gateways can't reduce network traffic.

Question 17

Answer c is correct. With demand priority, communications only take place among a sending computer, the hub, and a receiving computer, with all transmissions under the hub's control. Answers a and b are incorrect. Computers using the CSMA/CA access method send signals of their intent to transmit information. With CSMA/CD, computers monitor the network cable and only send messages when no other computer is transmitting information. Token passing relies on distributed control, not centralized control, because only the station that holds the token is permitted to transmit. Therefore, answer d is incorrect.

Question 18

Answer b is the correct choice. Amplifiers are used to boost signal strength on broadband networks. Repeaters strengthen baseband signals; therefore, answer a is incorrect. Passive hubs combine the signals of network segments with neither signal processing nor regeneration. Therefore, answer c is incorrect. Answer d is also incorrect; a time-domain reflectometer is a cable-testing tool, not a signal-boosting technology.

Question 19

Answers a and d are correct. Windows 95 and Windows For Workgroups allow you to assign passwords to shared resources through the use of File Manager or Explorer. Answers b and c are incorrect because Windows NT assigns rights to users and groups for resource access.

Question 20

Answer c is the correct choice, because DNS names use periods to indicate domains and subdomains. Answers a and b are incorrect because HOSTS and LMHOSTS files are used when a name server is not available to resolve fully qualified domain names (FQDNs) or NetBIOS names, respectively. NetBIOS names include backslashes, and are serviced by WINS, not DNS, so answer d is incorrect.

Question 21

Answer a is the correct choice. A high number of page faults per second, measured through Page Faults/sec, indicates that the operating system is being forced to move large amounts of data between the paging file and RAM. Answer b, Disk Reads/sec, is not a conclusive indicator of low memory, because the behavior of the storage subsystem impacts what it measures heavily. Answer c, % Processor Time, usually indicates CPU-bound bottlenecks, not RAM bottlenecks. Likewise, answer d measures network activity, not memory access.

Question 22

Answers b and d are correct. Windows 95 computers must be able to use NWLink, an IPX/SPX-compatible protocol. Likewise the Microsoft Client For NetWare Networks must also be installed for Windows 95 computers to access files and printers located on a NetWare server. The Gateway Service For NetWare runs on Windows NT, not Windows 95, which is not included in the question as stated; therefore a is an incorrect choice. File And Print Services For NetWare permits native NetWare clients to access a Windows NT Server, not Windows 95 clients to access a NetWare server; as this is irrelevant to the question, answer c is also incorrect.

Question 23

Answer d is correct; a mesh topology uses routers to evaluate multiple active paths and uses the best one for transmission. A star, a bus, and a ring all supply only one path between sender and receiver and do not meet the question's requirements. Therefore, answers a, b, and c are incorrect.

Question 24

Answer d is correct; the Presentation layer translates application data into an intermediary format for sending, and from the intermediary format into an application format upon receipt. In addition, it manages security issues and data compression. The Application layer (answer a) provides an interface between local applications and the network, but does no translation. The Data Link layer (answer b) handles packaging data into frames for transmission, and from frames into packets upon reception; again, no data translations are involved. Likewise, the Network layer (answer c) handles message routing, addressing, and quality-of-service information, but does no data translation either.

Question 25

Answer c is correct; most routers are not configured to transmit broadcast messages of any kind across wide-area links, or onto cable segments where such broadcasts do not apply. Answer a is incorrect because routers do not always transmit TCP/IP broadcasts. Answer b is incorrect because SNMP uses directed unicasts, not broadcasts, to send messages. Answer d is incorrect because the secret to dealing with broadcast storms is not to divide the load they impose, but to block such traffic from being forwarded elsewhere.

Question 26

Answer a is the correct choice; a protocol analyzer allows you to examine broadcast storms, network bottlenecks, and unusual network utilization patterns. Using a TDR (answer b) normally requires that the network be shut down while it's in use. A transceiver (answer c) is a simple medium-attachment device and offers no troubleshooting capabilities. A VOM (answer d) normally requires access to the conductors in a cable that carries network traffic; as such access requires the cable to be disconnected from its normal point of attachment, using a VOM typically renders one or more parts of a network inoperable during testing.

Question 27

Answer c is correct. DNS is used to resolve Unix host names into IP addresses. Answer a, DHCP, supplies IP addresses to clients dynamically, but provides no name-resolution services. Answer b, LMHOSTS, is an expanded version of a HOSTS file, which is designed to map between IP addresses, host names, and NetBIOS names. Because most Unix hosts do not need NetBIOS name support, this file plays no role in the process of translating a Unix host name into an IP address. For the same reason, WINS, answer d, is also uninvolved in resolving Unix host information.

Question 28

The correct choice is d. Advanced cable testers are able to display frame counts, collisions, and beaconing information. Answers a, b, and c all refer to devices that are not able to measure such information. Oscilloscopes can only measure and monitor waveforms; VOMs can only measure voltage, current, and basic electrical activity; and TDRs are used to check for cable faults or to measure cable lengths.

Question 29

Answer b is correct. By replacing the bridge with a switching hub, you can increase network performance while retaining your ability to use NetBEUI. Because this solution obtains the required result, and one of the optional desired results, it is an eminently satisfactory implementation.

Question 30

Answer c is the correct choice; machines that house network resources do take a performance hit when that resource is accessed. Answer a is incorrect because, if a machine in a peer-to-peer environment goes down, only the resources on that particular machine are unavailable; the rest of the network continues to work. A dedicated server only blocks access to network resources on server-based networks. Answer b is likewise incorrect, because it too describes a drawback of a server-based network. Answer d is incorrect; peer-to-peer networks are easy to implement, and no specialized staff is needed for full-time support. This is also a server-based network drawback, not one of a peer-to-peer network.

Question 31

Answer c is correct; the Network layer is responsible for determining the route from the source to the destination computer. The Transport layer is responsible for error-handling information and flow control. Therefore, answer a is incorrect. The Session layer maintains an ongoing session between computers. Therefore, answer b is also incorrect. The Physical layer is responsible for communication with the network media, and has nothing to do with route selection. Therefore, answer d is also incorrect.

Question 32

Answer b is correct. Of all the cable types mentioned in the answers, unshielded twisted-pair is the most susceptible to crosstalk (where electrical signals bleed over from one wire to another). Although coaxial (answer c) and STP (answer a) cables are susceptible to crosstalk, they have shielding to reduce its effects. Fiber optic cable (answer d) uses optical transmission technologies that are immune to crosstalk, as long as cable integrity remains unimpaired.

Question 33

Answer b is correct. The only situation that could cause an operating system to fail to detect a network card is an IRQ conflict. An erroneous protocol (answer d) and/or frame type (answer a) would only disable network communications; neither would render the card "invisible" to the OS. An incorrect IDE controller setting (answer c) might prevent the computer from booting, but it wouldn't affect the computer's ability to detect a NIC.

Question 34

Answer c is the correct answer. Using repeaters will stop the signal attenuation by regenerating the signal, but they have no ability to reduce or filter traffic in any way.

Question 35

The answers for this question are a, c, and d. Systems using user-level security assign each user a unique user name and password, and assign resources based on privileges associated with the user. Contrast this with share-level security, where resource owners place passwords on resources. Windows NT is designed to support user-level security. Windows 95 (answer b) is designed to support share-level security, which is why it's not included in the list of correct answers.

Question 36

Answer d is correct. A redirector intercepts requests for services, analyzes them, and forwards network requests to the correct hosts. Answer a is incorrect. A networked scheduling application manages group appointments, not a redirector. Answer b is incorrect. You map drives using network-aware file-management tools or utilities (like Windows Explorer). Answer c is incorrect because associating priorities is a services-management process.

Question 37

The correct answer is d. Only a gateway can translate from one protocol to another, and vice versa. A bridge (answer a) simply interconnects two cable segments; although a bridge can interconnect different cabling types, it requires that the protocols on both sides of the connection be the same. A router (answer b) can also connect multiple cable segments, but requires common protocols as well. As a brouter (answer c) combines the functions of a bridge and a router, it too is subject to the same limitation.

Question 38

The correct answer is c. During a boot, NTDETECT.COM attempts to identify all system peripherals. This includes sending a signal to all serial ports. This signal may shut off some manufacturers' UPS systems, so it makes sense to disable sending a signal to the port where the UPS is attached. Answer a is incorrect because bypassing the UPS will not fix the problem; it only circumvents it. Returning to the Last Known Good Configuration (answer b) will only restore the Registry to its previous settings; this will do nothing to alter Windows NT's bootup behavior. Answer d, reboot using the ERD, will not change this behavior either; it, too, is incorrect for that reason.

Question 39

Answer a is the correct choice. The Simple Network Management Protocol (SNMP) is able to obtain information from the management information base (MIB) maintained by a router. Although a protocol analyzer might be able to decode the packets that carry the MIB from one place to another, such devices are not able to interrogate MIBs. Therefore, answer b is incorrect. Network Monitor is a network-utilization and traffic-characterization tool, and has no ability to interrogate MIBs, either. Therefore, answer c is also incorrect. A TDR measures cable lengths and helps to locate cable breaks and faults, but has no ability to work with SNMP; thus, answer d is incorrect as well.

Question 40

The correct answer is d. Disk striping without parity spreads input/output activity across multiple drives, but works most quickly, because no parity information is calculated or written to disk. RAID level 2 (answer a) is noted for slow performance, so it is clearly unsuitable. Although RAID level 5 (answer b) is not as slow as level 2, it's not as fast as RAID 0 (disk striping without parity). Likewise, disk mirroring (answer c) is not as slow as RAID 2, but it's not as fast as RAID 0, either.

Question 41

The correct answers are IRQ 10 (answer c) and IRQ 11 (answer d). COM 1 uses IRQ 4 (answer b) and COM 2 uses IRQ 3 (answer a), so neither of those two IRQs is available.

Question 42

Choice c is the correct answer. Because X.25 uses telephone lines, it incorporates lots of error-checking overhead and requires packet assemblers and disassemblers to attach to the public data network. None of the other technologies mentioned—ATM (answer a), ISDN (answer b), or frame relay (answer d)—uses packet assemblers or disassemblers as part of the transmission and reception processes.

Question 43

Answer b is correct. Each trunk segment must be grounded at one end. Because there are six terminators, only three ends need to be terminated.

Question 44

Answer b is correct; all client computers must know the WINS server's IP address. Answer a is incorrect only because it says that all computers must have an LMHOSTS file; although it's not illegal for them to have one, WINS provides the same functions from a single centralized server. Answer c is true, but irrelevant. Answer d is just flat wrong: WINS uses directed unicasts (which is why each computer must have the WINS server's IP address), which are much less intrusive than NetBIOS broadcasts.

Question 45

The correct answer is a. A HOSTS file is a local text file that resolves DNS names into IP addresses. Thus, b is incorrect because HOSTS is equivalent to DNS, not WINS. Answer c is incorrect because LMHOSTS is equivalent to WINS, not DNS. Answer d puts the remote and local terms on the wrong sides, because a local LMHOSTS file is most commonly used as a remote WINS equivalent, not vice versa.

Question 46

Answer c is correct. The combination of a V.35 link with four 28.8 Kbps modems provides throughput equal to their sum; in fact, 4 times 28.8 Kbps equals 115.2 Kbps. Using simple mathematics, the other answers are obviously incorrect.

Question 47

Answer c is correct. Increasing the network packet size generally reduces the number of network reads and writes. TCP/IP has higher overhead than NetBEUI (which is one reason why NetBEUI is the faster of the two protocols), so it will increase the number of network reads and writes. Therefore, answer a is incorrect. Using Token Ring, with its 4 K and 16 K packet sizes, instead of Ethernet, with its maximum size of 1,564 bytes, would reduce the number of reads and writes, but is an incredibly expensive and time-consuming switchover for relatively little gain in performance. Thus, answer b is impractical and inefficient. Reducing the TCP window size, answer d, is the opposite of what you'd want to do—it too would increase the number of reads and writes and is wrong for that reason.

Question 48

Answer d is the correct response. After enabling auditing for unsuccessful login attempts in User Manager, you must inspect the Security log from within Windows NT's Event Viewer to see what IDs are involved in unsuccessful logins. Explorer, be it the Microsoft Internet or the file management variety, says nothing about logins; therefore, answer a is wrong. For the same reason, File Manager (answer b) is wrong as well. Although auditing must be enabled in the Policies menu of User Manager, this only permits auditing to occur; it collects no audit information. Because it cannot indicate what IDs are used for unsuccessful login attempts, answer c is also wrong.

Question 49

Answer c is correct. A Windows NT Server is required to provide user-level security to grant access to Windows 95 resources. A DNS server (answer a) only handles IP domain name and address resolution. A WINS server (answer b) only handles IP address and NetBIOS name resolution. The Master Browser (answer d) maintains a database of NetBIOS resources available on a network, which has only a tangential relationship with security information or control.

Question 50

Answer a is the correct choice. 10Base2 cable (or Thinnet) is able to transmit over segments that are up to 185 meters long. 10Base5 (answer b) can handle lengths up to 500 meters, which makes that an incorrect choice. 10BaseT (answer c) is limited to 100 meters, and falls short of the stipulated upper distance boundary. Fiber optic cable (answer d) for Ethernet can span distances up to 2,000 meters, well beyond the 185-meter ceiling.

Question 51

Answer a is the correct response. Only a gateway can perform protocol conversions by repackaging data packets in the form required by the protocol stack of a receiving computer. Neither a router, a bridge, nor a brouter can perform protocol translations. Therefore, answers b, c, and d are all incorrect.

Question 52

Answer d is correct. When a network error that interrupts token passing occurs, a signal called a beacon is transmitted to computers on a Token Ring network. Jitter refers to a variation in the timing between a network sender and receiver, or in the regularity of a particular source clock for sending signals. It has nothing to do with Token Ring, so answer a is incorrect. Crosstalk describes the phenomenon whereby signals traveling over one or more pairs of cable interfere with signals traveling over another set of one or more pairs, often within the same cable bundle. This has nothing to do with Token Ring, either, which explains why answer b is also wrong. Attenuation describes how signals weaken, owing to cumulative impedance across a cable, which increases as the cable gets longer. This is also unrelated to Token Ring networking, so answer c is wrong as well.

Question 53

Choice b is correct; a bridge can be used to segment traffic based on MAC addresses on a NetBEUI network. Gateways operate across all seven layers of the OSI Reference Model, but seldom (if ever) provide traffic control functions. For that reason, answer a is incorrect. Although routers can be used to segment network traffic, NetBEUI is not routable, so it's not a plausible solution for this situation. This makes answer c incorrect as well (but for routers with bridging capability, called brouters, they could provide such a service). Finally, a multiplexer aggregates multiple traffic streams (such as voice, video, and data), but also fails to manage traffic. For that reason, answer d is also incorrect.

Question 54

Answer a is correct. The Data Link layer of the OSI Reference Model is responsible for repackaging data bits from the Physical layer into frames. The Network layer (answer b) handles addressing and routing issues, not frames. The Physical layer (answer c) manages access to the networking medium and related signaling or reception issues, but does not manipulate frames either. Finally, the Presentation layer (answer d) handles translation from generic data formats to platform- and application-specific forms (and vice versa), but does not manipulate frames at all.

Question 55

Answer c is correct. An incremental backup backs up files that were created or changed since the last full backup and resets the archive bit. A daily backup (answer a) copies all files that were created or changed today (that is, whose creation or modification dates equal today's date) but leaves the archive bit alone. That's why it's an incorrect choice. A differential backup copies all files that have been created or changed since the last full backup, but leaves the archive bit alone, so answer b is incorrect. A normal backup (answer d) is the same thing as a full backup, which is to say that it backs up all files and then resets each one's archive bit. Because it copies all files, it too is an incorrect choice.

Sample Test #2

See Chapter 12 for Sample Test #1 and pointers to help you develop a successful test-taking strategy, including how to choose proper answers, how to decode ambiguity, how to work within the Microsoft testing framework, how to decide what you need to memorize, and how to prepare for the test. In this chapter, we include another sample test on subject matter pertinent to Microsoft Exam 70-058: "Networking Essentials." After this chapter, you'll find the answer key to this test.

Also, remember that you can take three adaptive practice exams on Networking Essentials online at www.coriolis.com/cip/core4rev/ (the password is NEPTOL61982) to help you prepare even more. Good luck!

Question 1

Some networking devices perform the same tasks as others. Which of the following devices can act like a router to segment network traffic?

○ a. Bridge

○ b. Decoder

○ c. Gateway

○ d. Multiplexer

Question 2

Which of the following operating systems allow you to assign a password to each shared resource? [Check all correct answers]

❏ a. Windows NT Server 4.0

❏ b. Windows NT Workstation 4.0

❏ c. Windows 95

❏ d. Windows For Workgroups 3.11

Question 3

Your company is based in Dallas. It has branch offices in Austin and San Antonio. Each of the three offices has a 10BaseT network. Users need to access resources in all three offices.

Required result:

- You must implement a networking solution, which will offer WAN communications between the three sites.

Optional desired results:

- The WAN connection needs to support about 256 Kbps of data and several analog telephone connections between sites.

- The WAN connection needs to be able to continue operations even if one of the WAN links should fail.

Proposed solution:

- Use three T1 connections: one between Dallas and Austin, one between Austin and San Antonio, and one between San Antonio and Dallas.

Which results does the proposed solution produce?

○ a. The proposed solution produces the required result and produces both of the optional desired results.

○ b. The proposed solution produces the required result and produces only one of the optional desired results.

○ c. The proposed solution produces the required result but does not produce any of the optional desired results.

○ d. The proposed solution does not produce the required result.

Question 4

Which of the following protocols can be used with a router? [Check all correct answers]

❏ a. AppleTalk

❏ b. IPX/SPX

❏ c. NetBEUI

❏ d. TCP/IP

Question 5

Which topology would you choose if you need to set up a temporary network for six computers in an office with no preinstalled wiring?

- ○ a. Bus
- ○ b. Star
- ○ c. Mesh
- ○ d. Ring

Question 6

Which of the following statements are true of a client/server network? [Check all correct answers]

- ❑ a. Tasks are divided between the back end and the front end.
- ❑ b. The back end fulfills the requests made by the front end.
- ❑ c. All processing occurs on the back end.
- ❑ d. All processing occurs on the front end.

Question 7

Which of the following connectivity devices typically works at the Physical layer of the OSI model?

- ○ a. Bridges
- ○ b. Gateways
- ○ c. Repeaters
- ○ d. Routers

Question 8

Which of the following devices can be used to resolve broadcast storms?

- ○ a. Bridges
- ○ b. Gateways
- ○ c. Repeaters
- ○ d. Routers

Question 9

Suppose that each of the following network interface cards fits your computer's data bus architecture and has the right type of cable connector for the cabling. Which card would you choose if performance (speed) is the most important consideration?

- ○ a. Bus type: EISA, memory transfer: shared memory
- ○ b. Bus type: ISA, memory transfer: shared memory
- ○ c. Bus type: EISA, memory transfer: I/O
- ○ d. Bus type: ISA, memory transfer: I/O

Question 10

What data transfer rate does T1 technology offer?

- ○ a. Up to 1.54 Mbps
- ○ b. Up to 45 Mbps
- ○ c. Up to 100 Mbps
- ○ d. Up to 622 Mbps

Question 11

You are replacing the old Windows NT Server on your network with a new Pentium II 450 MHz system. What tools can you use to gather performance data for your new server? [Check all correct answers]

- ❑ a. Oscilloscope
- ❑ b. TDR
- ❑ c. Windows NT Performance Monitor
- ❑ d. Windows NT Network Monitor

Question 12

Which of the following statements best describes a peer-to-peer network? [Check all correct answers]

- ❑ a. It requires a powerful, centralized, and dedicated server.
- ❑ b. It provides each user the ability to manage his or her own-shared resources.
- ❑ c. It provides extensive user and resource security.
- ❑ d. It is best for small networks with fewer than 10 users.

Question 13

Which of the following connector types is used to connect two pieces of cable on a linear bus topology?

- ○ a. RJ-45
- ○ b. BNC barrel connector
- ○ c. NIC
- ○ d. BNC terminator

Question 14

Your computer uses COM 1, COM 2, LPT 1, and LPT 2 with their default IRQ and I/O port settings. The 3Com NIC you are installing uses the following settings: IRQ 3, I/O 0x300. Which of the following will conflict with the 3Com NIC?

- ○ a. LPT 1
- ○ b. LPT 2
- ○ c. COM 1
- ○ d. COM 2

Question 15

Which layer of the OSI model provides flow control and ensures messages are delivered error free?

- ○ a. Physical layer
- ○ b. Network layer
- ○ c. Transport layer
- ○ d. Session layer

Question 16

Bridges are often called Media Access Control (MAC) bridges because they work at the MAC sublayer of the OSI model. In which layer of the OSI model does the Media Access Control sublayer reside?

- ○ a. Physical layer
- ○ b. Data Link layer
- ○ c. Network layer
- ○ d. Transport layer

Question 17

NetBEUI is a protocol that provides data transport services for NetBIOS sessions and applications. Which of the following statements describes the NetBEUI protocol? [Check all correct answers]

- ❑ a. It is the network protocol used on all Unix networks.
- ❑ b. It is a nonroutable protocol, used in Microsoft networks.
- ❑ c. It is a small, fast, and efficient Transport layer protocol.
- ❑ d. It is a standard, routable Application layer protocol.

Question 18

Several computers in your company store sensitive data that should not be accessed by everyone on the network. Which network model will be the most appropriate?

○ a. Complete standalone environment

○ b. Peer-to-peer network

○ c. Workgroup network

○ d. Server-based network

Question 19

You are implementing fault-tolerant systems for all the file servers on your network. You want to achieve the fastest possible read speed on the file servers. Which of the following would you implement?

○ a. Disk mirroring

○ b. Disk striping with parity

○ c. Disk striping without parity

○ d. Volume sets

Question 20

NDIS and ODI are specifications that define interfaces for communication between the Data Link layer and protocol drivers. What is the greatest benefit of NDIS and ODI?

○ a. Ability to dynamically bind a single protocol to multiple MAC drivers

○ b. Ability to bind multiple protocols to a single network adapter card

○ c. Ability for monolithic protocols to conform to the OSI model

○ d. Ability for monolithic protocols to be loaded into the upper memory area

Question 21

Which connectivity device should be used in a complex Ethernet 10BaseT network that uses both TCP/IP and NetBEUI protocols?

○ a. Amplifiers

○ b. Routers

○ c. Brouter

○ d. Gateway

Question 22

Which of the following refers to the signal overflow from an adjacent wire?

○ a. Attenuation

○ b. Beaconing

○ c. Chatter

○ d. Crosstalk

Question 23

Which of the following describe user-level security? [Check all correct answers]

❑ a. Passwords are assigned to different resources on a network.

❑ b. Passwords are assigned on a user-by-user basis.

❑ c. It provides a higher level of security on a network than share-level security does.

❑ d. It is also called password-protected shares.

Question 24

Which of the following best describes the purpose of the token in a Token Ring network?

- ○ a. The station that holds the token is allowed to transmit a message on the network.
- ○ b. Multiple tokens can be passed along different paths to improve performance.
- ○ c. The station that holds the token has the highest priority on the network.
- ○ d. A token contains information that is used to route messages between rings.

Question 25

WAN connections can use analog, digital, or packet switching technologies. Which of the following WAN technologies is intended to replace analog phone lines?

- ○ a. ATM
- ○ b. Frame relay
- ○ c. ISDN
- ○ d. T1

Question 26

A subnet mask is a bit pattern that specifies which portion of the IP address represents a subnet address. Which of the following is true of TCP/IP subnet masks?

- ○ a. They are used to mask a portion of the IP address so that TCP/IP can distinguish the network ID from the host ID.
- ○ b. They are used to mask a portion of the IP address so that TCP/IP can distinguish the DHCP server address from the default gateway address.
- ○ c. They are used to mask a portion of the IP address so that TCP/IP can distinguish the DNS address from the host address.
- ○ d. They are used to mask a portion of the IP address so that TCP/IP can distinguish the HOSTS name from the NetBIOS name.

Question 27

Frame relay is a form of packet switching technology that evolved from X.25. Which of the following best describes the frame relay technology?

○ a. It transmits fixed-length packets at the Physical layer through the most cost-effective path.

○ b. It transmits variable-length packets at the Physical layer through the most cost-effective path.

○ c. It transmits fixed-length frames at the Data Link layer through the most cost-effective path.

○ d. It transmits variable-length frames at the Data Link layer through the most cost-effective path.

Question 28

Your company has offices in two separate buildings. Each office is networked. You are responsible for connecting the two separate networks. The distance between the two buildings is approximately 450 meters. The current capacity for each network is 100Mbps. You want to have an efficient, secure backbone. What media is the best to use to connect the two buildings?

○ a. 10Base5

○ b. 100BaseT

○ c. Fiber optic

○ d. ATM

Question 29

What is the minimum category of UTP cable required to meet Ethernet 100BaseT standards?

○ a. Category 1

○ b. Category 2

○ c. Category 3

○ d. Category 5

Question 30

Which of the following uses 15-character names to identify computers on a network?

○ a. AppleTalk
○ b. IPX/SPX
○ c. NetBIOS
○ d. TCP/IP

Question 31

You are the administrator of your company's Windows NT network. Andy, the Director of Marketing for the company, comes to you after lunch and tells you that he forgot his password. What can you do to help Andy resolve his problem?

○ a. Edit Andy's password by using the Password option in the Server's Control Panel.
○ b. Delete Andy's password with User Manager For Domains and create a new one.
○ c. Assign Andy to the Administrator group and have him "fix" his own account.
○ d. Edit Andy's profile by using System Policy Editor.

Question 32

Which type of problem is most likely to be caused by increasing cable lengths?

○ a. Attenuation
○ b. Beaconing
○ c. Crosstalk
○ d. Jitter

Question 33

Which layer of the OSI model is responsible for translating the data format?

- ○ a. Application layer
- ○ b. Network layer
- ○ c. Presentation layer
- ○ d. Session layer

Question 34

Which of the following are transport protocols? [Check all correct answers]

- ❑ a. NetBEUI
- ❑ b. TCP
- ❑ c. IP
- ❑ d. IPX
- ❑ e. SPX

Question 35

Which type of LAN media access method is commonly used by Ethernet networks?

- ○ a. CSMA/CA
- ○ b. CSMA/CD
- ○ c. Token passing
- ○ d. DUN

Question 36

Which system component determines whether a print request is intended for the local machine or for a remote computer?

○ a. Transceiver

○ b. Redirector

○ c. Transport protocol

○ d. Server Service

Question 37

You want to connect a Token- Ring LAN with an Ethernet LAN. Both LAN segments use the IPX/SPX protocol. Which of the following devices would you use to connect the two network segments and provide traffic filtering?

○ a. Hub

○ b. Router

○ c. Brouter

○ d. Repeater

Question 38

Which topology would you implement for your WAN if you want to use routers to search among multiple active paths and determine the best path for a particular moment?

○ a. Bus

○ b. Ring

○ c. Star

○ d. Mesh

Question 39

Which of the following methods backs up files that were created or changed since the last full backup and marks the files as having been backed up?

- ○ a. Copy
- ○ b. Complete backup
- ○ c. Differential backup
- ○ d. Incremental backup

Question 40

Which of the following operating systems allow you to assign a password to each shared resource? [Check all correct answers]

- ❏ a. Windows For Workgroups 3.11
- ❏ b. Windows 95
- ❏ c. Windows NT Workstation
- ❏ d. Windows NT Server

Question 41

Your network consists of several Windows 95 computers. Which of the following is required to implement user-level security?

- ○ a. DNS server
- ○ b. WINS server
- ○ c. Windows NT Server
- ○ d. Master browser

Question 42

Which of the following protocols can be used to provide connectivity from PCs to IBM mainframe computers?

○ a. DLC

○ b. FTP

○ c. NCP

○ d. RIP

Question 43

Which type of cable can be used over a distance greater than 100 meters (328 feet), but cannot be used over a distance greater than 185 meters (607 feet) without a repeater?

○ a. 10BaseT (twisted-pair)

○ b. 10Base2 (Thinnet coaxial)

○ c. 10Base5 (Thicknet coaxial)

○ d. Fiber optic

Question 44

Your network includes several NetWare clients that need to access file and print resources on a Windows NT Server. Which of the following must be installed on the Windows NT Server? [Check all correct answers]

❑ a. NWLink

❑ b. Client Service for NetWare

❑ c. File and Print Services for NetWare

❑ d. File and Print Services for Microsoft Networks

Question 45

You have sent a TCP/IP packet over the Internet to the IP address 102.54.94.97. Where will this packet go if the destination host uses a subnet mask of 255.0.0.0?

○ a. To host ID 54.94.97 on network ID 102

○ b. To host ID 94.97 on network ID 102.54

○ c. To host ID 97 on network ID 102.54.94

○ d. To host ID 255 on network ID 0.0.0

Question 46

A sliding window size specifies how many packets can be received by a destination computer before an acknowledgment (ACK) is returned. Which of the following initial sliding window relationships is recommended to provide the best network performance?

○ a. The send window size should be greater than the receive window size.

○ b. The receive window size should be greater than the send window size.

○ c. The send window size should be the same as the receive window size.

○ d. Performance will be the same regardless of the relationship between the send window size and the receive window size.

Question 47

What is the standard cable type associated with ARCNet networks?

○ a. Twisted-pair

○ b. RG-58 /U coaxial

○ c. RG-58 A/U coaxial

○ d. RG-62 A/U coaxial

Question 48

Which of the following devices is most likely to use the same upper memory block addresses and conflict with a network adapter card when using Windows For Workgroups?

- ○ a. CD-ROM drive
- ○ b. Floppy drive controller
- ○ c. Hard drive controller
- ○ d. SCSI adapter card

Question 49

When will DNS be used instead of WINS to resolve a computer name to an IP address?

- ○ a. When the name being requested contains a period (".")
- ○ b. When the name being requested contains a backslash ("\")
- ○ c. When there is no LMHOSTS file
- ○ d. When there is no HOSTS file

Question 50

One way to browse (resolve) NetBIOS names on a TCP/IP network is by using a NetBIOS broadcast (or name query). Which of the following limitations applies to using this method?

- ○ a. MS-DOS computers cannot respond to NetBIOS name queries.
- ○ b. Computers on the local subnet receive only NetBIOS broadcasts.
- ○ c. NetBIOS broadcasts are passed through routers.
- ○ d. NetBIOS broadcasts are received only by WINS enabled hosts.

Question 51

Suppose the following situation exists:

You have been asked to select a TCP/IP naming standard and its related services for your organization's large internetwork. The computer names should be easy for users to understand and remember.

Required result:

- Users must be able to browse computer names across the company's routed internetwork.

Optional desired results:

- You must provide a centralized file or database that eliminates the need to maintain IP address mappings on each local machine.
- Users must be able to communicate with Windows Sockets applications using both HOSTS and NetBIOS names.

Proposed solution:

- Implement both a HOSTS and LMHOSTS file on each client workstation.

Which results does the proposed solution produce?

- ○ a. The proposed solution produces the required result and produces both of the optional desired results.
- ○ b. The proposed solution produces the required result and produces only one of the optional desired results.
- ○ c. The proposed solution produces the required result but does not produce any of the optional desired results.
- ○ d. The proposed solution does not produce the required result.

Question 52

HOSTS and LMHOSTS files are used under Windows NT to resolve computer names to IP addresses. Which of the following are true? [Check all correct answers]

- ❑ a. A local LMHOSTS file can be used as a local WINS equivalent.
- ❑ b. A remote LMHOSTS file can be used as a local DNS equivalent.
- ❑ c. A local HOSTS file can be used as a local DNS equivalent.
- ❑ d. A remote HOSTS file can be used as a local WINS equivalent.

Question 53

Which of the following is able to obtain performance information from a MIB (management information base) maintained by a router?

- ○ a. SNMP
- ○ b. TDR
- ○ c. Windows NT Performance Monitor
- ○ d. Windows NT Network Monitor

Question 54

You connect the leads from a volt-ohm meter (VOM) to each of the conductors in a twisted-pair. Which of the following settings should you use on the VOM to see if there is a short?

- ○ a. Current measured in amps
- ○ b. Impedance measured in ohms
- ○ c. Resistance measured in ohms
- ○ d. Voltage measured in volts

Question 55

There is a frame type mismatch on your Novell NetWare network. It is only affecting one computer. Which of the following needs to be reconfigured?

- ○ a. The frame type on the client machine
- ○ b. The frame type on the server machine
- ○ c. The frame binding setting on the client machine
- ○ d. The frame binding setting on the server machine

Answer Key #2

1. a
2. c, d
3. a
4. a, b, d
5. a
6. a, b
7. c
8. d
9. a
10. a
11. c, d
12. b, d
13. b
14. d
15. c
16. b
17. b, c
18. d
19. b
20. b
21. c
22. d
23. b, c
24. a
25. c
26. a
27. d
28. c
29. d
30. c
31. b
32. a
33. c
34. a, b, e
35. b
36. b
37. b
38. d
39. d
40. a, b
41. c
42. a
43. b
44. a, c
45. a
46. a
47. d
48. d
49. a
50. b
51. b
52. a, c
53. a
54. c
55. a

Question 1

The correct answer is a. Like a router, a bridge builds a routing table and uses it to filter packets based on their destination addresses. In this way, a bridge can reduce network traffic and utilization much like a router. A bridge can only see MAC (Media Access Control) or network interface card addresses provided by the Data Link layer. A router, on the other hand, can see information provided by the Network layer, and can therefore see network addresses. Because bridges can segment networks based on hardware addresses alone, they are usable with NetBEUI and other so-called "nonroutable" protocols. Answer b is an invalid answer; there is no such networking device as a decoder. Answer c does not segment network traffic; rather, it acts like a translator or converts information from one language into another (i.e., from Windows NT to mainframes). Answer d is incorrect because a multiplexer joins signals together to act as one. If you use two 28.8 Kbps modems with a multiplexer, then you are operating at 57.6 Kbps.

Question 2

The correct answers are c and d. Under Windows 95 and Windows For Workgroups 3.11, File Manager or Windows Explorer provides the ability to assign a password for each shared resource. Access to these resources is granted only when the user enters the appropriate password. Under Windows NT, all permissions are assigned to users and groups. When sharing a resource under Windows NT, you cannot specify an access password for that particular resource. Instead, you must specify the users and groups who can access the resource, making answers a and b incorrect.

Question 3

The correct answer is a. The proposed solution produces the required result and produces both of the optional desired results. You should use T1 links between the three sites because T1 lines can carry both voice and data simultaneously. The three T1 links offer redundancy so that if any one link fails, each site can still communicate with any other site. For example, if the T1 link between San Antonio and Dallas fails, San Antonio can still communicate with Dallas by going through Austin to relay the information.

Question 4

The correct answers are a, b, and d. Most protocols are considered "routable" protocols. AppleTalk, IPX/SPX, and TCP/IP are routable protocols. That is, they can be routed on a network through a router. NetBEUI is a nonroutable protocol—it does not pass through routers by default.

Question 5

The correct answer is a. The bus is the simplest and most commonly used topology. It is usually easier to install than a star or ring topology. Because only one computer at a time can send data on a bus network, the data transmission speed is directly related to the number of computers on the bus. The more computers on a bus, the slower the transmission speed. The bus topology is best suited for temporary networks or networks that have fewer than 10 computers. The ring topology gives much better performance but is fairly expensive to set up and is much more difficult to implement; therefore, answer d is incorrect. A star topology is not a bad choice because it is easy to implement, but it is not the best choice for this situation; therefore, answer b is incorrect. Cost of hardware for a temporary network will generally outweigh the ease of implementation. Answer c is incorrect because the mesh topology is not practical for a small, temporary network.

Question 6

The correct answers are a and b. In a client/server environment, all tasks are divided between a back end (the server), which stores and distributes data, and a front end (the client), which requests specific data from the server. Answers c and d are incorrect because in a true client/server environment, processing is shared between both the client and server.

Question 7

The correct answer is c. Repeaters are networking devices that are used to regenerate signals and work at the Physical layer of the OSI model. Bridges are networking devices that are used to filter traffic according to the hardware destination address of the packet and work at the Data Link layer of the OSI model; therefore, answer a is incorrect. Gateways are networking devices that translate information between protocols or completely different networks and work at the Application and Transport layers of the OSI model; therefore, answer b is incorrect. Answer d is incorrect because routers are network devices that segment networks, connect networks with different protocols, and can translate between different network architectures; routers work at the Network layer of the OSI model.

Question 8

The correct answer is d. Routers interconnect networks and provide filtering functions. They work at the Network layer of the OSI model to route packets across multiple networks based on specific network addresses. Routers can be used to prohibit broadcast storms because broadcasts are not forwarded. Bridges can segment network traffic, but they cannot filter broadcasts. If the destination address of a packet is not in the bridge's routing table (as in the case of a broadcast), the bridge forwards the packets to all of its nodes, and therefore possibly creates broadcast storms; therefore, answer a is incorrect. Answer b is also incorrect; gateways translate information but they do not filter packets. Repeaters do no filtering whatsoever; they simply regenerate signals and send them through to all nodes, making answer c incorrect.

Question 9

The correct answer is a. When choosing a NIC, there are many factors to consider, such as the bus width, bus type, and the memory transfer method used by the NIC. In general, NICs that use the EISA or the MCA bus types are faster than cards using the ISA bus type. Shared memory (either shared adapter memory or shared system memory) is a faster memory transfer method than the basic I/O method or DMA (direct memory access). Answer b is incorrect because ISA is a slower bus type than EISA. Answers c and d are incorrect because I/O memory transfer is slower than shared memory.

Question 10

The correct answer is a. T1 technology is one of the most widely used high-speed digital lines using two two-wire pairs to transmit data to a maximum of 1.54 Mbps. Answer b is incorrect because it refers to a T3 link, which is really 28 T1 lines. Answer c is incorrect because it refers to 100BaseT technology or fiber-optic technology. Answer d refers to Asynchronous Transfer Mode (ATM) technology, which is a high-speed packet-switching technology offering rates up to 622 Mbps with theoretical rates of 2.4 Gbps.

Question 11

The correct answers are c and d. Windows NT Performance Monitor is a tool used for gathering information on a server-by-server basis. The information gathered can be used for graphing trends, detecting bottlenecks, and monitoring general server health for four main subsystems: memory, processor, disk, and network. Performance Monitor also offers four methods for collecting information: chart, alert, log, and report. Windows NT Network Monitor is a software-based tool, which monitors and gathers information about packet types, errors, and packet traffic to and from each computer. Answer a is incorrect because an oscilloscope is a device that measures the signal voltage per amount of time and can also help define cable problems like shorts and breaks. Answer b is incorrect because a TDR is a device that is able to determine whether there is a cable break or short and the proximity of the cable break.

Question 12

The correct answers are b and d. In a peer-to-peer network, users are responsible for the administration of their resources and they act as both a client and a server, making answer b correct. A peer-to-peer network will only be appropriate if there are fewer than 10 users, making answer d correct. A peer-to-peer network does not require a powerful central server or a network administrator to provide centralized resource administration; therefore, answer a is incorrect. Answer c is incorrect because security is always an issue with peer-to-peer networking; users manage their own resources and there is no continuity of what is being shared and how it is being shared, and such networking does not provide extensive user and resource security.

Question 13

The correct answer is b. In a linear bus topology, coaxial cable—usually Thinnet—is used as the media. To extend the length of a Thinnet cable, a British Naval Connector (BNC) barrel connector is used, making answer b correct. An RJ-45 connector is used to connect UTP or STP to a repeater or hub and is not used with coaxial cabling, making answer a incorrect. A NIC is used to connect many nodes or computers together in a network environment; however, it cannot be used to simply connect pieces of cabling together, making answer c incorrect. Answer d is incorrect because a BNC terminator "soaks up" signals that arrive at the end of the cable and prevents them from reflecting off the end of the cable back onto the network; also, it can't be used to connect two pieces of cabling together.

Question 14

The correct answer is d. In most cases, COM 2 and COM 4 use IRQ 3, and COM 1 and COM 3 use IRQ 4. Because COM 2 is using its default IRQ setting of 3, it is conflicting with the NIC, making answer d the correct answer. Because COM 1 usually uses IRQ 4, answer b is incorrect. LPT 1 generally uses IRQ 7, and IRQ 5 is generally used for LPT 2 or a sound card, making answers a and b incorrect.

Question 15

The correct answer is c. The Transport layer provides error recognition and recovery, and it ensures reliable delivery of messages. It also repackages messages when necessary by dividing long messages into smaller packets for transmission. At the receiving end, it rebuilds the smaller packets into the original message. Answer a is incorrect because the Physical layer is the bottom-most layer of the OSI model and is where signals are transmitted and received; it also defines the media for the network. Answer b is incorrect because the Network layer handles addressing and routing of PDUs across internetworks in which multiple networks must be traversed between sender and receiver. Answer d is incorrect because the Session layer is responsible for setting up, maintaining, and ending ongoing sequences of communications (sessions) across a network.

Question 16

The correct answer is b. The Data Link layer is responsible for managing access to the networking medium and for ensuring error-free delivery of data frames from sender to receiver. The Data Link layer has two sublayers: LLC and MAC. The Logical Link Control (LLC) sublayer is the upper sublayer and is responsible for handling error-free delivery of data frames between sender and receiver. The Media Access Control (MAC) sublayer is the lower sublayer where the network interface can directly address the networking media. Answer a is incorrect because the Physical layer is the bottom-most layer of the OSI model and is where signals are transmitted and received; it also defines the media for the network. Answer c is incorrect because the Network layer handles addressing and routing of PDUs across internetworks in which multiple networks must be traversed between sender and receiver. Answer d is incorrect because the Transport layer provides error recognition and recovery, ensuring reliable delivery of messages.

Question 17

The correct answers are b and c. The NetBIOS Extended User Interface (NetBEUI) is a small, efficient, and fast protocol. For traffic within a LAN segment, NetBEUI is the fastest of the protocols shipped with Windows NT. NetBEUI does not require a lot of memory, and it offers good error protection. However, it is not routable and its performance across WANs is poor. Answer a is incorrect because UNIX uses TCP/IP as its default protocol. Because NetBEUI is a Transport layer protocol, answer d is also incorrect.

Question 18

The correct answer is d. A server-based network is the best network for sharing resources and data, and it provides extensive resource and user security. With a complete standalone environment, you lose the sharing of information through network technologies; therefore, answer a is incorrect. Answer b is incorrect because the environment described in the question needs security that you cannot get with a peer-to-peer network environment. A peer-to-peer network will only be appropriate if there are fewer than 10 users and security is not an issue. Because of how shares are created and managed in a peer-to-peer network, you cannot be assured that sensitive information is kept away from inappropriate users. The workgroup environment is similar to the peer-to-peer environment; therefore, answer c is incorrect.

Question 19

The correct answer is b. Fault-tolerant systems will ensure that data remains available despite accidental hardware failures. Disk striping with parity (RAID Level 5) is currently the most popular approach to fault tolerance design. A stripe set with parity allows concurrent read commands to be processed on all drives simultaneously, and is therefore faster than disk mirroring (RAID Level 1) or disk duplexing, making answer a incorrect. Disk striping without parity (RAID Level 0) does not provide any fault tolerance. However, if you want to achieve the greatest read performance and are not concerned about fault tolerance, then RAID level 0 is the best implementation. In fact, the only reason answer c is incorrect is because it does not provide any fault tolerance. Answer d is incorrect because volume sets are slow and do not provide any fault tolerance.

Question 20

The correct answer is b. NDIS (developed by Microsoft) and ODI (developed by Apple and Novell) are comparable specifications. Each provides a set of standards for protocols and network adapter card drivers to communicate. The primary benefit of NDIS is to allow multiple protocols to use a single network adapter card. ODI also uses a protocol-independent structure to support multiple protocols on the network. Answers a, c, and d are incorrect because neither NDIS nor ODI provides for the benefits listed.

Question 21

The correct answer is c. A brouter is a network component that combines the characteristics of both a bridge and a router. A brouter can act like a router for one protocol (such as TCP/IP) and like a bridge for another protocol (such as NetBEUI). NetBEUI is a nonroutable protocol and is not supported by routers. Answer a is incorrect because an amplifier is used in broadband networks to amplify signals and will not work in a 10BaseT network. Answer b is not the best answer because, although routers will work in this environment to route TCP/IP packets, they will not allow NetBEUI packets to go through. Answer d is incorrect because a gateway translates between two protocols; no such translation is required in the setting described.

Question 22

The correct answer is d. Crosstalk refers to the signal overflow from an adjacent wire. Crosstalk can distort information being transmitted on the cable and is a potential problem with all types of cabling. Attenuation is the degradation or distortion of an electronic signal as it travels from its origin; therefore, answer a is incorrect. Beaconing is the method that Token Ring networks use to identify and route network communications around a network error, making answer b incorrect. Chatter refers to a NIC that is sending a bunch of packets for no reason, usually indicating that a NIC is about to fail and should be replaced; therefore, answer c is incorrect.

Question 23

The correct answers are b and c. With user-level security, the server validates the user name and password combination when the user logs on to the network. This validation is used to grant or deny access to shared resources. User-level security provides a higher level of security on the network than share-level security because you don't have to provide each user with the password for a shared resource. Users gain access to the resource based on their user account permissions. Answers a and d are incorrect because they refer to share-level security.

Question 24

The correct answer is a. Token passing is a media access method that involves passing a data frame, called a token, from one station to the next around the ring. On a Token Ring network, computers must wait for a free token in order to transfer data, and only one computer at a time can use the token. The first computer initialized on a network generates the token. There can only be one token on a network; therefore, answer b is incorrect. Token passing gives equal access for the network to all nodes; the node that has the token is the only node that can present data to the network, and when the data has been transmitted the token becomes free for another node to use; therefore, answer c is incorrect. Answer d is incorrect because a token is used on a single ring, not for routing between multiple rings.

Question 25

The correct answer is c. Integrated Services Digital Network (ISDN) is a digital WAN technology that can accommodate voice and data transmission. One of the original goals of ISDN developers was to replace all current telephone lines, which require digital-to-analog conversions, with completely digital switching and transmission facilities. ATM, frame relay, and T1 links are all digital communication methods; however, they are all expensive and difficult to maintain. ISDN is very economical in comparison; in fact, many small businesses and home businesses are using ISDN links. The only drawback is that if you lose power, you lose your telephone connection. Therefore, answers a, b, and d are incorrect.

Question 26

The correct answer is a. The subnet mask is a method used by IP to determine which bits in an IP address denote the network ID and which bits denote the host ID. Bits that are masked represent the network ID. For example; if you have an IP address of 131.107.2.224 with a subnet mask of 255.255.255.0, then it is inferred that 131.107.2 is the network ID and 224 is the host ID. Subnet masks do not deal with HOSTS names, DNS names, NetBIOS names, or IP addresses of specific types of servers; therefore, answers b, c, and d are all incorrect.

Question 27

The correct answer is d. Frame relay uses a private virtual circuit (PVC) to transmit variable-length frames at the OSI Data Link layer. It does not have unnecessary accounting and error-checking functions, and therefore is much faster than X.25. Frame relay networks can also provide subscribers with bandwidth as needed. Answers a, b, and c are incorrect because none of them accurately describes the frame relay architecture.

Question 28

The correct answer is c. Fiber optic cable is faster and more secure than coaxial cable, but it is more expensive and requires expertise to install. Fiber-optic cable can support voice, data, and video transmission, and it is not susceptible to interference. It can transmit at 100 Mbps or more for up to 2,000 meters (or 6,562 feet). 10Base5 meets the distance requirements (500 meters) but is limited to 10 Mbps and is susceptible to noise interference; therefore, answer a is incorrect. 100BaseT is efficient for data transfer rates but is not capable of spanning 450 meters and is the most susceptible to noise interference; therefore, answer b is incorrect. ATM would not be suitable or practical for this implementation; therefore, answer d is incorrect.

Question 29

The correct answer is d. To meet 100BaseT, you have to use Category 5 cabling. Category 1 UTP can carry voice but not data; therefore, answer a is incorrect. Category 2 UTP can only transmit up to 4 Mbps and is not supported by 100BaseT standards; therefore, answer b is incorrect. The 10BaseT topology is defined by IEEE 802.3 specification, and it can use

Category 3, 4, or 5 UTP, but 100BaseT can use only Category 5 cabling; therefore, answer c is incorrect.

Question 30

The correct answer is c. Windows networking components rely on a naming convention known as NetBIOS. NetBIOS names are created when a computer is first set up or connected to a network. The NetBIOS name is usually the same as the computer name. There is a hidden sixteenth character that identifies services that use the NetBIOS name to advertise and communicate on the network. TCP/IP uses a 32-bit binary address to communicate across the network; therefore, answer d is incorrect. Other protocols, such as AppleTalk and IPX/SPX, use HOSTS names to communicate across the network; therefore, answers a and b are incorrect.

Question 31

The correct answer is b. The easiest way to correct Andy's password problem is to use the User Manager For Domains to delete his password and re-create a new one. Andy can change the password after he successfully logs in the first time. Assigning Andy to the Administrator group would not solve his problem because he would not be able to log in; besides, it is never a good idea to assign people to the Administrator group that do not have a need, so answer c is incorrect. Answer a is invalid, and answer d will not solve Andy's problem, so both are incorrect.

Question 32

The correct answer is a. Attenuation refers to the degradation of a transmitted signal as it travels farther from its source on the cable. Attenuation of a signal transmitted over a long cable can be corrected by a repeater, which regenerates an incoming signal before sending it farther along the cable. Answer b is incorrect because beaconing is the method that Token Ring networks use to identify and route network communications around a network error, making answer b incorrect. Answer c is incorrect because crosstalk refers to the signal overflow from an adjacent wire; crosstalk can distort information being transmitted on the cable and is a potential problem with all types of cabling. Answer d is also incorrect because jitter is the shift of digital signals over a transmission medium.

Question 33

The correct answer is c. The Presentation layer is where data may be encrypted and/or compressed to facilitate delivery, and where platform-specific application formats are translated into generic data formats for transmission, or from generic formats into platform-specific application formats for delivery to the Application layer. The Application layer provides interfaces to permit applications to request and receive network services; therefore, answer a is incorrect. The Network layer handles addressing and routing of PDUs across internetworks in which multiple networks must be traversed between sender and receiver; therefore, answer b is incorrect. The Session layer is responsible for setting up, maintaining, and ending ongoing sequences of communications across a network; therefore, answer d is incorrect.

Question 34

The correct answers are a, b, and e. NetBEUI, TCP, and SPX are all Transport layer protocols that are connection oriented (except for NetBEUI) and provide error control. IP and IPX are Network layer protocols that are connectionless protocols. Therefore, answers c and d are incorrect.

Question 35

The correct answer is b. Ethernet uses the Carrier Sense Multiple Access/Collision Detection (CSMA/CD) access method, in which computers avoid collisions by listening to the network before sending data. If a computer senses data on the network, it waits and tries to send its data later. Carrier Sense Multiple Access/Collision Avoidance (CSMA/CA) is a contention-based channel access method in which computers avoid collisions by broadcasting their intent to send data. CSMA/CA is commonly used in ARCNet environments; therefore, answer a is incorrect. Token passing is used in Token Ring networks, in which a token is sent around a ring; when a computer needs to send data, it grabs the token and sends its data. Therefore, answer c is incorrect. Dial-Up Networking (DUN) does not apply to LAN technology as much as it does to WAN technology; therefore, answer d is incorrect.

Question 36

The correct answer is b. The redirector is the software component responsible for intercepting requests from applications and determining whether the services are local or remote. The default redirector in Microsoft network is the Workstation Service (LanManWorkstation). The transceiver functions as a transmitter and a receiver to emit signals on a medium, as well as receive them, making answer a incorrect. The transport protocol is responsible for providing reliable communication sessions between two computers; therefore, answer c is incorrect. The Server Service is a service that allows a computer to share its resources and allows other computers to access those resources; therefore, answer d is incorrect. LanManServer is the Microsoft implementation of the Server Service.

Question 37

The correct answer is b. A router is a networking device that operates at the Network layer of the OSI model and is able to connect networks with different physical media, as well as translate between different architectures, such as Token Ring and Ethernet. Routers also provide filtering functionality to reduce overall network traffic. A hub is a central concentration point of a star network and basically functions like a repeater, which regenerates signals; therefore, answer a is incorrect. A brouter is a networking device that combines the best functionality of a bridge and a router. It is able to route packets that include Network layer information and bridge all other packets. For this question, it is not a recommended solution because you are only using a routable protocol and the cost would not be justified; therefore, answer c is incorrect. A repeater only regenerates signals, it does not route them; therefore, answer d is incorrect.

Question 38

The correct answer is d. Mesh is a topology commonly used in WANs. A mesh network connects remote sites over multiple telecommunication links. It relies on routers to search among different active paths and determine the best path. Bus, ring, and star topologies are generally considered for a local area network; therefore, answers a, b, and c are incorrect.

Question 39

The correct answer is d. The incremental backup backs up all files modified since the last complete backup or incremental backup and marks the file as being backed up. The copy command simply copies all files selected and does not mark the files as being backed up; therefore, answer a is incorrect. A complete backup backs up all files, whether they have been modified or not, and marks all files as having been backed up; therefore, answer b is incorrect. The differential backup backs up all files since the last full backup but does not mark the files as being backed up; therefore, answer c is incorrect.

Question 40

The correct answers are a and b. Under Windows For Workgroups 3.11 and Windows 95, File Manager or Explorer provides you with the ability to assign a password for each shared resource. Access to these resources is granted only when the user enters the appropriate password. Under Windows NT, all permissions are assigned to users and groups. When sharing a resource under Windows NT, you cannot specify an access password for that particular resource. Instead, you must specify the users and groups who can access the resource; therefore, answers c and d are incorrect.

Question 41

The correct answer is c. User-level security allows you to grant access to Windows 95 resources for users and groups defined in a Windows NT domain security accounts database. Such a database can be created only on a Windows NT Server domain controller or a NetWare server. When using this configuration under Windows 95 with File and Print Sharing for Microsoft Networks, the domain accounts and groups become visible by clicking on the Add Users button on the Sharing tab in the Resource Properties dialog box. None of the other options provide for user-level security; therefore, answers a, b, and d are incorrect.

Question 42

The correct answer is a. The Data Link Control (DLC) protocol is a nonroutable protocol. HP-series network interface print devices often use it to connect directly to the network. It can also be used to enable a computer to communicate with other computers running the DLC protocol stack, such as IBM mainframes. None of the other protocols listed are used for mainframe connectivity; therefore, answers b, c, and d are incorrect.

Question 43

The correct answer is b. 10Base2 has a distance limitation of 185 meters (607 feet). Answer a is incorrect because 10BaseT has a distance limitation of 100 meters (328 feet). Answer c is incorrect because 10Base5 has a distance limitation of 500 meters. Answer d is incorrect because fiber optic has a distance limitation of 2 kilometers.

Question 44

The correct answers are a and c. Both clients need to have the same protocol in order to talk to each other. NetWare's primary protocol is IPX/SPX, and Microsoft uses NWLink as an IPX/SPX-compatible protocol. For NetWare clients to access file and print resources on a Windows NT Server, Windows NT must be running File and Print Services for NetWare (FPSN). Client Services for NetWare (CSNW) are installed on a Windows NT client so they can access file and print resources on a NetWare server; therefore, answer b is incorrect. Answer d is invalid, so it is incorrect.

Question 45

The correct answer is a. The subnet mask defines which bits are used to distinguish the network ID and the HOST ID. Using a subnet mask of 255.0.0.0 for a class A address (102.0.0.0), the first octet is defined as the network ID and the remaining three octets are defined as HOST IDs. Therefore, answers b, c, and d are incorrect.

Question 46

The correct answer is a. If a sender on the network had to wait for an acknowledgment each time it sent a packet before sending another, network performance would be less than optimal. On the sending computer, the window size specifies how many packets will be sent before an acknowledgment must be received. On the receiving computer, the window size specifies how many packets will be received before an acknowledgment must be sent. To ensure that the sender will not be idle while waiting for an ACK, it is recommended that the send window size should always be greater than the receive window size. Therefore, answers b, c, and d are incorrect.

Question 47

The correct answer is d, RG-62 A/U coaxial. ARCNet (Attached Resource Computer Network) is a token passing network architecture designed for small workgroups. It can have a star bus or bus topology that passes data at 2.5 Mbps or more. Although it can support both twisted-pair and fiber-optic media, the standard cable type for ARCnet is RG-62 A/U coaxial cable. RG-62 A/U is not recommended for use with 50-ohm Ethernet networks because of its higher impedance characteristics. Answers a, b, and c are incorrect.

Question 48

The correct answer is d. Some network adapter cards use shared memory addresses located in upper memory blocks for their input and output buffers. This can cause conflicts with other devices, especially under 16-bit operating systems such as Windows For Workgroups 3.11. These problems are typically resolved by specifying an exclude ("x=") option in the EMM386.EXE command line in CONFIG.SYS or by placing special entries in the SYSTEM.INI file. Answers a, b, and c are incorrect because CD-ROM drives, floppy drives, and hard drive controllers are not likely to conflict with NIC addresses under Windows NT For Workgroups.

Question 49

The correct answer is a. The standard convention for recognizing fully qualified domain names (FQDNs) is by use of "." in the name, also called HOSTS name. DNS is generally used to resolve HOSTS names, FQDNs, and is used by TCP/IP utilities. The "\" is the Universal Naming Convention

(UNC) that Microsoft deploys with NetBIOS names; therefore, answer b is incorrect. NetBIOS names are resolved using WINS and/or LMHOSTS or HOSTS files; therefore, answers c and d are incorrect.

Question 50

The correct answer is b. NetBIOS uses broadcasts to do name queries when there is no WINS server configured. Because it is a broadcast packet, only computers that are part of the local network can receive the broadcast and clients on the remote side of a router will never receive the request, making answer b correct and answer c incorrect. Answers a and d are incorrect because MS-DOS clients, which are also non-WINs clients, use NetBIOS as a part of the operating system.

Question 51

The correct answer is b. Although the use of NetBIOS broadcasts alone will not provide for internetwork name resolution across routers, the use of local HOSTS and LMHOSTS files will. The HOSTS file will be used for DNS names and the LMHOSTS file will be used for NetBIOS names. However, without a WINS server, there is no central file or database that keeps IP address information, and the HOSTS and LMHOSTS files on each computer will have to be maintained locally, even if you created a central file and downloaded it to each client.

Question 52

The correct answers are a and c. LMHOSTS are synonymous with WINS; that is, an LMHOSTS file can replace a WINS server as a local means of resolving NetBIOS names to IP addresses. HOSTS files can also be used as a local DNS equivalent to resolve HOSTS names to IP addresses. Answers b and d are not true statements, and are therefore incorrect.

Question 53

The correct answer is a. MIB files are used by SNMP (Simple Network Management Protocol). Many operating systems (such as Windows NT) have SNMP management software built into them. SNMP uses MIB files to interrogate network devices such as routers, bridges, hubs, and file servers (such as Windows NT Server). Answers b and d are incorrect because neither TDR nor Network Monitor obtains performance information from a MIB. Answer c is incorrect because Windows NT Performance Monitor does not monitor routers; however, it does use the SNMP service to monitor TCP/IP related information on a server.

Question 54

The correct answer is c. Short circuits are most easily detected by measuring resistance in ohms between two conductors. You can also use a volt-ohm meter to detect an open circuit. A short circuit should measure zero resistance (in ohms) between two conductors and an open circuit should measure high or infinite resistance (in ohms) between two conductors. Volt-ohm meters normally do not test for impedance. Answers a, b, and d are incorrect.

Question 55

The correct answer is a. Because there is only one computer that is affected, you can assume that the server is not the problem. This leaves the client computer as the one needing to be reconfigured. Simply correct the frame type on the client computer and reboot the machine. Answers c and d are invalid choices because you do not have a binding setting for frame types, only for protocols and services.

Glossary

10Base2—A designation for 802.3 Ethernet thin coaxial cable (also called Thinnet, Thinwire, or Cheapernet). The "10" indicates bandwidth of 10 Mbps, the "Base" indicates it's a baseband transmission technology, and the "2" indicates a maximum segment length for this cable type of 200 meters (actually, it's 185).

10Base5—A designation for 802.3 Ethernet thick coaxial cable (also called Thicknet or Thickwire). The 10 indicates bandwidth of 10 Mbps, the Base indicates it's a baseband transmission technology, and the 5 indicates a maximum segment length for this cable type of 500 meters.

10BaseT—A designation for 802.3 Ethernet twisted-pair cable. The 10 indicates bandwidth of 10 Mbps, the Base indicates it's a baseband transmission technology, and the T indicates that the medium is twisted-pair (and that maximum segment length will be around 100 meters, but can only be precisely determined based on the manufacturer's testing results for the particular cable in use).

5-4-3 rule—Applies to Ethernet running over coaxial cable; states that a network can have a maximum of five cable segments with four repeaters, with three of those segments being populated.

802.1—The IEEE specification within Project 802 for the OSI Reference Model, and for internetworking and routing behavior at the Data Link layer (where logical addresses must be translated into their physical counterparts, and vice versa).

802.2—The IEEE specification within Project 802 for the Logical Link Control (LLC) sublayer within the Data Link layer of the OSI Reference Model.

802.3—The IEEE specification within Project 802 for Carrier Sense Multiple Access/Collision Detection (CSMA/CD, which means Ethernet users can attempt to access the medium any time it's perceived as "quiet," but they must back off and try to transmit again if they detect any collisions once transmission has begun) networks. It is more commonly referred to as an Ethernet network.

802.4—The IEEE specification within Project 802 for token bus LANs, which use a straight-line bus topology for the networking medium, yet circulate a token to control access to the medium.

802.5—The IEEE specification within Project 802 for Token Ring LANs, which map a circulating ring structure onto a physical star and circulate a token to control access to the medium.

802.6—The IEEE specification within Project 802 for metropolitan area networks (MANs).

802.7—The IEEE specification within Project 802 for the Broadband Technical Advisory Group's findings and recommendations for broadband networking technologies, media, interfaces, and equipment.

802.8—The IEEE specification within Project 802 for the Fiber Optic Technical Advisory Group's findings and recommendations for fiber optic networking technologies, media, interfaces, and equipment.

802.9—The IEEE specification within Project 802 that addresses hybrid networks that combine voice and data traffic within the same networking environment.

802.10—The IEEE specification within Project 802 for network security.

802.11—An IEEE standard for wireless networking.

802.12—The IEEE specification within Project 802 for high-speed networks, including Demand Priority and 100VG-AnyLAN technologies.

access control—A method to impose controls over which users are permitted to access network resources, usually based on permissions specifically granted to a user account, or to some group to which the user belongs.

access point device—The device that bridges between wireless networking components and a wired network. It forwards traffic from the wired side to the wireless side, and from the wireless side to the wired side, as needed.

account—The collection of information known about the user, which includes an account name, an associated password, and a set of access permissions for network resources.

account name—A string of letters, numbers, or other characters that names a particular user's account on a network.

active hub—Central hub in an ARCNet network that can retransmit the data it receives and can be connected to other hubs.

active monitor—Computer in a Token Ring network responsible for guaranteeing the network's status.

active topology—A network topology in which the computers themselves are responsible for sending the data along the network.

adapter slot—The sockets built into a PC motherboard that are designed to seat adapter cards; see also *ISA*, *EISA*, *MCA*, and *PCI* (all of which represent specific types of adapter slots).

analog—The method of signal transmission used on broadband networks; creating analog waveforms from computer-based digital data requires a special device called a digital-to-analog converter (d-to-a); reversing the conversion requires another device called an analog-to-digital converter. Broadband networking equipment must include both kinds of devices to work.

ANSI (American National Standards Institute)—The U.S. representative on the International Standardization Organization, a worldwide standards-making body. ANSI creates and publishes standards for networking, communications, and programming languages.

antenna—A tuned electromagnetic device that can send and receive broadcast signals at particular frequencies; in wireless networking devices, an antenna of some kind is an important part of their sending and receiving circuitry.

AppleTalk—The protocol suite developed by Apple for use with Macintosh computers.

Application layer—Layer 7 in the OSI Reference Model. It provides interfaces to permit applications to request and receive network services.

application protocol—This type of protocol works in the upper layers of the OSI model to provide application-to-application interaction.

application server—A specialized network server whose job is to provide access to a client/server application, and sometimes, the data that belongs to that application as well.

ARCNet (Attached Resource Computer Network)—An inexpensive and flexible network architecture created by Datapoint Corporation in 1977. It uses the token-passing channel access method.

ARCNet Plus—The successor to ARCNet. It supports transmission up to 20 Mbps.

ARP (Address Resolution Protocol)—A protocol in the TCP/IP suite used to associate logical addresses to physical addresses.

asynchronous—Communication method in which data is sent in a stream with start and stop bits indicating where data begins and ends.

attenuation—The degradation or distortion of an electronic signal as it travels from its origin.

auditing—The recording of selected events or actions for later review. Audits can be helpful in establishing patterns and in noting changes in those patterns that may signal trouble.

AWG (American Wire Gauge)—The standards by which cables are defined based on the wire diameter.

backbone—A single cable segment used in a bus topology to connect computers in a straight line.

back-end—A server in a client/server networking environment.

bandwidth—The range of frequencies that a communications medium can carry. For baseband networking media, the bandwidth also indicates the theoretical maximum amount of data that the medium can transfer; for broadband networking media, the bandwidth is measured by the variations that any single carrier frequency can carry, less the analog-to-digital conversion overhead.

barrel connector—Used in Ethernet 10Base2 (Thinnet) networks to connect two cable segments.

base I/O port—The memory address where the CPU and an adapter check for messages that they leave for each other (represents a kind of "mailbox" for the two to exchange short messages).

base memory address—The memory address at which the transfer area between the computer's main memory and a NIC's buffers begins, bounded by the size of its extent.

baseband—A transmission technology that uses digital signals sent over a cable without modulation, so that binary values (0s and 1s) are sent as pulses of different voltage levels.

baseline—A measurement of network performance over time against which current performance can be measured.

baud—Term used to measure modem speed, which describes the number of state transitions that occur in a second on an analog phone line.

Bayonet Nut Connector—The type of cable connector used for both Thinwire and Thickwire Ethernet (among other coaxial cable types); see also *BNC*.

bend radius—For network cabling, the maximum arc that a segment of cable may be bent over some unit length (typically one foot or one meter) without the risk of damage.

binding—The OS level association of NICs, protocols, and services to maximize performance through the correlation of related components.

bis—French term for *second*. It is used to describe the second version of an ITU standard.

bisync—Synchronous communications protocol.

BNC (British Naval Connector)—A matching pair of coaxial cable connectors, male and female. The female connector consists of a ferrule around a hollow pin with a pair of guideposts on the outside, and the male connector consists of a rotating, locking wire nut, with an inner sleeve with two channels that match the female connector's guideposts. A pin projects from the center of the male connector and mates with the hollow pin in the center of the female connector, while the guideposts and locking wire nut ensure a tight, well-seated connection.

Boot PROM—A special programmable chip that includes enough software to permit a computer to boot sufficiently and access the network, from whence it can download an operating system to finish the boot process.

braid—A woven mesh of metallic wires, usually either copper or steel, wrapped around the outside of one or more conductive cables, that provides shielding against EMI, RFI, and crosstalk from other cables.

BRI (Basic Rate Interface)—An ISDN implementation which provides two 64 Kbps B-channels. Generally used for remote connections.

bridge—Networking device which works at the Data Link layer of the OSI model which is used to filter traffic according to the hardware destination address of the packet.

bridging table—Reference table created by a bridge to track hardware addresses and which network segment each address is on.

broadband—This term describes an analog transmission technique in which multiple communication channels may be used simultaneously. Each data channel is represented by modulation on a particular frequency band, for which sending or receiving equipment must be tuned.

broadband optical telepoint network—An implementation of infrared wireless networking that supports broadband services equal to those provided by a cabled network.

broadcast—A technique for transmitting signals, such as network data, by using a transmitter of some kind to send those signals through a communications medium. For wireless networks, this involves sending signals through the atmosphere, rather than over some kind of cable.

broadcast packet—A packet type whose destination address specifies all computers on a network or network segment.

broadcast storm—Phenomenon that occurs when a network device malfunctions and floods the network with broadcast packets.

brouter—A networking device which combines the best functionality of a bridge and a router. It is able to route packets which include Network layer information, and bridge all other packets.

buffer—A temporary storage area a device uses to contain incoming data before it can be processed for input, or to contain outgoing data before it can be sent as output.

bus—A specialized collection of parallel lines in a PC. It is used to ship data between the CPU and peripheral devices and, occasionally, from one peripheral device to another (requires that one or both adapters involved have bus-mastering capabilities).

bus mastering—When an adapter card has sufficiently sophisticated circuitry that it can take possession of a computer's bus and coordinate data transfers without requiring any service from the computer's CPU.

bus width—The number of parallel lines that make up a particular kind of computer bus. For example, ISA supports 8- and 16-bit bus widths, EISA and MCA 16- and 32-bit bus widths, and PCI a 32-bit bus width.

cable modem—A device used to receive data from the Internet via a cable television cable.

cable tester—A network troubleshooting device which is able to test for cable defects, monitor network collisions, and monitor network congestion.

cascading IRQ controller—A multistep chip arrangement in which two or more IRQ controllers are connected to sequentially send an interrupt signal to each other and then to the CPU. For example, IRQ2 is tied to IRQ0 on a second controller, which becomes IRQ9 by convention. When a device with an IRQ value higher than 8 signals an interrupt, it sends the interrupt to IRQ2 on the first controller, which then forwards it to the CPU. When the CPU responds, IRQ2 forwards that to the initiating device.

Category 1 through 5—The EIA/TIA designations for unshielded twisted-pair cable are described in terms of categories, labeled Category 1, Category 2, and so on; often, these are abbreviated as Cat1, Cat2, and so on.

CDPD (Cellular Digital Packet Data)—A cellular communications technology that sends packets of digital data over unused cellular voice channels at a rate of 19.2 Kbps. CDPD is one of an emerging family of mobile computing technologies.

cellular packet radio—A communications technology that sends packets of data over radio frequencies different from those used for cellular telephones. It is a generic term for an emerging family of mobile computing technologies.

centralized administration—A way of controlling access to network resources, and managing network setup and configuration data from a single point of access and control. Windows NT Server's domain controllers provide this capability.

centralized computing—Computing environment in which all processing takes place on a mainframe or central computer.

channel access method—The rules used to determine which computer can send data across the network, thereby preventing data loss due to collisions.

Cheapernet—A synonym for 10Base2, also known as Thinnet or Thinwire Ethernet.

chip—A fixed-sized element of data that is broadcast over a single frequency when using the spread-spectrum radio networking technology called direct-sequence modulation.

CIDR (Classless Inter-Domain Routing)—A more efficient way to assign IP addresses than using IP address "classes."

cladding—A non-transparent layer of plastic or glass material inside fiber optic cable that surrounds the inner core of glass or plastic fibers; cladding provides rigidity, strength, and a manageable outer diameter for fiber optic cables.

client—A computer on a network that requests resources or services from some other computer.

client network software—A type of software designed for workstation computers that enables the use of network resources.

client-based multivendor solution—When multiple redirectors are loaded on a client, the client is able to communicate with servers from different vendors.

client/server—A model for computing where some computers request services (clients) and others respond to such requests for services (servers).

client/server relationship—A relationship by which applications can be divided across the network, so that a client-side component runs on the user's machine and supplies request and display services, whereas a server-side component runs on an application server, and handles data processing or other computationally intensive services on the user's behalf.

coaxial cable—A type of cable that uses a center conductor, wrapped by an insulating layer, surrounded by a braided wire mesh and an outer jacket or sheath, to carry high-bandwidth signals like network traffic or broadcast television frequencies.

collision—A condition that occurs on Ethernet networks when two nodes attempt to broadcast at the same time.

combination network—A network that incorporates both peer-to-peer and server-based capabilities.

communication server—A specialized network server that provides access to resources on the network for users not directly attached to the network, or that permits network users to access external resources not directly attached to the network.

communications carrier—A company that provides communications services for other organizations to use, like your local phone company and the long-distance telephone carriers. Most mobile computing technologies rely on the services of a communications carrier to handle the wireless traffic from mobile units to a centralized wired network of some kind.

concentrator—Used in an FDDI network to connect computers at a central point. Most concentrators connect to both of the available rings.

conduit—Plastic or metal pipe laid specifically to provide a protected enclosure for cabling of any kind.

congestion control—A technique for monitoring network utilization and manipulating transmission or forwarding rates for data frames to keep traffic levels from overwhelming the network medium; gets its name because it avoids "network traffic jams."

connectionless—A type of protocol that sends the data across the network to its destination without guaranteeing receipt.

connection-oriented—A type of protocol that establishes a formal connection between two computers, guaranteeing the data reaches its destination.

contention—A channel access method in which computers vie for time on the network.

cooperative multitasking—A form of multitasking where each individual process controls the length of time it maintains exclusive control over the CPU.

copy backup—Copies all selected files without resetting the archive bit.

CPU (central processing unit)—The collection of circuitry (a single chip on most PCs) that supplies the "brains" for most computers.

CRC (cyclic redundancy check)—A mathematical recipe that generates a specific value, called a checksum, based on the contents of a data frame. The CRC is calculated before a data frame is transmitted, then is included with the frame; on receipt, the CRC is recalculated and compared to the sent value. If the two agree, the data frame is assumed to have been delivered intact; if they disagree, the data frame must be retransmitted.

crosstalk—Interference that occurs when two wires are laid against each other in parallel. Signals traveling down one wire can interfere with signals traveling down the other, and vice-versa.

CSMA/CA (Carrier Sense Multiple-Access with Collision Avoidance)—A contention-based channel access method in which computers avoid collisions by broadcasting their intent to send data.

CSMA/CD (Carrier Sense Multiple-Access with Collision Detection)—A contention-based channel access method in which computers avoid collisions by listening to the network before sending data. If a computer senses data on the network, it waits and tries to send its data later.

daily backup—Copies all files modified on the day of the backup.

DAS (dual attachment stations)—Computers or concentrators connected to both rings in an FDDI network.

data channel—The cables and infrastructure of a network.

data frame—The basic package of bits that represents the PDU sent from one computer to another across a networking medium. In addition to its contents (payload), a data frame includes the sender's and receiver's network addresses, plus some control information at the head and a CRC at the tail.

Data Link layer—Layer 2 in the OSI Reference Model. This layer is responsible for managing access to the networking medium and for ensuring error-free delivery of data frames from sender to receiver.

datagrade—A designation for cabling of any kind that indicates that it's suitable for transporting digital data. When applied to twisted-pair cabling, it indicates that the cable is suitable for either voice or data traffic.

datagrams—The term used in some protocols to define a packet.

DBMS (database management system)—Client/server computing environment that uses the Structured Query Language to retrieve data from the server.

DECNet—Digital Equipment Corp.'s protocol suite.

dedicated server—A network server that acts only as a server, and is not intended for regular use as a client machine.

defragmentation—The process of reconstructing a larger PDU at a higher layer from a collection of smaller PDUs from a lower layer.

demand packet—Special packet sent by a computer in a 100VG-AnyLAN network informing the controlling hub that it has data to send.

demand priority—A high-speed channel access method used by 100VG-AnyLAN in a star hub topology.

demand signal—A signal sent by a computer in a demand priority network informing the controlling hub that it has data to send.

designators—Associated with drive mappings, by working in coordination with a redirector, it exchanges the locally mapped drive letter with the correct network address of a directory share inside a resource request.

desktop software—Sometimes called client software or productivity applications, this type of software is what users run on their computers (which are usually on the desktop—or at least, the monitor and keyboard, in any case).

device driver—A software program that mediates communication between an operating system and a specific device for the purpose of sending and/or receiving input and output from that device.

device sharing—Permits users to share access to devices of all kinds, including servers and peripherals such as printers or plotters.

DHCP (Dynamic Host Configuration Protocol)—A TCP/IP protocol that allows for automatic IP-address and subnet mask assignment.

diagnostic software—Specialized programs that can probe and monitor a system, or a specific system component, to determine if it's working properly, and if not, to try to establish the cause of the problem.

dictionary attack—A method of trying to determine an account's password by attempting to log on using every word in the dictionary for a password.

differential backup—Copies all files modified since the last full backup.

digital pulse—The use of specific voltage levels to send binary data across a cable, where one voltage level indicates a 1 and the other a 0, or where transitions from "high" to "low" are used to signal binary values.

DIP (dual inline package)—An integrated computer circuit that features two parallel rows of pins of equal length, offset approximately 1 cm.

DIP switch—An electrical circuit that consists of a series of individual two-way switches contained in a single chip; see also *DIP*, which explains the pin-outs for this kind of package.

directory server—A specialized server whose job is to respond to requests for specific resources, services, users, groups, and so on. This kind of server is more commonly called a domain controller in Windows NT Server networking environments.

direct-sequence modulation—The form of spread-spectrum data transmission that breaks data into constant length segments called chips and transmits the data on multiple frequencies.

discovery—Process by which dynamic routers learn the routes available to them.

disk duplexing—A fault tolerant disk configuration in which data is written to two hard disks, each with its own disk controller, so that if one disk or controller fails, the data remains accessible.

disk mirroring—A fault tolerant disk configuration in which data is written to two hard disks, rather than one, so that if one disk fails, the data remains accessible.

disk space—The amount of free space available on a computer disk drive, usually measured in megabytes (MB).

disk striping with parity—A fault tolerant disk configuration in which parts of several physical disks are linked in an array, and data and parity information written to all disks in this array. Should one disk fail, the data may be reconstructed from the parity information.

disk type—The type of disk controller and interface used to attach it to a computer. This usually refers to technologies like Integrated Drive Electronics (IDE), Extended IDE, or the Small Computer Systems Interface (SCSI).

distance-vector algorithm—One method of determining the best route available for a packet. Distance-vector protocols count the number of routers (hops) between the source and destination. The best path has the least number of hops.

distribution panel—The IBM cabling system term for a centralized wiring center, where twisted-pair networking cables congregate for interconnection, backbone access, and management.

DIX (Digital, Intel, Xerox)—The group which introduced the first Ethernet connector.

DMA (direct memory access)—A technique for addressing memory on some other device as if it were local memory directly available to the device accessing that memory. This technique lets a CPU gain immediate access to the buffers on any NIC that supports DMA.

DNS (Domain Name System)—A TCP/IP protocol used to associate a computer's IP address to a name.

domain—For Windows NT networks, a group of computers logically organized into a single security database.

domain controller—On a Windows NT Server-based network, this is a directory server that also provides access controls over users, accounts, groups, computers, and other resources on the network.

domain model—A Windows NT Server-based network whose security and access controls reside in a domain controller.

drive mapping—The convention of associating a local drive letter with a network directory share to simplify access to the remote resource.

driver—An abbreviation for "device driver," a small program that mediates between an operating system and the hardware device it knows how to access.

DUN (Dial-Up Networking)—Program included with Windows NT 4 and Windows 95 and 98 that allows connectivity to servers running RAS.

DVM (digital volt meter)—A network troubleshooting tool that measures resistance on a cable.

dynamic routing—Term used to describe the process by which routers dynamically learn from each other the paths available.

EIA (Electronic Industries Association)—An industry trade group of electronics and networking manufacturers that collaborates on standards for wiring, connectors, and other common components.

EISA (Extended Industry Standard Architecture)—A 32-bit PC bus architecture that is backward-compatible with the older, slower 16-bit ISA bus architecture.

electronic eavesdropping—The ability to "listen" to signals passing through some communications medium by virtue of detecting its emissions. This is especially easy to do for many wireless networking technologies, because they broadcast their data into the atmosphere.

email (electronic mail)—A computer-based messaging system where text and files can be distributed from a single user to one or more other users within the same network.

EMI (electromagnetic interference)—A form of electrical interference caused by emissions from external devices, such as transformers or electrical motors, that can interfere with network transmissions over an electrical medium.

enterprise network—A large-scale network usually connecting many LANs.

error-handling—The process of recognizing and responding to network transmission or reception errors, which usually consist of interminable delivery (time-out), incorrect delivery (fails a data integrity check), or lost information (data frames or PDUs needed to reassemble a higher-level PDU never show up and must be retransmitted).

Ethernet—A networking technology developed in the early 1970s, Ethernet is governed by the IEEE 802.3 specification, and remains one of the most popular types of networking technology in use today.

Ethernet 802.2—Ethernet frame type used by IPX/SPX on Novell NetWare 3.12 and 4.x networks.

Ethernet 802.3—Ethernet frame type generally used by IPX/SPX on Novell NetWare 2.x and 3.x networks.

Ethernet II—Ethernet frame type used by TCP/IP.

Ethernet raw—Ethernet frame type. Also called Ethernet 802.3.

Ethernet SNAP—Ethernet frame type used in Apple's EtherTalk environment.

EtherTalk—The standard for sending AppleTalk over Ethernet cabling.

Event Viewer—A Windows NT tool that records events in three logs based on type of event: security, system, and application.

Exchange Server—A BackOffice component from Microsoft that acts as a sophisticated email server.

extended LAN—LAN that can extend the span of a LAN as far as 3 to 25 miles. This is due to wireless bridges.

extent—The size of an area, usually used to describe the upper limit of a memory region on a PC named by a base address that indicates the starting point (upper bound equal base address plus extent).

fault tolerant disk configuration—An arrangement of physical or logical disks such that if one disk fails, the data remains accessible without having to be restored from backups.

fax server—A specialized network server that can send and receive faxes on behalf of the user community that it supports. A fax server can receive incoming faxes from phone lines and direct them to users across the network, as well as accept outgoing faxes across the network and redirect them out over a telephone line.

FCC (Federal Communications Commission)—A government organization which, among other responsibilities, regulates access to broadcast frequencies throughout the electromagnetic spectrum, including those used for mobile computing and microwave transmissions. Where these signals cover any distance (more than half a mile) and require exclusive use of a particular frequency, an FCC broadcast license is required. Many wireless networking technologies make use of so-called "unregulated frequencies" set aside by the FCC that do not require such licensing, but they must be shared with others using the same frequencies.

FDDI (Fiber Distributed Data Interface)—A network architecture that uses fiber optic cable and two counter-rotating rings to reliably send data at 100 Mbps.

fiber optic—A cabling technology that uses pulses of light sent along a light-conducting fiber at the heart of the cable to transfer information from sender to receiver. Note that fiber optic cable can send data in only one direction, so two cables are required to permit any two network devices to exchange data in both directions.

file and print server—The most common type of network server (and therefore not considered a specialized server), it provides file storage and retrieval services across the network, and handles print jobs on behalf of its user community.

flow control—An action designed to regulate the transfer of information between a sender and a receiver; is most often needed when a speed differential exists between sender and receiver.

fragmentation—The process of breaking up a long PDU from a higher layer to a sequence of shorter PDUs in a lower layer, ultimately for transmission as a sequence of data frames across the networking medium.

frame—Used interchangeably with "data frame," the basic package of bits that represents a PDU sent from one computer to another across the network. In addition to its contents, a frame includes the sender's and receiver's network addresses plus control information at the head and a CRC at the tail.

frame type—One of four standards that defines the structure of an Ethernet packet: Ethernet 802.3, Ethernet 802.2, Ethernet SNAP, or Ethernet II.

frequency-hopping—The type of spread-spectrum data transmission that switches data across a range of frequencies over time; frequency-hopping transmitters and receivers must be synchronized to hop at the same time, to the same frequencies.

front-end—A client in a client/server networking environment.

FTP (File Transfer Protocol)—Refers to a TCP/IP-based networked file transfer application, with an associated protocol, that's widely used on the Internet to copy files from one machine on a network to another.

full backup—A copy of data that resets the archive bit on all copied files.

gateway—Networking device that translates information between protocols or completely different networks, such as TCP/IP to SNA.

geosynchronous—An orbital position relative to the earth where a satellite orbits at the same speed as the earth rotates; this permits such satellites to maintain a constant, fixed position relative to earth stations, and represents the positioning technique used for microwave satellites.

global group—A group meant to be used in more than one domain.

Gopher—A TCP/IP-based network application, with an associated protocol, that provides a consistent, menu-driven interface to a variety of Internet files and information resources of many kinds, including text and application files, FTP-based resources, and more.

group—A named collection of user accounts, usually created for some specific purpose (for example, the Accounting group might be the only named entity permitted to use a bookkeeping application; then, by adding or removing individual users from the Accounting group, a network administrator could easily control who may access that application).

groupware—A type of network application where multiple users can simultaneously interact with each other and data files.

hard page fault—An exception that occurs when data a program needs must be called back into memory from its storage space on the hard disk. Hard page faults are relatively time-consuming to resolve.

Hayes-compatible—Modem standard based on the Hayes Smartmodem.

HCL (Hardware Compatibility List)—A vendor-maintained list of all hardware that is compatible with a particular operating system; in practice, it names a document maintained by Microsoft that names all the hardware compatible with Windows NT.

HDLC (High-Level Data Link Control)—Synchronous communication protocol.

hexadecimal—A mathematical notation for representing numbers in base 16; 10 through 15 are expressed as A through F; 10h or 0x10 (both are notations to indicate the number is hexadecimal) equal 16.

HMA (High Memory Area)—The region of memory on a PC between 640 K and 1,024 K (usually referred to in hex as A0000 through 1000000). This is the area where device driver buffer space and shared system memory are typically allocated.

HTML (Hypertext Markup Language)—The language used to create documents for the World Wide Web.

HTTP (Hypertext Transfer Protocol)—The protocol used by the World Wide Web to transfer files.

hub—The central concentration point of a network.

hybrid LAN—This is Microsoft's term for a LAN that includes both wireless and wired components.

IBM Type 1 through 9—These numeric cable designations represent the grades of cabling recognized by IBM's Cabling System. Types 2 and 9 are the most commonly used networking cables; Type 3 is voicegrade only, unsuitable for networking use.

ICMP (Internet Control Message Protocol)—A TCP/IP protocol used to send information and error messages.

IEEE (Institute of Electrical and Electronics Engineers)—An engineering organization that issues standards for electrical and electronic devices, including network interfaces, cabling, and connectors.

IIS (Internet Information Server)—A Microsoft BackOffice component that acts as a Web server in the Windows NT Server environment.

IMAP (Internet Message Access Protocol)—A developing standard soon to replace SMTP due to its advanced control and fault-tolerance features.

impedance—The resistance of a cable to the transmission of signals; impedance is what accounts for attenuation in a cable.

incremental backup—Copies all files modified since the last full or incremental backup.

infrared—That portion of the electromagnetic spectrum immediately below visible light; infrared frequencies are popular for short- to medium-range (10s of meters to 40 km) point-to-point network connections.

interference—The phenomenon that occurs when one type of signal or emission impinges on another, and either distorts or diminishes it.

Internet—An abbreviation of the term internetwork. When capitalized, this refers to the worldwide collection of networked computers that began with technology and equipment funded by the U.S. Department of Defense in the 1970s that today links millions of computers from nearly every known country in the world.

Internet browser—A graphical tool, such as Microsoft's Internet Explorer or Netscape's Navigator, designed to read HTML documents and access the World Wide Web.

internetwork—Literally, a network of networks. It describes a logical network that consists of two or more physical networks. Unlike a WAN, an internetwork may reside in only a single location, but because it includes too many computers or spans too much distance, cannot fit within the scope of a single LAN.

IP (Internet Protocol)—TCP/IP's primary Network layer protocol, which provides addressing and routing information.

IPX (Internetwork Packet Exchange)—A Network and Transport-layer protocol developed by Novell, most commonly associated with NetWare networks.

IPX/SPX—An abbreviation for Internet Packet Exchange, Sequenced Packet Exchange, this acronym names the set of protocols developed by Novell that is most commonly associated with NetWare, but is also supported in Microsoft networks, as well as those from other vendors.

IRQ (interrupt request line)—Any of 16 unique signal lines between the CPU and the bus slots on a PC. IRQs define the mechanism whereby a peripheral device of any kind, including a network adapter, can state a claim on the PC's attention. Such a claim is called an "interrupt," which gives the name to the lines that carry this information.

ISA (Industry Standard Architecture)—This acronym names the 16-bit PC adapter interface originally developed for use with the IBM PC/AT, but now included in nearly every PC available on the marketplace today.

ISDN (Integrated Services Digital Network)—Digital communication method that is able to transmit voice and data.

ISO (International Standardization Organization)—The international standards-setting body, based in Geneva, Switzerland, that sets technology standards for worldwide use.

ISP (Internet Service Provider)—A company that provides its clients with connectivity to the Internet.

ITU (International Telecommunications Union)—Standards body that developed the V-series modem standards.

jack coupler—The female receptacle into which a modular TP cable is plugged.

jacket—The outermost layer of a cable. It is also referred to as a sheath.

jumper—A small, special-purpose connector designed to make contact between two pins on an adapter card of some kind. Jumpers are sometimes used to establish configuration settings on network cards and other computer adapters.

jumper block—A collection of two or more sets of jumper pins, or a special connector designed to make contact between two or more sets of contiguous jumper pins at the same time.

LAN (local area network)—A collection of computers and other networked devices that fits within the scope of a single physical network. LANs provide the building blocks for internetworks and WANs.

laser—Actually an acronym for Light Amplification by Stimulated Emission of Radiation, lasers represent one of the most powerful techniques to transmit signals at optical frequencies, all the way from infrared to ultraviolet. Low-powered infrared lasers are often used in wireless LAN technologies; higher-powered infrared lasers are sometimes used for wireless bridges. Lasers are also used for high-powered, fiber optic-based data transmissions.

layers—The functional subdivisions of the OSI Reference Model in which each layer is defined in terms of the services and data it handles on behalf of its upper adjacent layer, and the services and data it depends on from its lower adjacent layer.

learning bridge—Another term for a transparent bridge which learns the hardware addresses of the computers connected to each network segment.

LED (light-emitting diode)—A lower-powered alternative for emitting data at optical frequencies, LEDs are sometimes used for wireless LANs and for short-haul, fiber optic-based data transmissions.

line of sight—A term that describes the requirement for narrowband, tight-beam transmitters and receivers to have an unobstructed path between the two. It is based on the idea that if sender and receiver can see each other, they can also exchange data.

link-state algorithm—A method used by routers to determine the best path for a packet to take. In addition to the number of routers involved, routers using link-state algorithms take into account network traffic and link speed in determining the best path.

LLC (Logical Link Control)—The upper sublayer of the IEEE Project 802 networking model for the Data Link layer (Layer 2) of the OSI Reference Model; handles error-free delivery of data frames between sender and receiver across a network, plus flow control.

local group—A group meant to be used in a single domain.

locally attached—This describes a device that's attached directly to a single computer, rather than a device that's available only over the network (which may be called network-attached or server-attached, depending on whether it has a built-in network interface, or must be attached directly to a server).

LocalTalk—The cabling system used by Macintosh computers. Support for LocalTalk is built into every Macintosh.

logon hours—The times during which a user is permitted to log on to his or her account. Logon hours may be restricted for security reasons.

MAC (Media Access Control)—A level of data communication where the network interface can directly address the networking media; also refers to a unique address programmed into network adapters to identify them on any network where they might appear.

MAN (metropolitan area network)—MANs use WAN technologies to interconnect LANs within a specific geographical region, such as a county or a city. In most cases, however, MANs are operated by a municipality or a communications carrier; individual organizations must sign up for service and establish a connection to use a MAN.

MAU (multistation access unit)—An active hub in a Token Ring network. Also referred to as an MSAU.

maximum segment length—The longest legal segment of cable that a particular networking technology permits; this limitation helps network designers and installers make sure that the entire network can send and receive signals properly.

MCA (Micro Channel Architecture)—IBM's proprietary 16- and 32-bit computer buses originally developed for its PS/2 PCs, now popular on its midrange RISC/6000 computers.

mesh—A hybrid topology used for fault-tolerance in which all computers are connected to each other.

MHS (Message Handling System)—A standard similar to X.400 developed by Novell.

MIB (management information base)—A set of objects used by SNMP to manage a networking device that contains information about the device.

MIC (medium interface connector)—One of a number of fiber optic cable connector types. MIC connectors feature a separate physical connector for each cable in a typical fiber optic cable pair.

Microsoft BackOffice—Microsoft's collection of software products that run on Windows NT and provide common office-oriented services and applications. IIS, RAS, and Windows NT Server are all BackOffice components.

Microsoft TechNet (Microsoft Technical Information Network)—A subscription service from Microsoft which supplies CD-ROMs on a monthly basis for technical information on networking and Microsoft-specific topics.

microwave—The broadcast frequency that operates between 1 GHz and 1 THz, between radio and infrared frequencies. Microwave transmissions are used for terrestrial and satellite transmissions.

MKB (Microsoft Knowledge Base)—An online reference for Microsoft and networking information.

mobile computing—A form of wireless networking that uses common carrier frequencies to permit networked devices to move around freely within the broadcast coverage area, yet remain connected to the network.

modem (modulator/demodulator)—Used by computers to convert digital signals to analog signals for transmission over telephone lines.

MSD.EXE—The Microsoft diagnostics program that ships with DOS, Windows 3.x, and Windows 95 and 98 operating systems; this program can document IRQs, base memory addresses, and HMA regions in use.

MSDL (Microsoft Download Library)—A bulletin board service on which Microsoft drivers and patches are available.

multitasking—A mode of CPU operation where a computer processes more than one task at a time. In most instances, multitasking is an illusion created through the use of time slicing.

NADN (nearest active downstream neighbor)—Used in a Token Ring environment to describe the computer to which a computer sends the token.

naming convention—A predetermined schema for naming objects within network space. The schema should simplify the location and identification of objects.

narrowband radio—A type of broadcast-based networking technology that uses a single specific radio frequency to send and receive data. Low-powered narrowband implementations do not usually require FCC approval, but are perforce limited to a 250 foot range or so; high-powered narrowband implementation does require FCC approval and licensing.

narrowband sockets—An emerging programming interface designed to facilitate communication between cellular data networks and the Internet.

NAUN (nearest active upstream neighbor)—Used in a Token Ring environment to describe the computer from which a computer receives the token.

NCP (NetWare Core Protocol)—Novell's upper-layer protocol that provides all client/server functions.

NetBEUI (NetBIOS Enhanced User Interface)—An enhanced set of network and transport protocols built in the late 1980s to carry NetBIOS information, when earlier implementations became too limiting for continued use. NetBEUI remains popular on many IBM and Microsoft networks.

NetBIOS (Networked Basic Input/Output System)—A venerable set of application programming interfaces designed by IBM in the late 1970s to provide easy access to networking services; NetBIOS remains a popular networking interface.

network adapter—A synonym for network interface card. It refers to the hardware device that mediates communication between a computer and one or more types of networking media; see also *NIC, network card*.

network administrator—An individual responsible for installing, configuring, and maintaining a network, usually a server-based network like Windows NT Server or something similar.

network applications—Enhanced software programs made possible through the communication system of a network; examples include email, scheduling, and groupware.

network card—A synonym for network interface card.

Network layer—Layer 3 of the OSI Reference Model. The Network layer handles addressing and routing of PDUs across internetworks in which multiple networks must be traversed between sender and receiver.

network medium—Usually, this refers to the cable, be it metallic or fiber optic, that links computers on a network. But because wireless networking is also possible, it can also describe the type of wireless communications used to permit computers to exchange data via some wireless transmission frequency.

network model/type—This refers to the kind of networking capabilities available on a network, which may be peer-to-peer, server-based, or a combination of the two.

Network Monitor—Software included with Windows NT which monitors network traffic and gathers information about packet types, errors, and packet traffic to and from each computer.

network news—The collection of discussion groups maintained on the Internet. Also referred to as Usenet.

network protocol—A set of rules for communicating across a network; a common protocol is required for any two computers to be able to communicate successfully across a network.

network resources—Any kind of device, information, or service that's available across a network. A network resource can be a set of files, an application or service of some kind, or a network-accessible peripheral device.

network services—Resources offered by a network not normally found in a standalone OS.

networking technology—Any of the recognized technologies defined to support networked communications. Popular networking technologies available today include Ethernet, Token Ring, FDDI, ATM, and ISDN.

newsgroup—A discussion group in which people share information via Usenet.

NIC (network interface card)—A PC adapter board designed to permit a computer to be attached to some sort of network medium. The NIC handles the translation of digital information into electrical signals for outgoing network communications, and translates incoming signals into their digital equivalent for delivery to the machine wherein it's installed.

NIC type—Used to categorize the type of bus a NIC supports.

NID (next station identifier)—The address of the next computer to which the token is passed.

NNTP (Network News Transfer Protocol)—The protocol used for distributing, retrieving, inquiring, and posting network news articles.

non-routable—A protocol that does not include network address information.

NOS (network operating system)—A specialized collection of software that gives a computer the ability to communicate over a network, and to take advantage of a broad range of networking services. Windows NT is a network operating system available in Workstation and Server versions; Windows 95, 98, and Windows For Workgroups also include built-in network client and peer-to-peer capabilities.

NT (network termination)—Part of the network connection device in an ISDN network.

NWLink (NetWare Link)—This acronym names a set of protocols developed by Microsoft that behave exactly like Novell's IPX/SPX (but named differently, to avoid trade name infringement).

ODI (Open Data-link Interface)—Part of the Novell protocol suite; it provides the ability to bind more than one protocol to a network card.

on-board co-processor—A microprocessor that may be special- or general-purpose that appears on an adapter card usually to offload data from a computer's CPU. NICs with on-board co-processors usually employ the special-purpose variety.

OS (operating system)—The basic program that runs on any computer that runs the underlying system and hardware; an operating system is required for any computer to enable it to work.

oscilloscope—A network troubleshooting device that measures the signal voltage per amount of time. When used with a TDR, it can help define cable problems.

OSI (Open Systems Interconnection)—The family of ISO standards developed in the 1970s and 1980s that were designed to facilitate high-level, high-function networking services among dissimilar computers on a global scale. The OSI initiative has largely failed owing to a fatal combination of "everything including the kitchen sink" in its standards-setting efforts, and a failure to develop standard protocol interfaces to help developers implement its manifold requirements.

OSI Reference Model—OSI Standard 7498, which defines a frame of reference for understanding and implementing networks that breaks the process down across seven layers. By far, the OSI Reference Model remains the OSI initiative's most enduring legacy.

OSPF (Open Shortest Path First)—TCP/IP's link-state routing protocol used to determine the best path for a packet through an internetwork.

packet—A specially organized and formatted collection of data destined for network transmission; alternatively, the form in which network transmissions are received following conversion into digital form.

packet header—Information added to the beginning of the data being sent. It contains, among other things, addressing and sequencing information.

packet switching—A transmission method wherein packets are sent across a networking medium that supports multiple pathways between sender and receiver; transmissions may follow any available path, and multiple packets may be under way simultaneously across the network. Thus, it's possible that packets may arrive in an order that differs from the order in which they were sent. X.25 is a common type of packet-switched network.

packet trailer—Information added to the end of the data being sent. It generally contains error-checking information such as the CRC.

parallel transmission—The technique of spreading individual bits of data across multiple, parallel data lines so they can be transmitted simultaneously, rather than according to some kind of ordinal and temporal sequence.

PARC—Xerox's Palo Alto Research Center.

parent hub—The central controlling hub in a 100VG-AnyLAN network to which child hubs are connected.

passive hub—Hub in an ARCNet network, which can connect only to active hubs and computers.

passive topology—Describes a network topology in which the computers listen to the data signals being sent, but do not participate in network communications.

password—A string of letters, numbers, and other characters that are intended to be kept private (and hard to guess); used to identify a particular user, or to control access to protected resources.

patch panel—An element of a wiring center where individual cable runs are brought together, so that, by making connections between any two points on the patch panel, the physical path of individual wires can be controlled and the sequence of individual wires managed. The so-called data path is particularly important in Token Ring networks, and this is where patch panels are frequently found.

payload—The data content within a PDU.

PCI (Peripheral Component Interconnect)—This acronym describes a 32-bit PC bus that offers much higher performance and more sophisticated capabilities than the 16-bit ISA bus.

PDU (packet data unit)—A data unit associated with processing at any layer in the OSI Reference Model; sometimes identified by the particular layer, as in "a Session or Layer 5 PDU."

PDU (protocol data unit)—A packet structure as formulated by a specific networking protocol; such a structure usually includes specific header and trailer information in addition to its data payload.

peer-to-peer—A type of networking where each computer can be a client to other computers, and act as a server as well.

Performance Monitor—A Windows NT tool used for graphing trends, based on performance counters for system objects.

peripheral device—Literally, this refers to any hardware component on a computer that's not the CPU. In a networking context, it usually refers to some kind of device, such as a printer or a plotter, that can be shared across the network.

Physical layer—Layer 1, the bottom-most layer of the OSI Reference Model. The Physical layer is where signals are transmitted and received and where the physical details of cables, adapter cards, connectors, and hardware behavior are specified.

plenum—The area between a false ceiling and the true one in most commercial buildings used to circulate heating and cooling air; it's called the plenum or the plenum space. Many types of cable, including networking cable, are also run through this space.

plenum-rated cable—A cable that has been burn-tested to make sure it does not emit toxic fumes or large amounts of smoke when incinerated. This designation is required for any cable to be run in plenum space by most building and fire codes.

Plug and Play—Microsoft's requirements for PC motherboards, buses, adapter cards, and operating systems. These requirements let a PC detect and configure hardware on a system automatically. For Plug and Play to work properly, all system components must conform rigorously to its specifications; currently, this architecture is supported in Windows 95 and Windows 98.

polling—A channel access method in which a primary device asks secondary devices in sequence whether they have data to send.

POST (power-on self-test)—The set of internal diagnostic and status-checking routines a PC and its peripheral devices always go through each time the computer is powered on.

power conditioning—A method of evening out the power input and reducing any spikes caused by noise on the power line, thus providing power that's better for delicate components such as computers.

PPP (Point-To-Point Protocol)—Remote access protocol that supports many protocols including TCP/IP, NetBEUI, and IPX/SPX.

preemptive multitasking—A form of multitasking where the NOS or OS retains control over the length of time each process can maintain exclusive use of the CPU.

Presentation layer—Layer 6 of the OSI Reference Model. The Presentation layer is where data may be encrypted and/or compressed to facilitate delivery, and where platform-specific application formats are translated into generic data formats for transmission, or from generic data formats into platform-specific application formats for delivery to the Application layer.

PRI (Primary Rate Interface)—An ISDN implementation that provides 23 64 Kbps B-Channels.

Project 802—The IEEE networking initiative that produced the 802.x networking specifications and standards.

propagation delay—Signal delay that is created when a number of repeaters are connected in a line. Because of this, many network architectures limit the number of repeaters on a network.

protocol—A rigidly defined set of rules for communication across a network. Most protocols confine themselves to one or more layers of the OSI Reference Model.

protocol analyzer—Combination of hardware and software that is able to capture network traffic and create reports and graphs from the data collected.

protocol suite—A family of related protocols in which higher-layer protocols provide application services and request handling facilities, while lower-layer protocols manage the intricacies of layers 1 through 4 from the OSI Reference Model.

protocol type field—Field used in the Ethernet SNAP and Ethernet II frames to indicate the network protocol being used.

PSTN (Public Switched Telephone Network)—Another term for the public telephone system.

punchdown block—A wiring center used for telephone and network TP cable where bare wire ends are inserted (punched down) into specific connectors to manage wiring layout and the data path (making a punchdown block a moral equivalent of a patch panel).

queued commands—Commands awaiting execution but not yet completed.

radio-frequency—That portion of the electromagnetic spectrum from 3 KHz to 1 MHz, used for radio communications and broadcast television, among other uses.

RAM (random access memory)—This refers to the memory cards or chips on a PC that provide working space for the CPU to use when running applications, providing network services, and so on. Where RAM on a server is concerned, more is usually better.

RAM buffering—A memory access technique that permits an adapter to use a computer's main memory as if it were local buffer space.

RAS (Remote Access Service)—A Microsoft BackOffice component that's bundled with Windows NT Server (a single-user version is also included with Windows NT Workstation). RAS acts as a communication server for the Windows NT Server environment.

raw data—Data streams unbroken by header information.

reassembly—The action of reconstructing a larger, upper-layer PDU from a collection of smaller, lower-layer PDUs where resequencing and recombining may be required to reassemble the original PDU.

receiver—A data communications device designed to capture and interpret signals broadcast at one or more frequencies in the electromagnetic spectrum. Receivers are necessary for both cable- and wireless-based transmissions.

redirector—The component in a protocol suite responsible for intercepting requests from applications and determining whether the service is local or remote (on the network).

reflective wireless network—An infrared wireless networking technology that uses a central optical transceiver to relay signals between end stations. All network devices must have an unobstructed view of this central transceiver, which explains why they're usually mounted on the ceiling.

registered jack—The expansion of the RJ acronym used for modular telephone and network TP jacks.

repeater—Networking device that is used to strengthen a signal suffering from attenuation. Using a repeater effectively doubles the maximum length of the network.

requestor—The term used by Novell for a redirector.

request-response—A way of describing how the client/server relationship works. This refers to how a request from a client leads to some kind of response from a server (hopefully, the service or data that's been requested, but sometimes an error message or a denial of service based on security).

RFI (radio-frequency interference)—Any interference that is caused by signals operating in the radio frequency range. This has become a generic term for interference caused by broadcast signals of any kind.

RG (Radio Government)—The expansion for the coaxial cable designation known as RG. This designation reflects coaxial cables original use as a conveyance for radio frequency data and signals. The cable designation for Thinnet is RG-58, for CATV RG-59, for ARCNet RG-62, and for Thicknet is either RG-8 or RG-11.

rights—The actions that the user of a particular account is permitted to perform.

ring—Topology consisting of computers connected in a circle, forming a closed ring.

RIP (Routing Information Protocol)—Used by TCP/IP and IPX/SPX; a distance-vector routing protocol used to determine the best path for a packet through an internetwork.

RJ-11—The four-wire modular jack commonly used for home telephone handsets; see also *registered jack*.

RJ-45—An RJ-45 is the 8-wire modular jack used for twisted-pair networking cables and also for PBX-based telephone systems (take care which connector you plug into an RJ-45 coupler).

routable—A protocol containing network address information.

router—Networking device that operates at the Network layer of the OSI model. A router is able to connect networks with different physical media, as well as translate between different network architectures, such as Token Ring and Ethernet.

routing table—Reference table that includes network information and the next router in line for a particular path.

SAP (Service Advertising Protocol)—Used by file and print servers on NetWare networks to inform computers of the services available.

SAS (single attachment stations)—Computers or concentrators in an FDDI network that are connected only to the primary ring.

satellite microwave—A microwave transmission system that uses geosynchronous satellites to send and relay signals between sender and receiver. Most companies that use satellite microwave lease access to the satellites for an exorbitant fee.

scatter infrared network—An infrared LAN technology that uses flat reflective surfaces like walls and ceilings to bounce wireless transmissions between sender and receiver. Because of the delays and attenuation introduced by bouncing, this variety of wireless LAN is the slowest, and supports the narrowest bandwidth of any of the infrared technologies.

scheduling—A type of network application where multiple users can share a single appointment book, address book, and calendar.

SDLC (Synchronous Data Link Control)—Synchronous communication protocol.

security—For networking, this generically describes the set of access controls and permissions in place that are used to determine if a request for a service or resource from a client can be granted by a server.

segmentation—The action of decomposing a larger, upper-layer PDU into a collection of smaller, lower-layer PDUs, that includes sequencing and reassembly information to permit the original upper-layer PDU to be reassembled on receipt of all the smaller, lower-layer PDUs.

serial transmission—A technique for transmitting data signals in which each bit's worth of data (or its analog equivalent) is set one at a time, one after another, in sequence.

server—A computer that provides shared resources (files and directories, printers, databases, and so on) to clients across a network.

server network software—A type of software designed for a server computer that enables the hosting of resources for clients to access.

server session—Connection between a network server and another node.

server-based—A type or model of networking where the presence of a server is required, both to provide services and resources, and to manage and control access to those same services and resources.

server-based multivendor solution—A server with the ability to readily communicate with clients from multiple vendors, such as Windows NT Server.

Session layer—Layer 5 of the OSI Reference Model. The Session layer is responsible for setting up, maintaining, and ending ongoing sequences of communications (called sessions) across a network.

SFD (Start Frame Delimiter)—Field in the Ethernet 802.3 frame that defines the beginning of the packet.

share—A network resource made available for remote access by clients.

share-oriented security—Security information based on the object being shared.

shared adapter memory—A technique for a computer's CPU to address memory on an adapter as if it were the computer's own main memory.

shared system memory—A technique for an adapter to address a computer's main memory as if it were resident on the adapter itself.

sharing—One of the fundamental justifications for networking is sharing of resources; in Microsoft's lexicon, this term refers to the way in which resources are made available to the network.

sheath—The outer layer of coating on a cable; also called the jacket.

shielding—Any layer of material included in cable for the purpose of mitigating the effects of interference on the signal-carrying cables it encloses.

SID (station identifier)—The hardware address for a computer in an ARCNet network.

signal bounce—A phenomenon that occurs when a bus is not terminated and signals continue to traverse the network.

SLIP (Serial Line Internet Protocol)—Dial-up protocol that was originally used to connect PCs directly to the Internet.

SMAU (smart multistation access unit)—An active hub in a Token Ring network.

SMB (Server Message Block)—A block of data comprising client/server requests or responses. SMBs are used in all areas of Microsoft network communications.

SMTP (Simple Mail Transfer Protocol)—The current standard protocol for Internet and other TCP/IP based email.

SNA (Systems Network Architecture)—IBM's native protocol suite for its mainframes and older minicomputers; SNA is still one of the most widely used protocol suites in the world.

sneakernet—A metaphorical description of a method of non-networked data exchange where files are copied onto a floppy on one computer, and then hand-carried (by someone wearing sneakers, presumably) to another computer.

SNMP (Simple Network Management Protocol)—A protocol in the TCP/IP suite that is used for management and monitoring of network devices.

soft page fault—An exception that occurs when data must be called back into a program's working set from another location in physical memory. Soft page faults take comparatively little time to resolve.

software agent—Part of the SNMP structure that is loaded onto each device that will be monitored.

source-route bridge—Type of bridge used in IBM Token Ring networks that learns its bridging information from information included in the packet's structure.

specialized server—Any of a number of special-function servers. A specialized server may be an application server, a communications server, a directory server or domain controller, a fax server, a mail server, or a Web server, among other roles.

spread-spectrum radio—A form of wireless networking technology that passes data using multiple frequencies simultaneously.

SPX (Sequenced Packet Exchange)—A guaranteed-delivery, connection-oriented protocol included in the original NetWare native protocol suite.

SQL (Structured Query Language)—Standard database query language designed by IBM.

SQL Server—A Microsoft BackOffice component. SQL Server provides a standard database management system for the Windows NT Server environment. SQL Server may be used as a standalone database server, but is also required to support other BackOffice components, most notably Systems Management Server.

standalone computer—A computer that's not attached to a network.

standby monitor—Computer in a Token Ring network that monitors the network status and waits for the signal from the active monitor.

star—Major topology in which the computers are connected via a central connecting point, usually a hub.

static routing—Type of routing in which the router is manually configured with all possible routes.

STP (shielded twisted-pair)—A variety of TP cable wherein each of one or more pairs of wires is enclosed in a foil wrap for additional shielding, and where the entire cable may be enclosed in a wire braid or an additional layer of foil for further shielding.

straight connection—A type of one-piece fiber optic connector. SC connectors push on, yet make a strong and solid contact to emitters and sensors.

straight tip—The most common type of fiber optic connector used in Ethernet networks with fiber backbones. ST connectors come in pairs, one for each fiber optic cable.

structured troubleshooting approach—A five-step approach to network troubleshooting recommended by Microsoft.

sublayers—The two components of Layer 2, the Data Link layer, of the OSI Reference Model; elaborated by the IEEE 802 Project, they are the Logical Link Control (LLC) sublayer and the Media Access Control (MAC) sublayer.

subminiature type A—A fiber optic connector. SMA connectors twist on, and also come in pairs.

surge protection—Power protection that prevents spikes or sags in the main current from affecting the computer.

synchronous—Communications type in which the computers rely on exact timing and sync bits to maintain data synchronization.

TA (terminal adapter)—Part of the ISDN network interface, sometimes called a digital modem.

TCP (Transmission Control Protocol)—The core of the TCP/IP suite; TCP is a connection-oriented protocol responsible for reformatting data into packets and reliably delivering those packets.

TCP/IP (Transmission Control Protocol/Internet Protocol)—This acronym represents the set of protocols used on the Internet, and has been embraced as a vital technology by Microsoft. At present, Windows NT and Windows 95 and 98 include outstanding support for TCP/IP; in the future, this support will only strengthen.

TDR (time-domain reflectometer)—A network troubleshooting device that is able to determine not only whether there is a break in the cable, but, if so, approximately how far down the cable the break or short is.

Telecommunications Industries Association (TIA)—An industry consortium of telephone equipment, cabling, and communications companies, that together, formulate hardware standards for equipment, cabling, and connectors used in phone systems and on networks.

Telnet—A TCP/IP protocol that provides remote terminal emulation.

terbo—French term used by the ITU to refer to the third revision of a standard.

terminator—A specialized end connector for coaxial Ethernet networks, a terminator "soaks up" signals that arrive at the end of a network cable and prevents them from reflecting off the end of the cable back onto the network, where they would interfere with real network traffic. Reflectance explains why coax Ethernet networks that lose their terminators cease to work.

terrestrial microwave—A wireless microwave networking technology that uses line of sight communications between pairs of earth-based transmitters and receivers to relay information. Because such equipment is expensive, microwave transmitters and receivers are usually positioned well above ground level, on towers, mountain tops, or atop tall buildings.

Thicknet—A form of coaxial Ethernet that uses a rigid cable about 0.4" in diameter. Because of its common jacket color and its rigidity, this cable is sometimes called "frozen yellow garden hose." Also known as Thickwire and 10Base5.

Thickwire—A synonym for Thicknet and 10Base5.

Thinnet—A form of coaxial Ethernet that uses a thin, flexible cable about 0.2" in diameter. Also known as Thinwire, 10Base2, and Cheapernet.

Thinwire—A synonym for 10Base2 and Thinnet.

time slicing—A method of granting different processes CPU cycles by limiting the amount of time each process has exclusive use of the CPU.

token—Used in some ring topology networks to ensure fair communications between all computers.

token-passing—A channel access method used mostly in ring topology networks, which ensures equal access to all computers on a network through the use of a special packet called a *token*.

Token Ring—A network architecture developed by IBM. It is physically wired as a star, but uses token-passing in a logical ring topology.

TokenTalk—The standard for sending AppleTalk over Token Ring cabling.

topology—Term used to describe the basic physical layout of a network.

transceiver—Literally, this is a compound word that takes the beginning of transmitter and the end of receiver. Thus, a transceiver combines the functions of a transmitter and a receiver, and integrates the circuitry needed to emit signals on a medium, as well as receive them, into a single device.

translation bridge—A bridge that is able to translate between network architectures.

transmitter—An electronic device that is capable of emitting signals for delivery via a particular networking medium.

transparent bridge—Generally used in Ethernet networks, these bridges build their bridging tables automatically as they receive packets.

Transport layer—Layer 4 of the OSI Reference Model. The Transport layer is responsible for fragmenting large PDUs from the Session layer for delivery across the network and for inserting sufficient integrity controls and managing delivery mechanisms to allow for their error-free reassembly on the receiving end of a network transmission.

Transport protocol—This protocol type is responsible for providing reliable communication sessions between two computers.

trust relationship—An arrangement in which a domain permits members of another domain to access its resources.

twisted-pair—A type of cabling where two copper wires, each enclosed in some kind of sheath, are wrapped around each other. The twisting permits narrow gauge wire, otherwise extraordinarily sensitive to crosstalk and interference, to carry higher bandwidth signals over longer distances than would ordinarily be possible with straight wires. Twisted-pair cabling is used for voice telephone circuits, as well as networking.

UDP (User Datagram Protocol)—A connectionless TCP/IP protocol that provides fast data transport.

UNC names—A standard method for naming network resources, it takes the form *servername**sharename*.

UPS (uninterruptible power supply)—A battery-backup system that will supply power in the event that building power is lost and can, in some cases, shut a server down gracefully to prevent data loss.

URL (uniform resource locator)—The specific address of an Internet resource.

user—An individual who uses a computer, either standalone or to access a network.

user-oriented security—Security information based on the account of the user accessing an object.

UTP (unshielded twisted-pair)—A form of TP cable that includes no additional shielding material in the cable composition, UTP cable encloses one or more pairs of twisted wires inside an outer jacket.

vampire tap—Consists of a two-piece apparatus with a set screw on the upper half that permits the pointed end of the screw to penetrate Thickwire coax to a precise depth, where it can tap into the center conductor without breaking it. This permits a transceiver to connect to the cable, and thereby enables devices to attach to the Thickwire segment. The set screw that penetrates the cable is called—in keeping with the name of the tap—the "fang."

virtual docking—Technology that permits laptops to exchange data with desktop machines, or permits data exchange between a computer and a handheld device or a printer.

voicegrade—A designation for networking cable—usually twisted-pair—that indicates it's been rated only to carry telephone traffic. Thus, voicegrade cable is not recommended for network use.

wall plate—A modular wall plate that includes couplers for telephone (RJ-11) and network (RJ-45, BNC, or other female connectors) jacks.

WAN (wide area network)—An internetwork that connects multiple sites, where a third-party communications carrier, such as a public or private telephone company, is used to carry network traffic from one location to another. WAN links can be quite expensive, and are charged on the basis of bandwidth, so few such links support the same bandwidth as that available on most LANs.

Web browser—The client-side software that's used to display content from the Web is called a Web browser, or just a browser, for short.

WINMSD.EXE—The Windows NT built-in diagnostics program; WINMSD.EXE can report on IRQs, base memory addresses, HMA use, and other system internal data.

wire braid—A woven mesh of wire that surrounds one or more conductive wires within a cable, the wire braid's job is to provide protection from interference (and sometimes, crosstalk).

wired—This term indicates that a network connection depends on access to a cable to carry the data transmissions from one networked device to another.

wireless—This term indicates that a network connection depends on transmission at some kind of electromagnetic frequency through the atmosphere to carry data transmissions from one networked device to another.

wireless bridge—A wireless bridge consists of a pair of devices, typically narrowband and tight beam, that are used to relay network traffic from one location to another. Wireless bridges that use spread-spectrum radio, infrared, and laser technologies are available, and can span distances from hundreds of meters up to 25 miles.

wiring center—A set of racks with associated equipment that generally includes hubs, punchdown blocks or patch panels, backbone access units, and other network management equipment, where TP wired network cables are brought together for routing, management, and control.

workgroup model—The Windows NT name for a peer-to-peer network that includes one or more Windows NT-based computers.

working set—The data that a program is actively using at any given time. The working set is only a small subset of the total amount of data that the program *could* use.

WWW (World Wide Web) —The TCP/IP-based collection of all Web servers on the Internet that, in the words of one of its originators, Tim Berners-Lee, comes as close to containing "the sum of human knowledge" as anything available on any network anywhere.

X.25—An international standard for wide-area, packet-switched communications.

X.400—Developed by CCITT (French acronym for the International Telegraph and Telephone Consultative Committee) as a hardware- and software-independent, message-handling protocol.

X.500—An improved message-handling protocol from CCITT. Able to communicate across networks and maintain a global database of addresses.

XNS (Xerox Network System)—A protocol suite developed by Xerox for its Ethernet LANs. The basis for Novell's IPX/SPX.

Index

Bold page numbers indicate sample exam questions.

10Base2 networks, 50, 55, **58**, 60–61, 64, 102, **259**, **328**
    coaxial cable, 101
    ISDN, **58**, 60
    nodes, 56
    restrictions, 103
10Base5 networks, 51, 55, **64**, **256**
    nodes, 56
10BaseF networks
    nodes, 56
    restrictions, 103
10BaseT networks, 47, 55, **58**, 60, 114, 230, 241, 321
    nodes, 56
    restrictions, 103
100BaseT networks, 55–56, **323**
802 specifications. *See* IEEE 802 specifications.

A

Access permissions, 107, **118**
Account lockouts, 139
Account Operators, user rights, 141
Accounts, 14, 156
Active hubs, 72–73
Active Monitor, 86
Adapters, 68
Adaptive exams
    versus fixed-length exams, 4–5, 7
    guessing at answers, 9
Administrators user account, user rights, 141, **150**, **228**
Advanced Program-to-Program Communication. *See* APPC.
Advantages and disadvantages, 102
    Ethernet networks, 102–103
    shielded (STP), 47–48, 55
    unshielded (UTP), 46–48, 55, **63**

AFP, 37
Amplifiers, 72, **72**
Analog connectivity, 187–189
Analog transmission, 188
AOL4FREE.EXE, 169
APPC, 38
Apple computers, protocols, 36–37, 87
AppleTalk, 37–38, 87, **315**
AppleTalk File Protocol. *See* AFP.
Application layer, OSI Reference Model, 31–32, **40**, 76, 157
Application protocols, 37, **42–43**
Application server, 14
Applications log, Windows NT Event Viewer, 146, **150**
ARCNet, 87–88, **329**
    cable, 49, 52, **63**, 101
    restrictions, 104
ATM (Asynchronous Transfer Mode), 196–198, **202–203**
ATP (AppleTalk Transaction Protocol), 37
Attached Resource Computer Network. *See* ARCNet.
Attachment Unit Interface. *See* AUI.
Attenuation, 48, **58**, **324**
Auditing, 140, 165–167, 219
    enabling, 167
    logon/logoff, 166, 212, **228**
    Windows NT, 166–167, 219
AUI, 51–52, **64**
Authentication, 164

B

Backbone, 77, 101
Backup, **178**, **183**, 214–218, **260**, **327**
    data recovery, 217
    hardware, 171
    operators, 172
    peer-to-peer network, 20
    Registry, 143
    schedule, 171–172

software, 218
tape backup, 171–172
Backup Operators, user rights, 141, **150**
Barrel connector, 101
Base memory address, 69–70
Baseband transmission, 72
Baselining, 211
Basic Rate Interface. *See* BRI.
Beaconing, 86, **91**, **259**
BNC (British Naval Connector)
  connectors, 50, **58**, **318**
Bootstrapping, 128
BRI, 193, 199, **201**, **203**, **205**
Bridges, 73, **94–95**, 109, **116–117**, 119,
  231, **246**, **247**, **260**, **314**
  disadvantages, 73
  network performance and, 109
  translation bridges, 73
  transparent bridges, 73
Broadcast storms, **244**, **250**
Brouters, 75, 109, **321**
Bus backbone, 77
Bus topology, 76–77, **90**, **96**, **316**
  disadvantages, 77
  installation, **118**
  selecting, 101

C

Cable tester, 223, **251**
Cables, **60–64**, 101–102, **114**, 241, 247,
  252, 259, 324, 328
  AppleTalk network, 87
  coaxial. *See* Coaxial cable.
  fiber optic, 52–55, **62**
  network security, 48, 54, 162–163
  shielded twisted-pair (STP), 47–48, 55
  testing, 223, **227**
  troubleshooting, 224–225, **227**
  unshielded twisted-pair (UTP),
    46–48, 55, **63**
Cache memory, 172
Carrier Sense Multiple Access with
  Collision Avoidance. *See* CSMA/CA.
CAT1 cabling, 46–47
CAT2 cabling, 46–47
CAT3 cabling, 46–47, **114**
CAT4 cabling, 46–47, **114**
CAT5 cabling, 59, **114**, **252**
Central processing unit. *See* CPU.
Centralized administration, 14
Channel Service Units/Data Service Units.
  See CSU/DSU.

CIR, 194
Circuit switching, 187–188
Client, 14
Client redirector, 125
Client software, 125–126
Client support, 112
Client/server networks, 21–22, **316**. *See
  also* Server-based networks.
  defined, 14
  network security, 21, 162
Coaxial cable, 48–49
  10Base2 network, 101
  advantages, 101
  ARCNet, 49, 52, **63**
  Broadband/cable TV, 49
  disadvantages, 101
  Ethernet networks, 47–49, 51, 55,
    102–103
  fire-resistant, 52
  plenum, 52
  Thicknet, 49, 51–52, 55, **64**, 77, 101
  Thinnet, 49–51, 55, **60–61**, **64**, 77, **96**,
    101–102, **114**
Collision detection, 85–86, **91**, 802
  standards
Collisions per second, 145
Committed Information Rate. *See* CIR.
Computers
  diskless workstations, 167–168
  naming, 156–159, **179**
Concentrators, 100, 105
Concept virus, 169
Configuration, NICs, 68, 71, **94**
Connectivity
  analog connectivity, 187–189
  digital connectivity, 187, 189–190, 199
  packet switching, 190–191
  standardization, 216
  troubleshooting, 225–226, **231**
Connectors, **243**, **318**
  barrel connector, 101
  BNC connectors, 50, **58**
  DB15 connector, 52
  RJ-11 connector, 47, **58**
  RJ-45 connector, 47, 70
  T-connectors, 50–51, 53, **58**, **61**, 101,
    116–117
Contingency planning, 215
Cooperative multitasking, 125, **132**
Copy backup, 171
CPU, 14

Crosstalk, 46–48, **63**, **252**, **321**
CSMA/CA network, 87, **91**
CSMA/CD network, **325**
  IEEE 802 specifications, 34, 83–84
  uses, 86, **91**
CSU/DSU, 190, 194

D

Daily backup, 171
Data, peer-to-peer network, 20
Data Datagram Protocol. *See* DDP.
Data encryption. *See* Encryption.
Data Encryption Standard (DES), 168
Data Link layer, **42**, **94**, **260**, **319**
  IEE 802 specifications, 35–36, 84
  OSI Reference Model, 32–34, 73
Data reads and writes, 144
Data recovery, 217
Data security. *See* Security.
Data striping, 175
Data transmission, 186–189. *See also*
  Cable, Connectivity.
  analog connectivity, 187–189
  circuit switching, 187–188
  digital connectivity, 187, 189–190
  packet switching, 190–200
DB15 connector, 52
D-channel, **201–202**, **205**
DDP, 36
DDS lines, 189
Dedicated lines, 188–189
Dedicated server, 14
Delete permission, 164
Demand priority, **247**
Demultiplexers (demux), **119**
Depends On Password access, 163
DES (Data Encryption Standard), 168
Design, principles, 108–110
Designators, 126
Device sharing, 14
DHCP services, 216
Dial-up lines, 188–189, 193
Differential backup, 171
Digital connectivity, 187, 189–190, 199
Digital Data Service lines. *See* DDS lines.
DIP switches, 87
Directory server, 15
Disaster recovery, 170, **232**. *See also* Fault
  tolerance.
  backup, 20, 171–172, **178**, **183**, 214–218
  importance of, 106
  RAID levels, 106, 173–177

sector sparing, 177, **180**
Uninterruptible Power Supply, 172–173
Windows NT, 144
Disk duplexing, 174–175, 177, **180**
Disk mirroring, 174–175, 177
Disk space, 15
Disk striping, **255**, **320**
  with ECC stored as parity, 175
  with error correction code, 175
  with large blocks, 175
  with parity, 175–176, **180**, **183**
  without parity, 173, 177, **181**
Diskless workstations, 167–168
DISKPERF, 148
DNS, 157–159, **180**, 216, **248**, **250**, **330**
Documentation, 111, 161, 220
  Applications log, 146, **150**
  hardware, 111
  network log, 161
  Security log, 146, **150**, **228**
  systems log, 146, **150**
Domain, 142
Domain controller, 15, 21–22
Domain Name Service. *See* DNS.
Domain Users account, 143
Domain-level security, **117–118**
Dual-In-Line Package switches.
  See DIP switches.
Duplexing. *See* Disk duplexing.
Dynamic routers, 74–75

E

E1, **201**
Eavesdropping, 54
Electromagnetic interference (EMI),
  cabling, 48
Email, 15
Emergency Repair Disk (ERD), 144
Encryption, 107, **113**, 168–169
Error Correction Code (ECC), 175
Ethernet networks, 15, 27, **241**, **245**, **251**, **321**
  10Base2, 50, 55–56, **58**, **60–61**, **64**,
    102–103
  10Base5, 51, 55–56, **64**
  10BaseF, 56, 103
  10BaseT, 47, 55–56, **58**, **60**, 102–103,
    114, **230**
  100Base, 55–56
  802 specifications, 34, **43**
  coaxial cable, 47–49, 51, 55, 102–103
  CSMA/CD, 34, 83–84, 86, **91**

European digital trunk line. *See* EI.
Event Viewer, Windows NT, 146, 149, 150, 211–21, 219, **258**
Execute permission, 164

F

Failed logons, 145, **228**
Fault tolerance, **178**, **180**, **320**
  defined, 173
  network topology and, 81–82, **91**, 106
  RAID levels, 106, **115**, 173–177
  sector sparing, 177, **180**
  Windows NT, 174, 177, **180**
Fiber Distributed Data Interface (FDDI), **202**, **204–205**
  cable, 52–54, 89
  data transmission, 52, 197–198
  network topology, 78, 88–89
Fiber optic cable, **241**, **245**, **323**
  advantages and disadvantages, **62**, 102
  comparison with other cable types, 55
  data transmission, 52–54
File And Object Access, auditing, 166
File server, 15, 106, 112
File Transfer Protocol. *See* FTP.
File-level permissions, **113**
File-system sharing, 131
Fixed-length exams
  versus adaptive exams, 4–5, 7
  guessing at answers, 8
FOIRL (Fiber Optic Inter-Repeater Link), 103
FQDNs (fully qualified domain names), 158, **180**
Fractional T1/T3 (FT1/FT3), 195
Frame relay, 194, **202–203**, **323**
Frame type, **230**, **246**, **333**
FTP, 37, **42**
Full access, 163
Full backup, 171–172
Full Control access, 165

G

Gateways, 75–76, **94**, **96**, 109, **117**, **119**, **231**, **254**, **259**
  characteristics, 76, 110
  selection, 76
Global groups, 141–143
Group accounts
  changes, 143–144
  global groups, 141–143
  local groups, 140–142

Groups, 15, 18
  permissions, 164–166
Guest user account, user rights, 141, **150**

H

Hard disk, monitoring, 148
Hard page faults, 148
Hardware, 100, 105, **116–117**, 119
  adapters, 68–71
  amplifiers, 72
  backup, 171
  bridges, 73, **94–95**, 109, **116–117**, 119, **231**
  brouters, 75, 109
  documenting, 111
  gateways, 75–76, **94**, 96, 109–110, **117**, **119**, **231**
  hubs, 72–73
  multiplexer/demultiplexer pair, 110, **119**
  network interface cards (NICs), 68–71
  network security, 48, 54, 162
  networking, 68–76
  peer-to-peer networks, 19–20
  repeaters, 72, **92**, 109, **116**, 119
  routers, 74–75, **93–95**, 109, **117**, **231**
  server-based networks, 22
  standardization, 216
  troubleshooting, 224–225
HDLC (High-Level Data Control), 39
Host names, 158
HOSTS files, 159, 216, **257**, **330**, **331**
Hubs, 72–73, 100
Hybrid mesh topology, 82, 84
Hybrid network, 15
Hybrid topologies, 81–82

I

ICMP, **232**
IEEE 802 specifications, 15, 30, 34–35, 40, 43, 83–87
  Data Link layer, 35–36, 84
  Ethernet network, 34, **43**
  FOIRL, 103
  Logical Link Control (LLC), 34–35, **43**, 83–84
  MANs, 34, **43**
  Media Access Control (MAC), 36, 57, 83–84
  multiple access, 85
  network security, **40**
  NICs, 34, 36, 56
  Token Bus LAN, 34, **43**
  Token Ring topology, 34, **43**, 83, 86–87

Incremental backup, 171–172, **260**, **327**
Industry Standard Architecture. *See* ISA.
Infrared data transmission, 54–55
Inherited-rights security, **117–118**
Installation
  bus topology, **118**
  network, 110–112
  network operating system (NOS), 127–129
  network printer, 130
  Windows NT Server, 128–129
Institute for Electrical and Electronic Engineers (IEEE), 83
Integrated Services Digital Networks. *See* ISDN networks.
Intelligent hubs, 73
Interfaces, 56–57
  Fiber Distributed Data Interface (FDDI), 52–54, 78, 88–89, 197–198, **202**, **204–205**
  NDIS, 57, **65**
  ODI, 57, **65**
International Standards Organization (ISO), OSI Reference Model, 30, 83
Internetwork, 15
Interrupt, 68–69
Interrupt Request Line. *See* IRQ.
I/O address, 68–69
IP address, **248**, **250**, **257**, **330**
  standardization, 216
  WINS, 158
IP (Internet Protocol), 36
IPX (Internetwork Packet Exchange), 36, **42**, 57, 75, **315**
IRQ, 68–69, **94**
IRQ conflicts, **242**, **253**, **256**, **318**
IRQ2, 69
ISA (Industry Standard Architecture), 15, 27
ISDN networks, 192–193, 199, **201**, **322**

J

Jumpers, 70

L

LANs, **26**, **254**, **325**
  defined, 16, 18
  microwave data transmission, 54
  need for WAN, 186
  radio data transmission, 54
  X.25 networks, 191
Layout, principles, 102–104
Learning bridge, 73

Leased lines, 188–189
Legacy systems, 105
Linear bus, 76
Link services, 36
LLC, 34–35, **43**, 83–84
LMHOSTS files, 159, 216, **230**, **257**, **330**, **331**
Local area networks. *See* LANs.
Local groups, 140–142
Locally attached device, 16
LocalTalk, 87
Logical Link Control. *See* LLC.
Logon hours, 138–140
Logon/logoff, auditing, 166, 212, **228**
LOPHTCRACK.EXE, 139

M

MAC address, 73, 156–157
Macro viruses, 169
Mail gateways, 76
Management Information Base. *See* MIB.
MANs
  defined, 16, 18
  IEEE 802 specifications, 34, **43**
MAU, 86–87, **91**, **116**
Media Access Control (MAC), 36, 57, 83–84
Memory, **330**
  cache memory, 172
  monitoring memory use, 148
  writing to disk, 172
Mesh topology, 80–81, **90–91**, **249**, **326**
Messages, network broadcast, **244**, **250**
Metropolitan area networks. *See* MANs.
MIB, 212, **232**, **332**
Microsoft certification exams
  adaptive testing versus fixed-length testing, 4–5, 7
  ambiguous questions, 237–238
  answer-elimination strategies, 236–237
  exam layout and design, 5–7
  exam readiness, assessing, 2–3
  exam strategies, 7–9
  guessing, on adaptive exams, 9
  guessing, on fixed-length exams, 8
  memorization as preparation, 239
  multiple-choice questions, 5–8
  practice exams, 11
  preparing for, 9–12, 239–240
  question types, 236
  scoring, 4
  setting, 3
  time given, 3

user interface to, 4
  Web sites for, 9–12
Microsoft Certified Professional site, 11–12
Microwave data transmission, 54
Mirroring. *See* Disk mirroring.
Monitoring
  auditing, 139–140, 165–167, 219, **228**
  hard disk, 148
  memory use, 148
  network performance, 146–147
  NT Performance Monitor, **119–120**, 146–149, 213, **227**
  power monitor, 223
  SNMP, 37, **42–43**, 212
Multiple access, 85, 802 standards
Multiplexer/demultiplexer pair, 110, **119**, 195
Multitasking, 124–125, **132**
Muxing, 195

N

NADN, 86
Name resolution standards, 157
NAUN, 86
NBP (Name Binding Protocol), 37
NCP, 37
NDIS, 57, **65**, **320**
Nearest Active Downstream Neighbor. *See* NADN.
Nearest Active Upstream Neighbor. *See* NAUN.
NetBEUI, **43**, 95, **116**, **244**, **247**, **260**, **319**, **325**
  defined, 36–37
  non-routable, 75, **95**, 106, **116**
NetBIOS, 36–37
NetBIOS computer names, 157, **180**, 225, **324**, **330**
NetWare, 124, 225, **245**, **249**, **328**
NetWare Core Protocol. *See* NCP.
Network adapter, 68
Network administration and support, 150–152, 200–211, **227–232**
  administrator, 16, 19, 22
  auditing, 139–140, 165–167, 219
  baselining, 211, 214
  changes to users and groups, 143–144
  client support, 112
  contingency planning, 215
  documentation, 111, 149, 161, 214, 220
  group accounts, 142–144, **150**
  monitoring. *See* Monitoring.
  network administrator, 16, 19, 22

network history, 149–**150**
network performance, 144–147, 213–214, 226
preventative maintenance, 214–215
security. *See* Network security.
SNMP, 37, **42–43**, 212
standardization, 216
total system management, 147–148
training, 220–221
troubleshooting, 221–226
upgrades, 219–220
user accounts, 138–142, **151**
utilities, 211
virus protection, 214
Network administrator, 16, 19, 22
Network analyzer, 222
Network applications, 131
Network architecture, selecting, 104–108
Network broadcast messages, **244**, **250**
Network Device Interface Specifications. *See* NDIS.
Network File System. *See* NFS.
Network history, 149
Network interface card. *See* NIC.
Network layer, OSI Reference Model, 31, 33, **41–42**, 74, **252**
Network log, 161
Network management. *See* Network administration and support.
Network medium, 16
Network Monitor, Windows NT, 147, 151–152, **227**, **317**
Network operating system (NOS), 16, 27, 27, 124–125, **132–134**, 219
  client software, 125–126
  combined client/server software, 127
  installation, 127–129
  selecting, 107, 111
  server software, 126–127
Network operations, 124–131, **132–134**
  client software, 125–127
  designator, 126
  multitasking, 124–125, **132**
  network operating system (NOS), 124–125
  network printing, 130
  network services, 129–130, **134**
  NT Server, 127–129
  redirector, 125–126, **133**
  server software, 126–127
  time slicing, 125
  UNC naming, 126, **133–134**

Network performance, 144, **258**, **332**
    collisions per second, 145
    data reads and writes, 144
    monitoring, 146–147
    queued commands, 145
    security errors, 145
    server sessions, 145
Network printing, 129–130
Network protocols, 16, 36, **42**. *See also* Protocols.
Network resource management, peer-to-peer network, 19
Network resources, 16
    client/server networks, 21–22
Network security, 17, **113**, **117–118**, 126, **178**, 218–219, **258**, **320**
    auditing, 139–140, 165–167, **228**
    cable, 48, 54, 162–163
    client/server networks, 21, 162
    diskless workstations, 167–168
    domain-level security, **117–118**
    eavesdropping, 54
    encryption, 107, **113**, 168–169, **180**
    failed logons, 145, **228**
    hardware, 48, 54, 162
    IEEE 802 specifications, **40**
    organizational considerations, 106–107
    peer-to-peer network, 106, 162
    permissions, 163–165
    planning, 160–161
    policy, 161
    routers, 162
    security log, 146, **150**, **228**
    servers, 162
    share-level security. *See* Share-level security.
    software, 126, 219
    user account information, 156
    user-level security. *See* User-level security.
    virus protection, 169–170
    wiretapping, 48
Network services, 129–130, **134**
Network topologies, 76, **90–91**, 102–104, **246**, **249**, **316**, **326**
    ARCNet, 49, 52, **63**, 87–88, 101, 104
    bus, 76–77, **90**, **96**, 101, **118**
    collisions per second, 145
    fault tolerance and, 81–82, **91**, 106, **116**
    hybrid mesh, 82, 84
    hybrids, 81–82
    mesh, 80–81, **90–91**
    ring, 78–79, **90**, **118**
    star, 79–80, **90**, **118**
    star bus, 81–82
    star ring, 81, 85
    Token Ring, 34, **43**, 78, 81, 83, 86–87, **91**, 104
Networking, **25–27**. *See also* Network administration and support, Network operations.
    computer software, 27
    concepts and terms, 13–24
    IEEE 802 specifications. *See* IEEE 802 specifications.
    infrared data transmission, 54–55
    interfaces, 56–57
    microwave data transmission, 54
    OSI Reference Model, 30–34
    planning and design, 100–112
    protocols, 36–39
    radio data transmission, 54
    wireless data transmission, 54–55
Networking standards, 82–87
    OSI Reference Model, 30–36, **40–42**, 56, 83
Networks
    cable, 46–55, 101–102
    choosing, 23–24
    defined, 18
    design principles, 108–110
    disaster recovery. *See* Disaster recovery.
    environmental considerations, 108
    fault tolerance, 81–82, **91**, 106, **115**
    hardware, 68–76
    information analysis considerations, 107–108
    installation, 110–112
    layout principles, 102–104
    models, 16, **40**
    naming schemes, 156–160
    selecting an architecture, 104–108
    software, 27, 105
    troubleshooting, 221–226
NFS, 37
NIC, 100, **253**, **317**
    base memory address, 69–70
    configuration, 68, 71, **94**
    defined, 16, 68
    IEEE 802 specifications, 34, 36, 56
    installation, 68
    transceiver settings, 70
No Access, 165
NT. *See* Windows NT.

NTDETECT.COM, 173, **181**
NWLink, 36–37, 57, **230**, **245**, **320**

O

OC-1, 197–198
OC-3, 198
ODI (Open Datalink Interface), 57, **65**, **320**
Operating system (OS), 17, 124–125. *See also* Network operating system.
Optical Carrier level, 197, 200, **205**
Optical TDR, 223
Oscilloscope, 223
OSI Reference Model, 30, **40–42**, 56, 83, **249**, **252**, **260**, **316**, **319**, **325**
   IEEE 802 specifications and, 34–35
   layers, 31–34
   NetBIOS computer names, 157
   protocols, 36
"Silver satin" cable, 46

P

Packet Assembler/Disassembler. *See* PAD.
Packet switching, 190–191
   asynchronous transfer mode (ATM), 196–197, **202–203**
   Fiber Distributed Data Interface (FDDI), 52–54, 78, 88–89, 197–198, **202–204**
   frame relay, 194, **202–203**
   ISDN networks, 192–193, 199–202
   SONET, 197–198, **203**, **205**
   switched 56, 190, 196, **201**, **203**
   Switched Multimegabit Data Services (SMDS), 199–200
   T1 and T3 lines, 190, 194–195, 200, **201–203**
   X.25 networks, 38, 191–192, 194, **203**
PAD, 191, **204**, **256**
Page faults, 148
Parity, disk striping, 174–176
Parity checking, 175
Passive hubs, 72
Password-protected shares, 107
Passwords, 17, **117–118**, 138–139, **151**, **248**, **314**, **324**, **327**
   account lockouts, 139
   changing, 139
   creating, 139, **151**
   LOPHTCRACK.EXE, 139
   peer-to-peer network, 19
   server-based network, 21–22
PCI, 17

PDNs, 191
Peer-to-peer networks, 17, 19–21, **26**, **252**, **318**
   advantages, 20
   backup, 20
   choosing, 23
   disadvantages, 19–21
   network security, 106, 162
Performance Monitor, Windows NT, **119–120**, 146–149, 213, **227**, **248**, **317**
Peripheral device, 17
Permanent Virtual Circuit. *See* PVC.
Permissions, 164–166
Personal computer interface. *See* PCI.
PGP, 168
Physical layer, OSI Reference Model, 32, 34–35, **41–42**, 72
Physical ring topology, 78–79, 86
PING, 232
Planning, 160–161, 215
Plenum cable, 52
Plug and Play adapters, 68
Power monitor, 223
Preemptive multitasking, 125
Presentation layer, OSI Reference Model, 31–32, **40**, **249**, **325**
Pretty Good Privacy. *See* PGP.
Preventative maintenance, 214–215
PRI (Primary Rate Interface), 193, 199, **203**, **205**
Print Operators user account, user rights, 141, **150**, **326**
Printing, network printing, 129–130
Process tracking, 167
Propagation delay, 72
Protocol analyzer, 222–223, **228**, **231–232**, **250**
Protocol stack, 36
Protocol suite, 36
Protocols, 36–39, **95–96**, **242**, **259**, **315**
   AFP, 37
   APPC, 38
   AppleTalk, 37–38, 87
   application protocols, 37, **42–43**
   ATP, 37
   DDP, 36
   FTP, 37, **42–43**
   gateways, 75–76, **94**, **96**, 109–110, **231**
   HDLC, 39
   ICMP, 232
   IP, 36
   IPX, 36, **42**, 57, 75

NBP, 37
NCP, 37
NetBEUI, 36–37, **43**, 75, **95**, 106, **116**
network protocols, 16, 36, **42**
non-routable protocols, 75
NWLink, 36–37, 57, **230**
RARP, 168
routable protocols, 75
SMTP, 37, **42–43**, 230
SNMP, 37, **42–43**, 212, **232**
SPX, 37, **42**
TCP, 37
TCP/IP, 38, 75, 225–226, **229**
Telnet, **42**
transport protocols, 37, **42–43**
X.25, 38, 191–192, 194, **203**
XNS, 39
PSTN (Public Switched Telephone Network), 188, 192
Public Data Networks. *See* PDNs.
PVC, 194

Q

Queued commands, 145

R

Radio data transmission, 54
RAID Level 0, 173, 177, **180–181**
RAID Level 1, 106, **115**, 173–175
RAID Level 2, 175
RAID Level 3, 175
RAID Level 4, 175
RAID Level 5, 175–175, **183**
RAID levels, **243**
RAID (Redundant Array of Inexpensive Disks), 106, 173, **178**
RAM (Random Access Memory), 17
RARP, 168
RDISK utility, 144
Read Only access, 163–164
Read permission, 164
Redirectors, 125–126, **133**, 254, **326**
Repeaters, 72, **92**, 109, **116**, **119**, 241, **253**, 316
Replicator group, user rights, 140, **150**
Request-response, 17
Restart, auditing, 167
Reverse Address Resolution Protocol. *See* RARP.
RG cables, **329**
RG-8 cable, 49
RG-11 cable, 49
RG-58 cable, 49, **63**, 101, **114**
RG-59 cable, 49, 101
RG-62 cable, 49, 52, **63**, 88, 101
Ring topology, 78–79, **90**, **118**
RJ-11 connector, 47, **58**
RJ-45 cable, **60**, **63**
RJ-45 connector, 47, 70
Routers, 74–75, **93–95**, 109, **117**, 231, 246, 250, 255, 314–315, 326
    network security, 162

S

Sector sparing, 177, **180**
Security. *See* Network security.
Security errors, 145
Security log, 146, **150**, 228
Sequenced Packet Exchange. *See* SPX.
Server Message Block. *See* SMB.
Server Operators user account, user rights, 141, **150**
Server redirector, 125
Server sessions, 145
Server software, 126–127
Server-based networks, 17, 21–23, **25**, **320**
    advantages, 21–23
    choosing, 23–24
    disadvantages, 22–23
Servers, 22
    defined, 17, 21
    network security, 162
Session layer, OSI Reference Model, 31, 33, **40–41**
Shared devices, 14
Shared resources, 17. *See also* Share-level security.
    client/server networks, 21
    naming scheme, 159–160
    network operating system, 130
    peer-to-peer networks, 20
    permissions, **118**
Share-level security, **117–118**, 163–164, **178**, **182**, 219
    defined, 107, 163
Sharing, 17
Shielded twisted-pair cabling. *See* STP cabling.
Shutdown, auditing, 167
SID, 87
Signal attenuation, 48, **58**
SMAU (Smart Multistation Access Unit), 86–87
SMB, 37

SMDS, 199–200
SMTP (Simple Mail Transport Protocol), 37, **42–43**, 230
SNMP (Simple Network Management Protocol), 37, **42–43**, 212, **232, 255**, 330
Soft page faults, 148
Software
 auditing, 219
 backup, 218
 client software, 125–126
 combined client/server software, 127
 designators, 126
 network security, 126, 219
 networking, 27, 105
 redirectors, 125–126, **133**
 server software, 126–127
 UNC pathnames, 126, **133–134**
 upgrades, 219–220
SONET, 197–198, **203, 205**
Specialized server, 18
SPX, **42, 315, 325**
Standalone applications, 18, 131
Standardization, 216
Standby monitors, 86
Star Bus hybrid topology, 81–82
Star Ring hybrid topology, 81, 83
Star topology, 79–80, **90, 118, 246**
Star-wired Ring topology, 81
Static routers, 74
Station Identifier. *See* SID.
STP cabling, 47–48
Stripe sets, 175, 177, **243**
Striping. *See* Disk striping.
Switched 56, 190, 196, **201**, 203
Switched connections, 187, 190
Switched Multimegabit Data Services. *See* SMDS.
Switching, 187
System log records, Windows NT Event Viewer, 146, **150**

T

T1 lines, 105, 194–195, 200, **201–203, 315, 317**
T3 lines, 195, 200, **201**
Tape backup, 171–172
T-connectors, 50–51, 53, **58, 61**, 101, **116–117**
TCP, 37, **325**
TCP/IP, 38, 75, 225–226, **229**, 315
TDR, 223, **228**
Telecommunications, 105–106. *See also* Connectivity.

WANs, 187–188
Telephone lines
 ISDN, 192–193, 199, **201**
 plenum cabling, 52
 T1 lines, 105, 194–195, 200, **201–203**
 T3 lines, 195, 200, **201**
 twisted-pair cable, 46–47
Telnet, **42**
Terminators, 49, **61**, 77, **96, 256**
Thicknet cable, 49, 51–52, 55, **64**, 101
 bus topology, 77
Thinnet cable, 49–51, 55, **60–61, 64, 96**, 101–102, **114**
 bus topology, 77
Time slicing, 125
Time-domain reflectometer. *See* TDR.
Token Bus LAN, IEEE 802 specifications, 34, **43**
Token Ring topology, 78, **91**, 106, **259, 322**
 IEEE 802 specifications, 34, **43**, 83, 86–87
 restrictions, 104
 Star Ring hybrid topology, 81
Topologies. *See* Network topologies.
Total system management, 147
 hard disk, 148
 memory use, 148
TRACERT, **232**
Training, 220–221
Transceiver, 70
Translation bridge, 73
Transmission Control Protocol. *See* TCP.
Transparent bridge, 73
Transport layer, OSI Reference Model, 31, 33, **40–42, 94**, 319
Transport protocols, 37, **42–43, 244, 325**
Trojan Horse virus, 169
Troubleshooting, 221, **227–232**
 cable, 224–225, **227**
 hardware, 224–225
 methods, 222
 network performance problems, 226
 software connection problems, 225–226
 support resources, 223–224
 tools, 222–223

U

UNC pathnames, 126, **133–134**
Uninterruptible Power Supply (UPS), 172–173, **255**
Unshielded twisted-pair cabling. *See* UTP cabling.

Upgrades, 219–220
User accounts, 156
   account lockouts, 139
   auditing, 139–140, 167
   changes to, 143–144
   creating, **151**, 138–139
   global, 141–142
   local groups, 140–142
   logon hours, 138–140
   managing, 138
   passwords, 138–139, **151**
User groups, 141, **150**
   global, 141–143
   local groups, 140–142
   Windows NT, 141
User-level permissions, **113**
User-level security, 107, **113**, **117–118**,
   163–165, **178**, **182**, **254**, **258**, **321**, **327**
   User rights, 140–142. *See also* Auditing.
Users, 18, 107
UTP cabling, 46–48, 55, **63**, 323

V

Vampire tap, 51–52, **64**
Virus protection, 169–170
Viruses, defined, 169

W

WANs, 18, 186, **201–205**, 243, **322**
   analog connectivity, 187–189
   asynchronous transfer mode (ATM),
      196–197, **202–203**
   circuit switching, 187–188
   digital connectivity, 187, 189–190, 199
   Fiber Distributed Data Interface
      (FDDI), 52–54, 78, 88–89,
      197–198, **202–204**
   frame relay, 194, **202–203**
   ISDN networks, 192–193, 199–200,
      201–202
   packet switching, 190–191
   service types, 199–200
   SONET, 197–198, **203**, **205**
   switched 56, 190, 196, **201**, **203**
   Switched Multimegabit Data Services
      (SMDS), 199–200
   T1 and T3 lines, 190, 194–195, 200,
      201–203
   terminology, 186–187
   X.25 networks, 38, 191–192, 194, **203**
Wide area networks. *See* WANs.

Windows 95
   Device Manager, 70–71
   share-level security, **178**
Windows Internet Name Service.
   See WINS.
Windows NT, 124, 127
   auditing capabilities, 166–167
   base memory address, 70
   disaster recovery, 144
   disk duplexing, 174, 177
   disk mirroring, 174, 177
   disk striping, **183**
   domain model concept, 21–22
   Event Viewer, 146, 149, **150**,
      211–212, 219
   fault tolerance, 174, 177, **180**
   group accounts, 142
   installation, 128–129
   logon hours, 140
   monitoring hard disk, 148
   monitoring network performance,
      146–147, 213
   Network Monitor, 147, **151–152**, **227**
   NTDETECT.COM during startup,
      173, **181**
   password, 139
   Performance Monitor, **119–120**,
      146–149, 213, **227**
   permissions, 163–165
   pre-defined user groups, 141, **150**
   preventative maintenance, 214
   Registry database, 143
   Services applet, 129–130
   tools, **119–120**
   user groups, 141, **150**
   WINS, 158
WINMSD.EXE, 70
WINNT32.EXE, 128
WINNT.EXE, 128
WINS, 157–159, **180**, 216, **230**, **248**,
   257, **330**
Wireless data transmission, 54–55
Wiretapping, 48
Workgroup model, 18
Worm programs, 159
Write permission, 164

X

X.25 networks, 38, 191–192, 194, **203**, **256**
XNS (Xerox Network System), 39

CERTIFIED CRAMMER SOCIETY

A breed apart, a cut above the rest—a true professional. Highly skilled and superbly trained, certified IT professionals are unquestionably the world's most elite computer experts. In an effort to appropriately recognize this privileged crowd, The Coriolis Group is proud to introduce the Certified Crammer Society. If you are a certified IT professional, it is also our pleasure to invite you to become a Certified Crammer Society member.

Membership is free to all certified professionals and benefits include a membership kit that contains your official membership card and official Certified Crammer Society blue denim ball cap emblazoned with the Certified Crammer Society crest—proudly displaying the Crammer motto "Phi Slamma Cramma"—and featuring a genuine leather bill. The kit also includes your password to the Certified Crammers-Only Website containing monthly discreet messages designed to provide you with advance notification about certification testing information, special book excerpts, and inside industry news not found anywhere else; monthly Crammers-Only discounts on selected Coriolis titles; *Ask the Series Editor* Q and A column; cool contests with great prizes; and more.

GUIDELINES FOR MEMBERSHIP

Registration is free to professionals certified in Microsoft, A+, or Oracle DBA. Coming soon: Sun Java, Novell, and Cisco. Send or email your contact information and proof of your certification (test scores, membership card, or official letter) to:

Certified Crammer Society Membership Chairperson
THE CORIOLIS GROUP, LLC
14455 North Hayden Road, Suite 220, Scottsdale, Arizona 85260-6949
Fax: 602.483.0193 • Email: ccs@coriolis.com

APPLICATION

Name:

Address:

Society Alias:
Choose a secret code name to correspond with us and other Crammer Society members. Please use no more than eight characters.

Email:

Coriolis introduces

EXAM CRAM INSIDER™
A FREE ONLINE NEWSLETTER

Stay current with the latest certification information. Just email us to receive the latest in certification and training news for Microsoft, Java, Novell, A+, and more! Read e-letters from the Publisher of the Exam Cram series, Keith Weiskamp, and Exam Cram Series Editor, Ed Tittel, about future trends in IT training and education. Access valuable insider information on exam updates, new testing procedures, sample chapters, and links to other useful, on-line sites. Take a look at the featured program of the month, and who's in the news today. We pack all this and more into our *Exam Cram Insider* online newsletter to make sure *you* pass your next test!

To sign up for our twice monthly newsletter, go to www.coriolis.com and click on the sign up sheet, or email us at eci@coriolis.com and put "subscribe" in your subject header.

EXAM CRAM INSIDER – Another reason Exam Cram is *The Smartest Way To Get Certified*.™ And it's free!

CORIOLIS HELP CENTER

Here at The Coriolis Group, we strive to provide the finest customer service in the technical education industry. We're committed to helping you reach your certification goals by assisting you in the following areas.

Talk to the Authors

We'd like to hear from you! Please refer to the "How to Use This Book" section in the "Introduction" of every Exam Cram guide for our authors' individual email addresses.

Web Page Information

The Certification Insider Press Web page provides a host of valuable information that's only a click away. For information in the following areas, please visit us at:

www.coriolis.com/cip/default.cfm

- Titles and other products
- Book content updates
- Roadmap to Certification Success guide
- New Adaptive Testing changes
- New Exam Cram Live! seminars
- New Certified Crammer Society details
- Sample chapters and tables of content
- Manuscript solicitation
- Special programs and events

Contact Us by Email

Important addresses you may use to reach us at The Coriolis Group.

eci@coriolis.com

To subscribe to our FREE, bi-monthly on-line newsletter, *Exam Cram Insider*. Keep up to date with the certification scene. Included in each *Insider* are certification articles, program updates, new exam information, hints and tips, sample chapters, and more.

techsupport@coriolis.com

For technical questions and problems with CD-ROMs. Products broken, battered, or blown-up? Just need some installation advice? Contact us here.

ccs@coriolis.com

To obtain membership information for the *Certified Crammer Society*, **an exclusive club for the certified professional.** Get in on members-only discounts, special information, expert advice, contests, cool prizes, and free stuff for the certified professional. Membership is FREE. Contact us and get enrolled today!

cipq@coriolis.com

For book content questions and feedback about our titles, drop us a line. This is the good, the bad, and the questions address. Our customers are the best judges of our products. Let us know what you like, what we could do better, or what question you may have about any content. Testimonials are always welcome here, and if you send us a story about how an Exam Cram guide has helped you ace a test, we'll give you an official Certification Insider Press T-shirt.

custserv@coriolis.com

For solutions to problems concerning an order for any of our products. Our staff will promptly and courteously address the problem. Taking the exams is difficult enough. We want to make acquiring our study guides as easy as possible.

Book Orders & Shipping Information

orders@coriolis.com

To place an order by email or to check on the status of an order already placed.

coriolis.com/bookstore/default.cfm

To place an order through our on-line bookstore.

1.800.410.0192

To place an order by phone or to check on an order already placed.